MAHAN'S

PERMANENT FORTIFICATIONS.

REVISED AND ENLARGED

BY

JAMES MERCUR,
PROFESSOR OF CIVIL AND MILITARY ENGINEERING,
UNITED STATES MILITARY ACADEMY.

SECOND EDITION.

FIRST THOUSAND.

The Naval & Military Press Ltd

Published by

The Naval & Military Press Ltd
Unit 10 Ridgewood Industrial Park,
Uckfield, East Sussex,
TN22 5QE England

Tel: +44 (0) 1825 749494
Fax: +44 (0) 1825 765701

www.naval-military-press.com
www.military-genealogy.com
www.militarymaproom.com

In reprinting in facsimile from the original, any imperfections are inevitably reproduced and the quality may fall short of modern type and cartographic standards.

PREFACE.

IN revising this work for the use of the cadets at the Military Academy, it has been my object to retain the arrangement and so far as practicable the identical language of the original text. I am prompted to this not only by an affectionate respect for my former instructor, but more especially by a wish to give the cadets an opportunity to profit by Professor Mahan's clear, concise, and comprehensive statements, which are the result of the native ability, the education, started in America, continued in France under Gen. Noizet, and completed by a life-long study; and the rare experience gained in over forty years' service as Assistant-professor and Professor at the Military Academy.

The parts omitted and the new matter introduced have been selected with a view to rejecting only that which has become obsolete through the introduction of improved weapons and methods, and to explaining and illustrating the new features developed from the same causes.

In making these selections it has seemed better to omit the details of the Bastioned system as worked out by Noizet, notwithstanding its value as a problem in fortification-drawing, and to replace it by fuller treatment of detached works, sea-coast defence, and constructions in iron and steel as used at the present day.

My thanks are due to Lieut. G. J. Fiebeger, Corps of Engineers, for translations from the German, and for collecting the information contained in Appendix II.; and to Lieut. Geo. W. Goethals, Corps of Engineers, for compiling Appendix I.

WEST POINT, N. Y., March, 1887.

CONTENTS.

CHAPTER I.

PRELIMINARY CONSIDERATIONS AND COMPONENT ELEMENTS OF PERMANENT DEFENCES.

ART.	I. *PRELIMINARY CONSIDERATIONS.*	PAGE
1–4.	Permanent fortification: its object and means of attainment,	1

II. *GENERAL PROFILE.*

5–7	Description and analysis of the general profile,	2
8.	Description of modern profile,	5
9.	Command,	5
10.	Description and discussion of scarps,	6
11.	" " " counterscarps,	9
12.	" " " ditches,	10
13.	" " " face covers,	11
14.	General remarks on general profile,	12

III. *OPEN DEFENCES.*

15.	Classes of open defences,	13
16.	Loop-holed walls,	13
17.	Exterior corridors,	15
18.	Barbette batteries,	15
19.	Embrasure batteries,	16
20.	Machicoulis defences,	16

IV. *COVERED DEFENCES.*

21.	Detached scarp walls,	17
22.	Semi-detached scarp walls,	18
23.	Scarp galleries,	18
24.	Counterscarp galleries,	20
25.	Bastionnets,	21
25a.	General remarks on covered defences,	21
26.	Caponnière defences for the enceinte ditch,	22
27.	Casemates on land fronts,	24

ART.		PAGE
28.	Mortar casemates,	25
29.	Casemates for water fronts,	26
30.	Turrets,	27
31.	Embrasures of casemates,	27
32.	Bomb-proof buildings,	28
33.	Powder magazines,	29

V. COMMUNICATIONS.

34.	General remarks on communications,	30
35.	Particular conditions that communications should satisfy,	30
36.	Ramps,	31
37.	Stairs,	32
38.	Posterns,	32
39.	Gateway,	33
40.	Portcullis and other defences of gateway,	33

VI. ENCEINTES.

41.	Classes of enceintes,	35
42.	Systems and methods of fortification,	35
43.	General remarks upon systems of fortification,	36

VII. OUTWORKS.

44.	General remarks on outworks,	36
45.	General conditions outworks should satisfy,	37
46.	Classes of outworks,	38
47.	Covered way,	38
48.	Places of arms,	38
49.	Traverses,	38
50.	Tenaille,	39
51.	Demi-lune,	39
52.	Counterguard,	39
53.	Redoubts,	40
54.	Tenaillon,	40
55.	Horn work,	40
56.	Crown work,	40

VIII. ADVANCED AND DETACHED WORKS.

57, 58.	Advanced works: definition and discussion,	40
59.	Detached works: " " "	41

IX. INTERIOR RETRENCHMENTS.

60, 61.	Interior retrenchments: description and discussion,	42
62.	Cavaliers: " " "	43

CHAPTER II.

Systems of Fortification.

62a.	General considerations,	44

CONTENTS. vii

I. BASTIONED SYSTEM.

ART.		PAGE
63.	Description and analysis of the bastioned system,	44
64.	Principal objections to the bastioned system,	45

II. METHODS OF VAUBAN.

65–75.	Description of Vauban's First Method,	46
76.	Analysis " " " "	49

III. CORMONTAIGNE'S METHOD.

77–79.	Development of method and principles applied,	51
80–88.	Description of Cormontaigne's Method,	52
89.	Analysis of Cormontaigne's Method,	56
90–94.	Use of the counterguard by Vauban, Cormontaigne, Coehoorn, Carnot, Haxo, and Noizet,	57

IV. METHOD OF THE SCHOOLS OF MEZIÈRES AND METZ.

95–98.	Development of the method,	58

V. NOIZET'S METHOD.

99–104.	Description of Noizet's Method,	59
106.	General remarks upon and objections to Noizet's Method,	61
107.	Modifications adopted or suggested,	61
108.	Considerations determining the method to be selected,	62

VI. CHOUMARA'S METHOD.

109.	Principles upon which it is based,	62
110–119.	Description of Choumara's Method,	64
120–122.	Remarks upon Choumara's Method,	68

CHAPTER III.

TENAILLED SYSTEM.

123.	Description and analysis of the system,	70

CHAPTER IV.

POLYGONAL SYSTEM.

I. POLYGONAL SYSTEM IN GENERAL.

124.	Polygonal system: description and analysis,	71

II. MONTALEMBERT'S METHOD.

125.	Development of and principles involved in Montalembert's Method,	72
126–128.	Description of Montalembert's Method,	73
129.	Modifications introduced by Gen. Brialmont,	74
130.	Polygonal system exemplified by the defences of Antwerp,	74

CHAPTER V.

EXISTING GERMAN FORTIFICATIONS.

I. *RECENT GERMAN FORTIFICATIONS.*

ART.		PAGE
131.	System adopted,	77
132.	General conditions imposed,	77
133.	Independent works,	78
134.	Defensive barracks,	78
135.	Profiles of unmodified works,	79
136.	Casemates,	79
137.	Posterns,	79
138.	Mines,	79
139.	Powder magazines, guard-rooms, store-rooms, etc.,	79
140.	Revetments, scarps, and counterscarps,	79
141.	Casemates for cannon and mortars,	80
142.	Casemated traverses,	82
143.	Caponnières for enceinte ditch,	82
144.	Bastionets for ditch defence,	83
145.	Details of defensive barracks,	83
146.	Remarks upon German fortifications,	84
147.	Changes required to fit these works to modern requirements,	85

II. *FRONTS OF POSEN.*

148–151.	Outline description of front,	86

III. *FORT ALEXANDER AT COBLENTZ.*

152–158.	Description of Fort Alexander,	88
159–162.	Remarks upon the polygonal system as applied by the Germans, with analysis of the relative advantages and defects of the polygonal and bastioned systems,	90
163.	Recent modifications in the bastioned and polygonal systems,	92
164.	Considerations determining the character of future fortifications and systems to be adopted,	92

CHAPTER VI.

DETACHED FORTS.

165.	Now the main line of defence,	94
166.	Tracé adopted; dimensions; garrison; armament; profiles and revetments,	94
167.	Bomb-proof covers and use of turrets,	95
168.	Communications,	95
169.	Small but important works entirely bomb-proof,	96
170.	Outworks,	96
171.	Glacis or wing batteries,	96
172.	Intermediate works,	96

CONTENTS.

CHAPTER VII.

INFLUENCE OF IRREGULARITIES OF SITE ON THE FORMS AND COMBINATIONS OF THE ELEMENTS OF PERMANENT WORKS.

ART.		PAGE
173–175.	General conditions to be satisfied,	97
176.	Conditions of command,	98
177, 178.	Rule to be observed in adaptation of plan to site,	98
179.	Remarks upon foregoing subjects,	100

II. DEFILEMENT OF PERMANENT WORKS.

180.	Remarks upon defilement of permanent works,	101
181.	Data for the " " " "	102
182–185.	Limits of defilement,	103
186.	Dangerous zones of the site,	104
187.	Portions of zones that may be disregarded,	104
188.	Defilement of masonry,	104
189.	Limits of defilement for small works,	104
190.	Front and lateral limits,	104
191.	Remarks,	105

III. PROBLEMS OF DEFILEMENT.

192.	Cases of defilement,	105
193.	Front defilement of a redan, the command being given,	106
194.	Reverse defilement of a redan,	108
195.	Position of traverse for reverse defilement,	109
196.	Forms and arrangement of traverses,	109
197.	Combinations of several traverses,	109
198.	Precautions to be taken in locating traverses,	110
199.	Remarks upon defilement by traverses,	110
200.	General case of the defilement of a bastion,	110
201.	Defilement of retired from advanced works,	112
202.	Defilement by parados and conclusions drawn from experiments,	112
203.	General remarks upon defilement—Recapitulation,	113

CHAPTER VIII.

ACCESSORY MEANS OF DEFENCE.

I. WATER AS AN ACCESSORY.

204, 205.	Marshy sites,	115
206.	Artificial inundations,	115
207.	Water applied as an active means of defence,	116

II. OTHER MATERIALS AS ACCESSORIES.

208.	Natural and artificial beds of rock as an accessory,	116
209.	Stumps of trees as an obstruction,	117
210.	"Obstacles" as an accessory,	117

CONTENTS.

III. *MINES AS ACCESSORIES.*

ART.   PAGE
211. General considerations in their use,   .   .   .   117

CHAPTER IX.

Sea-coast Defence.

I. *BATTERIES ON LAND.*

212. General conditions of sea-coast defence,   .   .   118
213. Use of stone casemates abandoned,   .   .   .   118
214–217. Earthen batteries, ...   118
218–221. Disappearing gun carriages, ...   119
222–224. Use of traverses, ...   120
225. Gun pits, ...   120
226, 227. Mortar batteries, ...   120
228. Batteries on elevated sites,   .   .   .   121
229, 230. The use of armor, ...   121

II. *FLOATING BATTERIES.*

231. Conditions requiring their use,   .   .   .   121

III. *OBSTACLES, SUBMARINE MINES, AND TORPEDOES.*

232. Their use a necessity in the defence of harbors,   .   122
233. General considerations to be fulfilled by passive obstacles, ...   122
234. Different kinds of passive obstacles,   .   .   122
235. First use of submarine mines and torpedoes,   .   123
236. General conditions to be fulfilled by submarine mines, ...   123
237–239. Uses of submarine mines and torpedoes,   .   123
240–244. Classification and general description of submarine mines, ...   124
245. Conditions to be fulfilled by the electrical system,   .   125
246, 247. Construction of mine cases,   .   .   .   125
248. Explosives used, ...   125
249. Movable torpedoes, general description,   .   125
250. Destructive range of submarine explosions,   .   125
251–255. Organization of fortifications, mines, and torpedoes for the defence of harbors,   .   .   126
256. Remarks, ...   127

CHAPTER X.

The Defensive Organization of Frontiers with Permanent Fortifications.

257. Opinions held by prominent military authorities on the necessity of fortified frontiers,   .   .   128
258. Remarks on the organization of the frontier defences of the United States,   .   .   .   129

BOOKS FOR

ARMY AND NAVY OFFICERS

PUBLISHED BY

JOHN WILEY & SONS.

ORDNANCE AND GUNNERY.
For the use of the Cadets of the U. S. Military Academy. By Captain Henry Metcalf, Ordnance Department, U. S. Army Instructor of Ordnance and Gunnery, U.S.M.A. 12mo, 500 pp., cloth, with separate atlas containing 350 cuts, . . $5.00

MODERN FRENCH ARTILLERY.
The St. Chamond, De Bange, Canet and Hotchkiss systems, with illustrations of French War Ships. By James Dredge. 4to, half morocco, ... $20.00 *net*

HANDBOOK OF PROBLEMS IN DIRECT FIRE.
By James M. Ingalls, Captain First Artillery, U. S. A. 8vo, cloth, ... $4.00

BALLISTIC TABLES.
Reprinted from the Handbook for West Point Cadets. By Capt. Jas. M. Ingalls. 8vo, cloth, ... $1.50

SUBMARINE MINES AND TORPEDOES.
As applied to Harbour Defense. By John Townsend Bucknill, Honorary Lieutenant-Colonel (late Major Royal Engineers) Reserve of Officers. With illustrations. 8vo, cloth, . $4.00

PRACTICAL SEAMANSHIP.
By John Todd, Master Mariner, and W. B. Whall, Extra Master Younger Brother Trinity House. Royal 8vo, full cloth, with 243 Illustrations and Diagrams, ... $7.50

NOTES ON MILITARY HYGIENE.
For Officers of the Line. A Syllabus of Lectures at the U. S. Infantry and Cavalry School. By Alfred A. Woodhull, Major of Medical Dep't., Bvt. Lt. Col. U. S. Army. 12mo, morocco, $2.50

SIMPLE ELEMENTS OF NAVIGATION.
By Lucien Young, U. S. Navy. Pocket-book form, . $2.00

THE SOLDIERS' FIRST AID HANDBOOK.
Comprising a Series of Lectures to Members of the Hospital Corps and Company Bearers. By William D. Dietz, Late Captain and Assistant Surgeon U. S. Army. 18mo, morocco, $1.25

PERMANENT FORTIFICATIONS.
By Prof. D. H. Mahan, Revised and brought up to date by Col. James Mercur, U. S. Military Academy, West Point. Numerous plates, 1887. 8vo, half morocco, . . . $7.50

ELEMENTS OF THE ART OF WAR.
By James Mercur, Professor of Civil and Military Engineering, United States Military Academy. Illustrated with full-page and folding plates. Third edition. 8vo, cloth, . . $4.00

PRACTICAL MARINE SURVEYING.
By Harry Phelps, U. S. Navy. 8vo, cloth, . . $2.50

"WRINKLES" IN PRACTICAL NAVIGATION.
By S. T. S. Lecky, Master Mariner, Commander R. N. R. Second edition. 80 illustrations. 8vo, cloth, . . . $6.00

AN ABRIDGEMENT OF MILITARY LAW.
By Lt. Col. W. Winthrop, Deputy Judge Advocate-General U. S. Army, late Professor of Law, U. S. Military Academy. Second and revised edition. 12mo, red cloth, . . . $2.50

A MANUAL FOR COURTS-MARTIAL.
Prepared by Lt. Arthur Murray, 1st Artillery, late Acting Judge Advocate-General, U. S. A. Third edition. 18mo, morocco, flap, ... $1.50

CAVALRY OUT-POST DUTIES.
By F. De Brack, translated from the French (third edition, 1863) by Major Camillo C. C. Carr, 8th Cavalry, U. S. A. 18mo, morocco, flap, ... $2.00

GUNNERY FOR NON-COMMISSIONED OFFICERS.
Compiled by Lt. Adelbert Cronkhite, 4th Artillery, with BallisticTables, by Capt. James Chester, 3d Artillery, 18mo, morocco, flap, ... $2.00

ART OF SUBSISTING ARMIES IN WAR.
By Capt. H. G. Sharpe, U. S. A. 18mo, cloth, . . $1.25
morocco, ... $1.50

THE ARMY OFFICER'S EXAMINER.
By Lt. Col. W. H. Powell, U. S. A. 12mo, cloth, . $4.00

ELEMENTARY NAVAL TACTICS.
By Commander Wm. Bainbridge-Hoff, U. S. N. 8vo, cloth, (in preparation.)

Fort St. Marie, Antwerp.

CONTENTS.

ART.		PAGE
259.	Important points to be fortified,	130
260.	Rivers and mountain ranges as natural defensive lines.	130
261.	Advantages offered both in defensive and offensive operations by fortified points on rivers,	131
262.	Points to be fortified in mountain ranges,	131
263.	Defensive means adopted for the coasts of the United States,	131
264.	Character of the works necessary for sea-coast defence,	132
265.	Defences for important commercial marts and naval depots,	132
266.	Defence of important extensive roadsteads,	134
267.	Opinions entertained by foreign military authorities on the fortification in a permanent manner of important inland centres of population,	134
268.	Fortifications of Paris and Lyons in France,	135
269.	Objections to the adoption of European practice for the defences of the large cities of the United States,	135.

CHAPTER XI.

SUMMARY OF THE PROGRESS AND CHANGES OF FORTIFICATION.

I. *PROGRESS OF THE DEFENCE.*

270.	Fortification as seen in its earliest stages,	137
271.	Enclosures of simple stone walls and towers,	137
272.	Insufficiency of these against improved means of offence,	138
273.	Introduction of ditches and wide ramparts as defensive features,	138
274.	Examples of the great strength and extent of some ancient fortifications,	139
275.	Methods of attack used by the Ancients,	139
276.	Defensive methods employed by the Ancients,	140
277.	Rise and fall of the art under the Romans,	140
278.	Progress of the art under the Western Empire,	141
279.	Conditions of the art under the Feudal System,	141
280.	Castellated fortifications of the Feudal Period,	142
281.	Fortifications of cities during the same period,	142
282.	Changes in the art occasioned by the invention of gunpowder,	143
283.	First appearance of the bastioned system and the changes consequent upon it,	143
284.	Italian school of engineers,	144
285.	Spanish school,	145
286.	Dutch school,	145
287.	German school,	146
288.	Swedish school,	146
289.	French school,	147

CONTENTS.

II. *PROGRESS OF THE ATTACK SINCE THE INVENTION OF FIREARMS.*

ART.		PAGE
290.	Methods and progress of the attack from the invention of gunpowder to the time of Vauban,	148
291.	Changes and improvements made in the methods of attack by Vauban,	149
292.	Present condition of the art in the United States,	150
293.	Probable changes in the immediate future,	151

CHAPTER XII.

MODERN CONSTRUCTIONS IN IRON AND STEEL.

294.	Introduction of armor,	152
295.	Its development,	152
296–299.	Its behavior under impact and relative cost,	153
300.	Application of armor to land defences comparatively free from difficulties,	154
301.	English armored forts,	154
302.	English turrets,	155
303, 304.	Dover turret,	155
305, 306.	French turret (Mougin),	155
307, 308.	German turret (Schumann),	156
309.	Competitive trials of French and German turrets,	157
310.	Revolving turret caponier,	158
311.	Fixed turret caponier,	158
312.	Disappearing turret,	159
313.	Cost of small turrets,	159
314.	Application of small turrets,	159
315.	Grüson casemates,	160

APPENDIX I.

PENETRATION OF PROJECTILES AND THICKNESS OF PARAPETS.

Formulas for penetration in iron,	161
Calculated penetration into clay, sand, and granite,	162
Actual penetrations into earth, granite, concrete, etc.,	163
Prescribed thicknesses of German parapets,	164

APPENDIX II.

Frontier and interior fortifications of France, Germany, Italy, Austria-Hungary, and Russia in Europe,	165

APPENDIX III.

Books of reference,	170

LIST OF PLATES.

PLATE No. 1. Typical modern profiles.
" 2. Mortar battery.
" 3. Profiles of older forts.
" 4. Scarps, counterscarps, and galleries.
" 5. Sea-coast fronts, caponnière and bastionet.
" 6. Sea-coast and land-front casemates.
" 7. Barbette battery and disappearing gun-carriages.
" 8. Machicoulis, posterns, Totten embrasures, and outline plans of different systems of fortification.
" 9. Outworks.
" 10. Vauban and Cormontaigne's fronts.
" 11. Brialmont's method.
" 11a. Noizet's front.
" 12. Choumara's method.
" 13. Montalembert and Carnot's methods.
" 14. Fort Alexander and front of Posen.
" 15. Tête de pont opposite Germersheim.
" 16. Detached work (German).
" 17. Problems of defilade.
" 18. English, French, and German turrets.
" 19. Disappearing turrets, fixed and revolving iron caponiers.

FRONTISPIECE—Grüson chilled iron casemated battery near Antwerp.

ELEMENTS

OF

PERMANENT FORTIFICATION.

CHAPTER I.

PRELIMINARY CONSIDERATIONS AND COMPONENT ELEMENTS OF PERMANENT DEFENCES.

I.

PRELIMINARY CONSIDERATIONS.

1. The term *permanent fortification* is applied to those defences which, constructed of materials of a durable nature and designed for permanent occupancy by troops, receive such a degree of strength that an enemy will be forced to the operations either of a siege or a blockade to gain possession of them.

2. These defences differ from temporary fortification but in degree; the general principles of defensive works being alike applicable to both.

3. The object of such defences is to secure the permanent military possession of those points, either on the frontiers or in the interior of a state, which must at all times have a well-defined bearing on the operations of a defensive or an offensive war.

4. For the attainment of this object the following general conditions should be fulfilled in the arrangement of such defences:

1st. *They should be of sufficient strength to resist with success all the ordinary means resorted to by an assailant in an open assault.*

2d. *Be provided with suitable shelters to protect the troops, the armament, and the magazines of provisions and munitions of war required for their defence against the destructive measures of the assailant.*

3d. *Be so planned that every point exterior to the defences within cannon range shall be thoroughly swept by their fire.*

4th. *Have secure and easy means of communication for the movement of the troops, both within the defences and to the exterior.*

5th. *And, finally, be provided with all such accessory defensive means as the natural features of the position itself may afford, to enable the garrison to dispute with energy the occupancy by the assailant of every point both within and exterior to the defences.*

The defensive branch of the military engineer's art consists in the knowledge of the means which are employed to fulfil the above conditions, and of their suitable adaptation to the natural features of the positions he may be called upon to fortify.

II.

COMPONENT ELEMENTS OF PERMANENT WORKS.

GENERAL PROFILE.

5. The first condition laid down for permanent defences, security from open assault, supposes a strength of profile greatly superior to that which is given to temporary works.

6. The usual and most simple form of profile for permanent works consists of a *rampart*, a *parapet*, and a *ditch*, exterior to which a *glacis* is usually thrown up.

The Rampart, A, Plates 1 and 3, is an earthen mound, raised above the natural level of the ground, and upon which the parapet B is placed.

The rampart thus serves to give the troops and armament, which are placed on top of it and behind the parapet, a commanding view over the ground to be guarded by the fire of the defences; whilst at the same time it increases the obstacle to an open assault by the additional height it gives to the scarp.

The top surface of the rampart, b c, in rear of the parapet, termed the *terre-plein*, affords the troops and armament a convenient position for circulation from point to point, where they are sheltered from the direct view of the assailant.

The rampart is usually terminated on the interior, a b, by

allowing the earth to assume either its natural slope, or one somewhat less steep, termed the *rampart-slope*.

In cases where this slope would take up too much of the ground within the defences it is replaced by a wall, termed the *parade-wall*, which rises from the level cf the interior ground, termed the *parade*, to the interior line of the *terre-plein*.

Inclined planes of earth, termed *ramps*, lead from the parade to the terre-plein, and serve as communications between them.

7. The Parapet, B, Pl. 3, Fig. 4, serving the same purposes in permanent as in field works, receive the same general form as in the latter.

The essential properties of the parapet, as in field-works, are to afford cover from the enemy's missiles, and every facility for sweeping his positions by the fire of its artillery and small-arms.

To afford perfect cover against direct fire, at short range, a thickness of parapet equal to once and a half the penetration of the gun brought against it is usually used. (For penetrations, see Appendix I.) It is not always practicable to give this full thickness, nor is it in the general case necessary, since the penetration of elongated projectiles into parapets of the usual form is less than into experimental butts. The projectile will generally be deflected from its direct course, turn upward, and pass out from the superior slope before passing through the parapet. These considerations have led the German engineers to give to the parapets of their new inland forts, Plate 1, Figs. 1 and 3, a thickness varying from 17 to 23 feet, and to sea-coast works 40 feet.

The French consider 20 to 26 feet necessary for land fronts, and our own engineers have recommended in special cases 70 feet thickness in sea-coast batteries. The most of the parapets of existing works have received only from 18 to 20 feet, and these will doubtless be found to give efficient cover against any ordinary attack.

In small works of less importance and not liable to be breached the thickness may be reduced to 12 or 15 feet.

In some cases the exterior slope, Pl. 3, Fig. 12, is replaced by a wall, which, resting on the top of the scarp wall, rises to the level of the superior slope.

The exterior slope of the parapet usually rises from the top of the scarp wall, leaving a narrow berm between it and the scarp, or face of the wall.

In some cases, however, it is thrown so far to the rear of

the scarp, Pl. 1, Figs. 2 and 5, as to leave sufficient room for a communication c, in front of the parapet, in which the troops can circulate under cover from fire, being masked either by an earthen parapet, or by a wall, D. This covered communication, c, is termed an *exterior corridor* or *chemin-de-ronde*.

For the superior slope, the rule, so long in use, of making it six base to one perpendicular, or $\frac{1}{6}$, is still generally followed.

This rule has not been adopted because cannon cannot be fired under a greater depression than $\frac{1}{6}$, although, from the inconveniences attending greater depressions than this, artillerists are unwilling to resort to them; but from a greater depression necessitating the employment of very deep embrasures, or else that of platforms raised so high to the rear that the men serving the guns will be very much exposed to fire.

Still, where a greater or less plunge is necessary to bring the exterior ground better under fire it should be adopted, as it is to be observed that the strength of the parapet at the angle of the interior crest should be increased where the assailant can have a plunging fire on it; whereas when exposed to a fire from a level much below this crest the angle at it will be less exposed, and the plunge of the parapet can be increased without injury.

Until within a recent period, the interior slope, the banquette, and banquette slope received the same forms and dimensions as in field works; the top of the rampart falling, from the foot of the banquette slope to the crest of the rampart slope, one foot, to drain off the surface-water.

In the later profile the interior slope is $\frac{1}{4}$, and has a banquette tread of only 2 feet, with a banquette slope of only $\frac{1}{4}$. Where guns are mounted either in barbette or embrasure the interior slope is increased to $\frac{3}{4}$, and the banquette and its slope removed; the earth taken off by these modifications serving to form the merlons between the shallow embrasures cut into the parapets.

When the foot of the exterior slope rests on the top of the scarp wall, a berm of two feet in breadth is left between it and the edge of the coping. This breadth of berm is objectionable, as giving a good landing-place for a scaling-party in an open assault; and it is proposed, when the work is in danger of an attack, to reduce the berm to 18 inches or one foot, by increasing the thickness of the parapet 6 inches or one foot.

The exterior slope, for the reasons given in discussing the parapets of field-works, should not be greater on land fronts than the natural slope of the earth of which the parapet is formed.

8. The profiles now used are shown in Plate 1, Figs. 1, 2, 3, 4. and 5. The part of the terre-plein used as a general barbette for heavy guns has a width and height suitable for the carriages used; that used as a road in rear is given a breadth sufficient for communication (20 to 25 feet), and is placed low enough to be screened from a trajectory falling at an angle of $\frac{1}{4}$, if this is consistent with a sufficient cover over the arches of the bomb-proofs.

In the older works the terre-plein received a breadth of 40 to 50 feet, estimated between the interior crest and the top of the rampart slope. From motives of economy, and sometimes to enlarge the parade, this breadth was reduced to 20 or 24 feet, and a parade wall substituted for the rampart slope. The great length of modern guns and the necessity for increased room for bomb-proofs under the terre-plein have caused a return to a greater width. The minimum is now about 40 feet.

The great command and low scarps of modern works make the exterior slope much longer than it formerly was. It is sometimes broken up by introducing two or more berms between its crest and foot.

9. The *command*, or height of the parapet above the site, has a very important bearing in the close defence of permanent works.

In the first place, the greater the command, the greater will be the plunge of the guns on the exterior ground, and the more difficulty will the assailant meet with in obtaining cover in his trenches from this plunge; being obliged to make them deeper than usual, and to increase the height of their parapets.

In the second place, having to fire under greater angles of elevation, as the command is greater, he will only be able to reach the terre-pleins by the use of diminished charges and a corresponding decrease in accuracy of fire. For defence against the distant attack by long-range guns these considerations have less weight, the advantage of command in this case arising principally from its giving a better view of the enemy's works.

Motives of economy, however, require the command to be restricted within quite narrow limits. When the work consists of a simple enceinte enveloped by a covered-way the command may be reduced to 16 feet, which allows a sufficient command above the glacis crest. The height of the latter is so fixed that a projectile falling at an angle of ¼ and just grazing it shall not strike the scarp wall at a distance less than sixteen feet above its bottom.

10. SCARP.—Scarp walls are *full, detached,* or *semi-detached.* A *full scarp wall* is a retaining-wall extending from the bottom of the ditch to the foot of the exterior slope, which rests upon its top (Plate 3, Figs. 2 and 4).

A detached scarp wall (Plate 1, Figs. 1, 2, and 3) rises from the bottom of the ditch. leaving between its back and the foot of the rampart behind it a breadth of several feet, either on the same level as the bottom of the ditch, or raised a few feet above this level. In some cases the wall is built with several tiers of arched recesses on its back, the portions of the wall in front of which are pierced with loop-holes, each recess being of sufficient size to give shelter to several men serving the loop-holes, and firing into the ditch and on the top of the counterscarp.

A *semi-detached* scarp wall (Plate 1, Fig. 5) has its lower portion made as retaining-wall, generally built with relieving arches, either closed or open in rear; the upper portion for a height from 8 to 12 feet being detached from the rampart and prepared for defence like the preceding example.

Detached and semi-detached scarp walls have evident advantages over the full scarp. They are better covered by the glacis from the plunging fire of the assailant; they offer the same obstacle to an escalade as the latter, and when the assailant has gained the top of the wall they present the further difficulty of his getting down on the other side; they give a good fire upon the ditch, and are thus favorable to the safety of sortie parties in retreat; and when a wide space is left between them and the parapet, room is afforded for the formation of a column on each side of any breach made in the wall, to charge in flank an assaulting column entering the breach.

On the other hand, these walls favor an assaulting column rushing through a breach in them, as the assailants can spread along the corridor on the right and left, and assault the work on a wider front. Should the assailant not choose this course, he has the alternative of establishing himself securely upon the exterior slope in trenches; and if it suits his purposes better, to drive a mine gallery from the breach into the rampart, to blow it up and open a breach into the work.

ELEMENTS OF PERMANENT FORTIFICATION.

But a very marked defect in all of these detached scarps is the exposed condition in which the men behind them are from the splinters from the walls when the corridor can be enfiladed, and from the splinters of exploding shells, which either lodge and explode in the rampart, or roll down it and explode in the corridor.

To break in some measure the effects of this enfilade, and also to prevent an assaulting column from spreading to the right and left along the corridor, traverse walls, having doors in them for communication and loop-holed to fire along the corridor, are placed from point to point, running from the scarp wall back to the exterior slope across the corridor. But these cross-walls would soon be destroyed by an ordinary enfilade, and the splinters from them would render the corridor untenable.

Notwithstanding this defect, on account of their many advantages, detached and semi-detached walls are now very generally adopted by engineers. Since their object is to prevent escalade and stop assaulting columns and lines, they would ordinarily only be manned by the defenders when the assailants were so close to them as to preclude the use of their artillery against the defence.

In order to protect dry ditches against escalade a scarp wall 30 feet high was until recently considered necessary. This height had been established from long experience in sieges preceding the introduction of the breech-loading small arms and metallic ammunition. With the increased rapidity of fire resulting from these improvements, and machine guns, engineers are all of the opinion that a less height will now afford ample security.

The French engineers consider the maximum height necessary for full scarps for main works to be from 23 to 26 feet, and for outworks from 16 to 20. With detached scarps they reduce these heights to 20 feet for the main work and 16 or even 13 for the outworks. The German and Belgian engineers adopt about the same heights.

Some engineers have shown a tendency to do away with either the revetted scarp or counterscarp, and in some instances with both; trusting to entanglements and other obstacles combined with the fire of the work to repel assault.

While these means may be sufficient in works fully garrisoned and protected against surprise by constant watchfulness, a restriction to their use would be fraught with freat danger to works having small garrisons if suddenly attacked, and would add greatly to the fatigue of the defence by the additional guard duty and the constant state of readiness to repel assault required of the garrison. As the object of all fortifications is to compensate for numeri cal weakness on the part of the defence, the safer practice would seem to be to do this by placing such an obstacle in the way of an open assault that but a few men promptly availing themselves of it might hold back the assailant until a sufficient force could be gathered at the point assailed to render the attack abortive.

Besides securing the place from an escalade, full and semi-detached scarp walls act as retaining-walls, to hold up the excavated side of the ditch towards the rampart, the rampart itself, and the parapet. This requires that they should receive a thickness and form of profile adapted to this end.

The top stone of the wall, k, Pl. 3, Fig. 4, termed the *cordon* or *coping*, projects beyond its face, and serving as a *larmier* or *drip*, protects it from the effects of the rain-water, which runs from the parapet upon the coping.

The line in which the face of the scarp wall if prolonged would intersect the coping is termed the *magistral*. This is a very important line in drawing the plans of permanent works, serving as the directing line to fix, both upon the drawing and upon the ground in setting out the work, the dimensions and relative positions of all the bounding lines of the parapet and other parts.

Although no ordinary scarp walls can resist breaching, and have to be covered by earthen masks to screen them from the distant fire of the assailed, they should be so constructed as to render breaching a difficult operation; limiting the breach made to the part of the wall actually destroyed by the assailant's projectiles.

In the scarp walls of Vauban and Cormontaigne, and in many of the more modern fortifications of Europe, the scarp walls are built solid, with counterforts on their back, of the forms and dimensions adopted by Vauban. This engineer gave his scarps a thickness of about $\frac{1}{3}$ their height and a batir of $\frac{5}{1}$. Cormontaigne, finding that the faces of these walls were soon injured by the weather, adopted a batir of $\frac{6}{1}$. This for the same reason was increased by some to $\frac{1.2}{1}$, by others to $\frac{2.0}{1}$; and in our climate, where the action of the weather on masonry is very injurious, our engineers have varied their batir from $\frac{2.4}{1}$ to $\frac{4.8}{1}$.

To give greater efficacy to the resistance offered to breaching, and to prevent the breach from taking a gentle slope when formed, it has been proposed by some to back the wall and counterforts by a kind of pisé work, or with beton with but little lime in it, of several feet in thickness.

Others have proposed, for the same purpose, to connect the end of the counterforts by vertical arches, and to fill the cells thus formed either with pisé, or with this poor beton.

Others prefer long thin counterforts sustaining several tiers of relieving arches; the cells thus formed being left open for defence, for bomb-proof shelters, and for magazines for provisions, etc.

All these expedients have been tried, though not fully tested by experiment; the last under all points of view having the most advantages in its favor.

11. Counterscarp Wall. A revetted counterscarp is regarded as adding to the difficulty of descending into the ditch, and as offering greater security against an open assault. For this purpose the wall should not be less than 12 or 15 feet in height to offer a serious impediment; in any case, where motives of economy do not imperiously forbid it, the counterscarp wall of the enceinte should be from 18 to 24 feet in height. This height will not only give great security to the ditch, but, as will be seen in the description of the siege works of the assailant, it will delay considerably his progress, as the gallery by which he must generally reach the bottom of the ditch from the level of the covered-way terre-plein is one of the slowest and most laborious of his operations.

Besides giving greater security against a surprise, a revetted counterscarp enables the assailed to circulate through the ditches even when the assailant has established his trenches along the glacis crest, as the top of the counterscarp wall will screen the troops passing along the bottom of the ditch.

It also affords facilities for forming a counterscarp gallery behind it loop-holed for the defence of the ditch against an open assault, *which for small works without thorough flanking arrangements will be found very serviceable.*

Besides, this gallery will be found of great utility where a system of defensive mines is to form a part of the defences.

But as counterscarp galleries, if seized upon by the assailant, may be turned against the defences, it is important that they should be placed in positions where they will be of little value to the assailant if seized upon.

The necessity for revetting with a wall of masonry the scarp and counterscarp of a wet ditch in which the water can be retained at a level of six feet in depth, is not so obvious, as when the ditch is wide the obstacle of the water alone would seem to be sufficient to secure the place from a surprise. Many works under this condition have been built with simple earthen scarps and counterscarps; in some instances a chemin-de-ronde being formed by leaving a wide berm between the foot of the exterior slope and the crest of the scarp, and planting a loop-holed stockade near the crest.

But in rigorous climates, where the water freezes hard, a wet ditch is no longer a security in winter; and a dry ditch with the usual revetted scarp and counterscarp is a better security against a surprise than the expedients proposed, of keeping an open channel along the middle of the ditch of 12 feet in width, piling up on each side of it the ice taken from the channel and throwing water over the exterior slopes to freeze and form a slippery surface to an assaulting column.

12. Ditch. The width and depth of the enceinte ditch depend mainly upon the amount of embankment required for the enceinte and the glacis, and therefore will result from the calculation for equalizing the excavation and embankment which these demand.

A deep and narrow ditch offers the advantage of presenting more difficulty to the assailant in reaching the bottom of it, either in an open assault, or by a gallery in the attack by regular approaches, thus prolonging the defence.

It masks better the sally-ports from the enemy's fire by allowing them to be placed so low that the projectiles coming over the glacis cannot reach them.

In like manner by drawing in the crest of the glacis nearer to the scarp the latter will be better masked by it from the plunge of the distant fire of the assailant's batteries, and cannot be breached so low down from his batteries placed along the glacis crest.

On the other hand, when the ditch is too narrow it may be partly filled by breaching the scarp, and then blowing in the counterscarp so as by the united *débris* to form an easy roadway for an assaulting column to enter the work.

A wide ditch, on the other hand, requires more labor to construct the trench across it by which the assailant can reach the foot of the breach under cover. This is a consideration of some importance in wet ditches, where the assailant is obliged to construct a dike upon which the parapet of his cover is placed.

In the most recently constructed forts the main ditch is limited to a depth of about 30 feet and a width of from 13 to 16 yards. Wet ditches have a width of from 20 to 80 yards and a depth of water from 6 to 10 feet. The dimensions are reduced to a minimum where the embankments are not great and circumstances are unfavorable to an attempt at escalade.

The bottom of the ditch, when dry, usually receives a slight slope from the foot of the scarp and counterscarp to its centre, where a small drain, termed a *cunette*, is dug to receive the surface-water and keep the ditch dry. In some cases, from motives of economy, the difference of level between the cunette and the foot of the counterscarp wall is increased, thus giving a less height of wall. This practice, however, can only be followed where the foundations of the wall will be secure, from the soil of the bottom of the ditch being of such a nature as not to yield from the effects of the weather upon it.

13. Face Covers. Engineers since the times of Cormontaigne have until recently adopted his method of placing the top of the scarp wall on a level with the crest of the glacis, or a little below this crest, to give the wall cover from the assailant's distant batteries. But this is evidently only a partial remedy, since the plunge of projectiles fired from a distance is very great in the descending branch of the trajectory, and with the rifled guns now used, these projectiles fired from a distance may pass over the glacis crest and strike the wall quite low down, thus effecting serious damage, particularly in the case of wide and shallow ditches.

Various expedients have been proposed by engineers to remedy this defect. Choumara, an engineer of celebrity, has proposed to form what he terms an interior glacis within the ditch, the crest of which shall rise so high above the bottom of the ditch, that it shall mask the scarp wall from the plunge of the distant batteries, and shall force the assailant to establish his breaching batteries on this interior glacis to enable him to fire low enough to effect a practicable breach in the wall.

Brialmont, a more recent writer, proposes a like plan for the same purposes; and in one of our own works, Fort Warren, Boston Harbor, a heavy earthen face-cover masks a portion of the scarp wall, from a position from which a breaching fire might have been brought against the part thus masked.

The latest practice, when face-covers are not used, is to give the crest of the glacis the depth and width of the ditch, and the height of the scarp wall such relations that at least 16 feet of the scarp wall is covered by the glacis from a plunging fire of $\frac{1}{4}$. See Plate 1, Figs. 1, 2, 3, 4, and 5.

14. General Remarks. The command of the parapet over the exterior ground and any outworks of the defences, its *relief*, or height above the bottom of the ditch, and its height above the top of the scarp wall, are all points which call for a careful consideration on the part of the engineer in any combination of these that he may be called upon to make.

First, it is important that the parapet should thoroughly sweep all the ground within range of its guns, at least up to the glacis crest; and the more so as the closer the assailant's trenches approach the work, the greater will be the plunge obtained upon them, and the more difficult it will be for the assailant to cover himself by his trenches.

That the parapet should command all outworks within range of its fire is obvious, otherwise when seized upon by the assailant these outworks would have a plunging fire upon the main work.

The rule is laid down by some authorities, that the projectiles of the parapet should clear the crest of the glacis by at least 2 feet. But this is by no means necessary, for if the glacis has a covered-way for troops in its rear, it will be impracticable to keep these troops in the covered-way with missiles passing in such close proximity to them, particularly as they are subjected to danger from the blast, gas checks, and unburned powder-grains, as well as from the bursting of shells in their rear.

The relief of the parapet of the flanking parts of the work should evidently be such that every point along the foot of the scarp wall shall be swept by its fire. This supposes also a certain correlation between the relief and the length of the lines flanked, so that this condition shall be satisfied; a relation that can always be easily found, either by calculation, or a very simple geometrical construction from given *data*.

In like manner the height of the interior crest of the parapet above the top of the scarp wall can be easily ascertained by the same methods, with assumed *data*. It should evidently be at least such that a gun, on any kind of carriage, firing through an embrasure of assumed depth and under a given depression, should clear the coping of the wall about one foot.

A mere geometrical diagram will show that as the height of the interior crest above the top of the wall, supposing the position of the latter fixed, is increased, the whole parapet will be thrown further back from the wall, and the interior space of the work will be in the same degree lessened.

All of these considerations therefore suggest that nothing like absolute rules can be laid down so as to give a routine character to the practice of this branch of the military art.

The rules here given with respect to the form and dimensions of the general profile of the enceinte are founded upon reasons growing out of the nature of the question, and as such have served as guides to engineers in the practice of their profession. As they have stood besides the test of long experience, it is safe to follow them, whilst at the same time the engineer should not hesitate to vary from them when satisfied, after careful examination, that the case before him requires it. Fortification, it must be remembered, is like all other arts: it has its canons, which are founded upon the nature of the question, and its rules of practice based upon these and upon experience. As the latter presents to the engineer new facts, his practice must be made to conform to them; but the general principles of his art must ever remain the same, and be his invariable guide.

III.

OPEN DEFENCES.

15. By this term are understood the dispositions made for the action of the troops and armament which afford cover only from the direct fire of the assailant.

To this class belong the arrangement of the parapet which has already been described; simple *loop-holed walls* for musketry used as inclosures of gorges. detached scarps, etc.; *exterior corridors* which are covered either by a wall or an earthen parapet; and *barbettes and embrasures* for artillery.

16. Loop-Holed Walls. Walls of this class, when used as the inclosures of the gorges of lunettes or other isolated works, placed in advance of the enceinte, but within the reach of its artillery fire, should be high enough to secure the work from an open assault, and sufficiently thick to resist the occasional shot which may reach them over the parapet by which they are covered. For these purposes the height, Plate 4, Fig. 24, should be from 12 to 15 feet, and the thickness from 4 to 5 feet. The loop-holes are not placed nearer to each other than from 3 to 4 feet, estimated between their axes. They should be at least 6 feet above the exterior foot of the wall, and $4\frac{1}{2}$ feet above the ground or banquette within. The loop-holes are usually placed at regular intervals along the line of the wall, or only opposite that portion of the exterior ground upon which a fire is to be brought to bear.

The form and dimensions of the loop-hole will depend upon the thickness of the wall and the field of view, both vertically and horizontally, which is to be covered by its fire. The plan is either trapezoidal, Plate 4, Figs. 17, 20, widening from the front of the wall inwards, or else it widens from the centre each way to the front and back; or, as is the more usual form in our works, the interior portion from the centre widens inwards, whilst the exterior part is rectangular in plan, and of the same width as the width on the interior or back of the wall. The first form is best adapted to walls not more than $2\frac{1}{2}$ feet thick, the others to heavier walls; the object being to lessen, as far as practicable, the weakness which loop-holes necessarily cause to the wall; this defect increasing as the exterior or interior opening is greater.

For thin walls, where the plan of the loop-hole is trapezoidal, the width of the exterior opening may be from 2 to 4 inches, and that of the interior from 15 to 18 inches. These dimensions, however, may vary according to the field of fire to be brought within the range of the loop-hole, the more or less cover to be given to the troops, and the strength of the masonry of which the wall is formed. The vertical dimensions of the loop-hole, both on the interior and the exterior, will depend upon the field of fire to be embraced in this last direction, and they will be regulated accordingly; the top and sole of the loop-hole receiving a suitable slope or direction for this purpose.

The foregoing details can only be well determined upon from the special object to which the loop-holed defences are to be applied. Care only is to be taken that in attempting to give cover to the troops their field of view be not too restricted by too narrow an opening for the use of the fire-arms.

Where the throat or narrowest part of the loop-hole is within the wall, the exterior opening leaves a wider mark for the missiles of the assailed, and when the sides of the loop-hole gradually widen outwards, a shot striking one of them may glance inward and do injury.

To prevent this accident, the sides, and sometimes the sole, are made in offsets. A more convenient form for construction, and one better adapted for arresting the enemy's balls, is to make the exterior portion rectangular in plan for half the width of the wall as already described.

The best form is a modification of this made by placing at the throat a plate of iron or steel pierced by an opening generally 2 by 5 inches.

17. Exterior Corridors. In open exterior corridors the troops are covered in front either by an earthen parapet, which is usually only musket-proof, the scarp wall being run up to the superior slope; or else the scarp wall serves as the cover, in which case it is pierced either throughout its length or at suitable points with loop-holes. The floor of the corridor, c, Plate 4, Fig. 27, serves as a banquette tread for the loop-holes, and is therefore placed with reference to the direction of the fire from the loop holes. The height to which the scarp wall rises above the floor of the corridor will depend upon the level of the floor, and that of the bottom of the ditch; this height, however, should not be less than $6\frac{1}{2}$ feet to afford a sufficient cover to the troops.

The preceding Fig. 27 is given as an example of a semi-detached scarp, A, an earthen counterscarp and covered-way, D; being a section of an outwork of one of our sea-coast forts.

18. Barbette Batteries. For guns mounted on the ordinary field and siege carriages, the barbettes are constructed in the same manner and with the same dimensions as in field-works; the arrangement of the ramps and the slopes being determined by the position in which the barbette is placed, and its relative position with respect to the terre-plein and parapet.

For the heavy guns used, both for land and sea fronts, a solid foundation of concrete and stone, with the necessary iron work, is laid to receive the gun with its carriage, and to allow it to be worked efficiently. To protect the guns against flank fire, large traverses (generally containing bomb-proof constructions) are used. These traverses are extended upon the parapet so as to form *bonnets*, affording the greatest cover consistent with a wide field of fire.

16   ELEMENTS OF PERMANENT FORTIFICATION.

Carriages have been designed which allow the gun to be lowered behind the parapet for loading, and raised above it for firing (see Plate 7).

The modifications of parapet, already referred to, to suit special carriages and guns, are very marked when this class of carriage is used, also when arrangements are made for loading the guns under cover. This cover is obtained by making bomb-proof communications and chambers, opening toward the gun, under the parapet and traverses, in which the machinery for loading the guns is placed, and which allow the ammunition to be safely carried from the magazines to the guns.

These, or similar protections, have become absolutely necessary to prevent barbette guns being silenced, if they are exposed to the close fire of small-arms and machine guns.

Where ample space exists for placing batteries of heavy guns, with considerable command, and a favorable soil, particularly for coast defence, the modification of parapet may extend even to sinking a pit for each gun and constructing bomb-proof underground communications, magazines, quarters, store-rooms, etc., for their service.

19. Embrasure Batteries. The embrasures cut in the parapets for guns on field and siege carriages differ in no essential point from those for field-works. It is well, however, to observe, as the parapet is weakened by receiving embrasures, the splay given to them should, in all cases, be carefully regulated by the field of fire it is desirable to command, so as to leave as large a mass of merlon between them as practicable, to resist the assailant's fire.

20. Machicoulis. For the purpose of attaining, by musketry, the foot of a scarp wall without flank defences, resort must be had to a machicoulated arrangement at the top of the scarp.

The usual mode adopted for this purpose, Pl. 8, Figs. 67, 68, is to form a parapet wall which rests upon a solid horizontal band of stone, near the top of the scarp, which is supported on corbels or projecting blocks, firmly built into the wall. The back of the parapet wall is placed a few inches in advance of the scarp, leaving room for the slanting loop-holes pierced in the horizontal band through which the fire is to be delivered on the foot of the scarp. The top of the parapet wall is also arranged to admit of firing on more distant points.

In the example given, which is from an Austrian authority, Fig. 67 is a front elevation, and Fig. 68 a section through a loop-hole.

Figs. 65, 66 are a front elevation and section through a loop-hole, from the same authority. This is a semi-detached scarp wall, the top portion of which is arranged on the back with loop-hole recesses; the lower portion having very inclined arched recesses in front, with slanting loop-holes to fire on the foot of the scarp from the upper recesses.

Where from the irregularity of the site the ordinary machicoulis cannot be made efficient, resort may be had to small polygonal chambers of stone, open at top, and having the sides and bottom pierced with loop-holes and machicoulis. These constructions may be made just of sufficient size to hold a single sentinel. They are placed at the angles of the works where they will not be exposed to artillery, and are supported on a corbel work projecting from the top of the scarp wall.

These devices will be rarely if ever used in works constructed in the future, since they are absolutely useless if exposed to artillery fire, and can generally be replaced by cheaper and simpler constructions, which are equally efficient upon fronts not so exposed.

IV.

COVERED DEFENCES.

21. Detached Scarp Walls. When the scarp walls are entirely detached, leaving an open corridor between them and the rampart, they are pierced with one or two tiers of loop-holes, from which a fire can be brought upon the ditch and in some cases upon the terre-plein of the covered-way, or any work in front of the enceinte.

To give cover to the men at the loop-holes arched recesses, Pl. 4, Figs. 25, 26, are made in the thickness of wall, or else short counterforts are built back from the wall, which serve as the piers of covering arches. The width of the recesses should admit of three or four loop-holes at the usual distance apart, their height and depth being sufficient to give the men shelter from vertical fire and allow them to handle their arms with convenience.

The two Figs. above are sections of this description of scarp wall taken through the crowns of the arches, as shown in an Austrian work. A is a section of the wall; B and D, elevations of the sides of the recesses; c, an elevation and section of the recess arch.

22. Semi-detached Walls, Fig. 28, are also in some cases built with recesses. Besides these, traverse walls, H, are built back from the scarp wall into the parapet, at intervals, to afford cover to troops, circulating in the corridor, from enfilading fire, and to admit of a defence of the corridor if the assailant should enter it between any two of these traverses. For this purpose they are pierced with loop-holes, and have door-ways for circulation throughout the corridor.

23. Scarp Galleries. In the permanent works of more recent construction in our own country and in Europe revetment walls with relieving arches, Pl. 4, Fig. 15, have in most cases been introduced instead of the ordinary thick walls with counterforts, which had been hitherto the usual mode of retaining the earth of the rampart and parapet.

The piers of the relieving arches, which also serve as counterforts to the revetment-wall, are rectangular in plan, and usually run back from 12 to 16 feet. They are from 4 to 6 feet thick, and placed from 12 to 18 feet apart between their centre lines. The arches are usually full centre and 2 feet thick, with a rough shaped capping which adds an additional thickness from 9 to 12 inches over the crown of the arch.

The preceding Fig. is a section of a revetment wall of this kind, of one of our forts, through the curtain in front of which is a mask of which D is the section. B is an elevation of the face of the pier; C, the relieving arch; and A, the scarp wall.

This mode of construction offers the advantages of a more stable structure and rendering it more difficult for the assailant to make a practicable breach in the wall, whilst by a suitable arrangement of the relieving arches and their piers with the earth of the rampart, a sufficient space can be secured behind the scarp wall to form a gallery for defensive purposes.

The arches and piers form the top and sides of the gallery, the scarp wall forming the front, and the back or rear being either partly or wholly closed by a wall which retains the earth behind it. The gallery is thus divided up into chambers, the communication between which is effected by doorways made through the piers.

The width and height of the gallery should in all cases be sufficient to allow the men ample room for handling their fire-arms, and to admit of a circulation through the gallery when the troops for the defence are posted in it.

From three to four loop-holes are made in the portion of the scarp wall that forms the front of each chamber. The dimensions and forms of the loop-holes are the same as already described, and they are otherwise arranged for defence as in detached scarp walls.

In Pl. 4, Fig. 16, a section of a scarp gallery constructed in one of our older forts is shown. A is the scarp wall; B the pier of the relieving arch C; D the rear wall which closes the gallery and sustains the earth behind it. The section also shows the parts of the rampart and parapet and the breast-high wall E.

In Figs. 17, 18, 19, the plan, section, and rear elevation of a gallery are shown as given in French authorities. The peculiarity of this example, Fig. 19, consists in the arrangement of the rear of the gallery, which, instead of being entirely closed by a wall, is only partly so; a small wall, a, which rests upon an arch, b, built between the two piers, is placed parallel to the back of the scarp wall and at a distance from it equal to the width of the gallery, the top of the wall being raised to the level of the surface of the earthen slope which falls in behind from the top of the arch. The section, Fig. 18, through r s, and elevation, Fig. 19, show the position of the loop-holes, and the vent for the escape of the smoke is pierced in the scarp wall just below the crown of the arch. B, are the piers; A the arches with their capping; D the doorways through the piers.

Figs. 20, 21, represent the plan and section of a scarp gallery in two tiers, as given in an Austrian work. The rear of the gallery is closed by a simple wall. Besides the vent holes for the escape of smoke, drains are made in the scarp wall at the level of the gallery floor to convey off any water that may collect in it.

Figs. 22, 23, are a plan and section, from the same authority, of a gallery behind the lower portion of the scarp wall, the upper portion being connected with relieving arches so arranged that, being open to the rear, the foot of the slope of earth will just touch the back of the wall at its foot within. In this example the pressure of the earth being supposed to be great, the gallery is closed in the rear by arched walls; the arches being built into the vertical piers B, of the relieving arches C. This example also shows the manner of barricading the doorways through the piers by vertical grooves, made in the opposite faces of the piers, to receive the scantling forming the barricade.

In Fig. 28 is shown the section of a gallery behind the lower portion of the scarp, with the upper portion arranged with recesses for loop-holes.

These same methods of construction are now adopted, with changes in dimensions resulting from the different height of scarp walls and the need of an additional depth of protection against vertical fire.

The galleries are now made, almost exclusively, one tier in height, the arches receive a thickness of 3 feet of brick or concrete and a capping of 12 to 18 inches covered with from 5 to 15 feet of earth, according to their exposure.

24. Counterscarp Galleries. Pl. 4, Fig. 35. The most simple method of arranging a gallery behind a counterscarp wall for the defence of a ditch is to build another wall parallel to that of the counterscarp, and to throw an arch over between the two to cover the top of the gallery. The counterscarp wall is pierced with loop-holes arranged in the same way as in scarp galleries.

The example selected is from one of our works, and shows a section of the gallery through a loop-hole. A, counterscarp wall ; D, parallel wall ; C, arch and capping ; E, glacis mask covering the scarp wall.

In Figs. 29, 30, 31, are shown a plan, section on $r\ s$, and a section and interior elevation on $o\ p$, of a counterscarp gallery taken from a French authority. In this case counterforts, square in plan, are built along the back of the counterscarp wall, leaving 8 feet between them. Parallel to the counterscarp wall and 4 feet in rear of the counterforts another wall is built, which, with the counterforts, serves as the support of a series of arches perpendicular to the counterscarp wall sprung between the counterforts, and another parallel to it and resting on the counterforts and parallel wall. The arches between the counterforts form with them recesses, A, for the men serving the loop-holes pierced in the counterscarp wall ; whilst the covered space, B, in rear serves for circulation without disturbing the men engaged in firing.

Counterscarp galleries may also be arranged for a ditch defence with artillery ; howitzers, rapid-firing and machine guns are used for this purpose. A plan, Fig. 32, a vertical section and side elevation on D C, Fig. 33 ; and a section and back elevation on A B, Fig. 34, taken from one of our works, show a disposition of this kind in the reëntering angle of the counterscarp.

25. Bastionnets. In small works, where a flanking disposition cannot be obtained from the enceinte, as in lunettes and redoubts, the ditches may be swept by covered chambers, Pl. 5, Fig. 39, attached to the scarp wall either at the centre of the sides of the work, or at the angles.

These chambers, Pl. 5, Fig. 39, are usually of a pentagonal form, the sides which join the scarp wall serving to flank it, and the two exterior sides, forming a salient angle, delivering their fire on the opposite counterscarp and its crest. From their form and purposes they have received the name of bastionnets.

The dimensions of these constructions will depend upon the amount and kind of fire to be delivered. Their scarps should be as high as that of the main work. The entrance to them is either directly from a parade by a postern, or from a scarp gallery which flanks them.

Fig. 39 shows a plan of bastionnet, D, at an angle communicating with a scarp gallery, E. In rear of the scarp gallery and opposite to the bastionnet, is placed a small powder-magazine for its service. The example is from an Austrian authority, and is arranged for one small gun on each flank, besides the loop-holes for small-arms.

As a general rule, it may be laid down that the salient angles of the redoubt are the most suitable positions for the bastionnets, as they will thus form small bastioned fronts, in which both the faces of the main work and those of the bastionnets will be swept by the flanks of the latter. The only danger in this arrangement is that the loop-holes in one flank may be fired into from the opposite one. This, however, may be guarded against by a suitable position given to the loop-holes.

As the main object of covered defences is protection against shells, it is essential that the arches of the galleries and bastionnets should be bomb-proof. The thickness previously given is generally thought necessary, but where the span of the arch is very small the thickness of the brick may be reduced to 2 feet.

With regard to the front walls of these constructions, as they are too weak to withstand the direct action of artillery, they must either be covered by earthen masks, as a glacis raised beyond the counterscarp for example, or be used only in positions where they are not exposed to this fire.

General Remarks. It should be observed that whatever advantages covered defences afford as shelter from the assailant's fire, they present the inconveniences of a comparatively narrow and obstructed field of view to the assailed, which is further obscured by the smoke which may gather within the gallery, and in front of the loop-holes. From these causes the assailed having to aim at a venture, his fire is likely to be less effective than in open defences, where the smoke disperses rapidly and leaves a clear field of view. The same may be said of loop-holed walls covering exterior corridors where the space to the rear is confined.

Owing to these considerations, loop-hooled and covered defences of the kind in question should be restricted to special defensive purposes, where an object within the field of fire can be attained with some certainty whether seen or not by the assailed; as, for example, the protection of a ditch, or a scarp wall which cannot be flanked from within the work; for sweeping a covered-way, or the interior of any outwork which cannot be brought well under the fire of the parapet of the main work.

26. Caponnière Defences for the Enceinte Ditch. These works are classed under the head of what are termed *defensive casemates*, which are bomb-proof arched structures for receiving cannon, firing through embrasures pierced in the front or mask wall of the casemates. Defences of this class, when used to flank the ditch, are usually termed *casemated caponnières*.

These defences are usually placed in the ditch at the middle point of the side or front to be flanked. The outline of their plan is mostly that of a lunette, Pl. 5, Fig. 36, the flanks being perpendicular to the line of the scarp, and the two faces making a salient angle of 60°. The caponnière is either built in juxtaposition with the enceinte, or else detached from it. In the latter case an inclosure is formed between the two by a loop-holed wall which connects the flanks with the scarp wall. Each flank consists of one or two tiers of arched chambers, the piers of the arches being perpendicular to the back of the walls of the flank. Each chamber is of sufficient dimensions for the service of a single gun with a contracted field of fire. (Pl. 5, Figs. 36, 37.) In some cases loop-holes are pierced for small-arms on each side of the embrasure; in others the casemates of one story are pierced for cannon, and the other for small-arms.

The casemates are closed in rear by a thin wall, which is provided with windows for light and ventilation; and the piers are pierced with doorways to form a communication between the chambers and to assist the ventilation. Flues

ELEMENTS OF PERMANENT FORTIFICATION. 23

or vents, Fig. 37, are made in the front wall, just under the arches, for a like purpose. Where it may be necessary, the lower floor is drained by a conduit through the front wall.

An open court is left between the flanks, and each flank is covered at top with from 6 to 12 feet of earth. The flanks are separated from the faces by a closed corridor which serves as a communication.

In front of the corridor and on each side of the axis of the caponnière on second floor, a casemated chamber, which is open in front, is arranged for one mortar, Figs. 36, 38. The arches of these chambers rise towards the front the better to subserve the object in view.

On one side of the chambers on first floor the powder magazine is placed, with a store-room. On the other side a stairway between the stories is built.

The space within the salient angle, inclosed by the walls of the faces and the front of the mortar casemates, is open at top. It has an open corridor on the second story for communication, and the front walls are arranged with loop-holed recesses for small-arms, Figs. 36, 38.

The enceinte, in the rear of the flanks of the caponnière, is arranged with a scarp gallery, to flank the caponnière flanks and the court between them. A break is in some cases made in the line of the scarp wall, perpendicular to the caponnière faces, and casements for cannon and small-arms arranged behind the scarp wall, to flank these faces. In some cases these flanking dispositions are placed in front of the scarp wall, the casements being open to the rear, looking on a narrow court between them and the scarp which is closed on the sides by a loop-holed wall.

The example here given of a casemated caponnière is from an Austrian authority. Fig. 36 is the plan; Fig. 37, a section and elevation on AB of one flank, and the end wall of the corridor looking towards the court between the flanks; Fig. 38, a section and elevation along c′ d′ of the corridor, mortar casemate, and triangular court. Figs. 37, 38, are on an enlarged scale.

This construction, if subject to artillery fire, as it will be in the close attack, is readily destroyed. It is valuable only to resist escalade or assault in the early stages of the attack.

To preserve it in condition to be effective for the last stages of the defence has been the study of the advocates of the polygonal system.

The latest forms differ from that described in having but one tier of casemates, covered with earth which may be arranged as a parapet, or simply as a protection to the arches. The face wall of the casemates is protected from fire by being set back so far from the heads of the arches, that a shot coming from the crest of the glacis and passing just under the crown of the arch will strike the ground below the embrasure. (Plate 1, Fig. 7.)

This requires, when the exterior side is great, an arch of considerable length, which by retaining the smoke of discharge obstructs the view, and interferes with the ventilalation of the caponnière.

This difficulty is alleviated by leaving an opening between the face wall and the tunnel-shaped arches for the escape of smoke, and shielding the face wall by giving additional height to the earth cover of the tunnel arches. (Plate 1, Fig. 8.)

When these arches are subject to accurate battering fire the *débris* from their heads will obstruct the fire of the caponnière guns, and when the heads are battered away the face wall will be easily breached and rendered useless. The advantage of the new over the old form consists in adding to the time necessary for the reduction of the work.

For important works which justify the expense, armored caponnières, either stationary or revolving turrets, are proposed. Their faces may be of sufficient strength to withstand the besieger's guns, or they may be raised to work their guns and lowered in a pit to shield them from fire. Their tops can only be struck obliquely in either case. They will be more fully described hereafter.

27. Casemates on Land Fronts. Various modes have, from time to time, been proposed for arranging defensive casemates for the exterior defence of land fronts. The difficulty in covering the masonry from the batteries of the assailant has been the chief objection to these structures, and is the more prominent as the fire of artillery becomes more accurate, as such casemates would soon be ruined or rendered untenable by embrasure shots.

The Haxo casemate, named from its designer, Gen. Haxo, has been extensively used. These casemates consist (Plate 6, Figs. 45, 46, 47, 48, and 49) of a series of arched bombproof chambers closed in front by a thin mask wall which, except around the embrasures through it, is covered from the assailant's artillery by the parapet. To present but a small surface of masonry to fire, the arches, which are horizontal and perpendicular to the mask wall for the greater portion of their length, descend towards the front, leaving where they join the mask wall just sufficient height within for the service of the gun. To effect this the anterior portion of the arch must be conoidal in shape.

The piers of the arches are pierced with wide arched openings which serve the double purpose of a communication between the casemates and to give the gun a wider traverse for firing.

Embrasures are pierced in the parapet in prolongation of those of the mask wall, and it is proposed to cover the small portion of the masonry necessarily exposed by this arrangement by placing several thicknesses of heavy timber in front of it to receive the shot, or to case it with wrought-iron.

When the casemates serve simply for the cover of the cannon, the arches are covered with from 4 to 6 feet thickness of earth, and are left open to the rear for the more prompt escape of the smoke, and a ditch is sometimes made just in rear of the casemates to catch bombs and limit the effects of their explosion. When the arches are made longer than for the service of the guns alone, the earthen covering is sometimes arranged with a parapet to cover cannon in barbette, or for small-arms.

The example shown by the Figs. is from a French authority. Fig. 45 is a plan on m n, Fig. 47; Fig. 46 a section and interior elevation towards the mask wall on o p, Fig. 47; and Fig. 47 a section and side elevation on r s, Figs. 45, 46.

In Figs. 48, 49 is shown an arrangement of two casemates of the Haxo kind from an Austrian authority. In this case the masonry is covered on the flanks from enfilading fire by earth. Fig. 48 is an interior elevation of the arches, and the back wall that retains the earth on the sides. Fig. 49 is a longitudinal section, and shows the manner of covering the masonry in front and securing the earthen embrasure by a timber facing.

The attempt to remedy the defects of the Haxo casemate by strengthening the face wall with iron and removing the objectionable embrasure in the earthen parapet has led to the development of the iron and steel constructions which are applied to sea-coast works, but which have been used more sparingly on land fronts owing to their great expense and the difficulty of finding a metal which will resist long-continued direct battering. The latter difficulty may be overcome by the use of inclined armor.

28. Mortar Casemates. In Fig. 50, Pl. 6, is shown a longitudinal section of a mortar casemate placed in rear of a parapet, by which it is covered from direct fire. The arch is covered, as in the preceding case, by earth, to break the shock of shells. It rises towards the front to give ample room for the shell in its flight. The casemates are covered on their flanks from enfilading fire by an embankment, and are partly closed by a wall in the rear. A small ditch is made in front of the chamber, and a slight wall built within it, to give cover from the splinters of shells falling between the parapet and the casemate. Arched chambers are in some cases made beneath the mortar chambers which serve as store-rooms and temporary magazines.

When these casemates are placed in rear of a portion of the parapet but little exposed to direct fire, the thickness of the parapet in front of them may be reduced, and the interior slope be replaced by a breast-high wall along the front of the casemates, in order to give better cover in flank and from slant fire, by throwing forward the casemates more under cover of the parapet.

The example given is from the same authority as in the preceding example of casemated caponnières.

On faces exposed to plunging fire this casemate must be lowered so that its arch is protected by the parapet from projectiles passing over it.

29. Casemates for Water Fronts. In the casemated batteries for sea-coast and harbor defences, the scarp or mask walls of the chambers for the guns, being exposed to the fire of ships alone, are not subject to the accurate breaching fire which land fronts may be called upon to sustain. Masonry walls could be built strong enough to resist single shots from the ships' guns in use prior to about 1865–70. Under these conditions were built our existing casemated masonry forts, whose details are shown in Plates 5 and 6, Figs. 40 to 44, inclusive.

With the increase in the power of ships' guns these walls are easily penetrated, and they are no longer effective as a defence. No modifications of these works have been made in this country; but in some English and Continental forts the masonry fronts of the gun chambers only have been replaced by iron shields, leaving the rest of the scarp wall of masonry (a construction of doubtful value), and in others the entire scarp wall has been built of iron, the original masonry of the interior of the work only being retained.

In the newer casemated works, which are made with one tier of artillery fire, the parts exposed to fire are of iron or steel, the thickness of which is determined by the intensity and greater or less obliquity of the blow to which they are liable to be subjected.

30. Turrets. The field of fire from casemates being limited, and the exposure to hostile fire of the embrasures and muzzles of the guns while loading objectionable, revolving turrets have been adapted to fortifications to remedy these defects.

Turrets are particularly valuable for sites exposed to fire from all sides, as by their construction they occupy little space, give protection against plunging and reverse as well as front fire. They command a wide field of fire, are incommoded by smoke no more than open defences, and lend themselves to the use of the best possible appliances for loading and working their guns. For fortifications, their weight (which is objectionable on ships) is an advantage when they are struck by heavy projectiles. The principal objection to them is the great cost not only of the turret itself, but of the machinery for working it and of the substructure.

They have been made in the form of a vertical cylinder or a truncated cone with a flat top, an oblate spheroid, with the embrasures just above the equatorial circumference and a spherical segment with the embrasures pierced horizontally through the dome-shaped top.

The first forms have the advantage of an easy mechanical construction with either rolled or forged plates, and the disadvantage that they may be struck in a direction nearly or quite normal to the surface.

The spheroid can only be made of cast metal.

The dome can be made of wrought-iron, steel, or compound plates.

The last two forms can only be struck obliquely by direct fire. More detailed descriptions of some of these will be given farther on.

31. Embrasures. The form, dimensions, and construction of embrasures in mask walls present a problem which has offered to engineers no little difficulty in finding a satisfactory solution by which the best cover could be given to the guns and men by exposing the least surface to embrasure shots, whilst the guns should receive a suitable traverse to command a wide field of fire.

The most perfect type of masonry embrasure was that used in the latest casemates constructed in this country; it was designed by General Totten, of the U. S. Engineers, and is known by his name. It is shown in Plate 8, Figs. 61, 62, 63, and 64.

In iron construction, the problem is more simple, and has been solved in several ways, all having in view the greatest field of fire with the smallest opening. This object is best accomplished by pivoting the gun, for both horizontal and vertical movement, as nearly as possible at the centre of the embrasure.

When the gun is allowed to recoil, the carriage must be so constructed as to allow it to move back without jamming in the embrasure. Some of the most recently devised carriages hold the gun in position and prevent recoil by suitable strong recoil bars and arcs, and secure the muzzle in the embrasure either with a ring and trunnions (Grüson's method), or by a spherical enlargement on the gun and corresponding socket in the embrasure (Krupp).

In others the recoil is prevented by the direct resistance of the pintle or platform. The muzzle of the gun should project in all cases not less than one foot beyond the embrasure; frequently it projects much more.

In revolving turrets the gun needs no horizontal traverse, and can be worked in an embrasure of the Grüson pattern, whose height is about once and a half the diameter of the gun at the embrasure, and whose breadth is about two inches greater than this diameter.

The guns are aimed by sights on the chase, by sighting through the bore, by peep holes over the embrasure, or by sights placed on top of the turret or casemate. All the guns of a battery are sometimes pointed by using fixed horizontal and vertical arcs properly graduated, and pointers attached to the gun; the sighting being done by the use of a sight-bar or telescope mounted on a suitable lookout, and provided with an arc and pointer, whose readings, properly corrected for parallax and tabulated, give for each gun its correct pointing.

32. Bomb-proof Buildings. Casemated bomb-proof quarters are indispensable to the safety and comfort of the garrison during siege, or any prolonged attack for the annoyance or reduction of the work by a bombardment. In some cases advantage is taken of a scarp wall, on a land front, which is well covered by a glacis or other face cover to form in its rear quarters of this character. In others they are made under the terre-plein and traverses where their entrances and face-walls are not exposed to fire; and when sufficient room cannot be obtained in these places constructions similar to traverses may be built to cover additional space. The arches to resist splinters only may be 3 feet thick, covered with 6 feet of earth. If subject to a fire of "torpedo shells," Brialmont recommends a thickness of arch of from 6 to 10 feet. Whenever the plan of the work admits of it, quarters of this kind should be arranged for defence, by being pierced with loop-holes and even with embrasures for cannon. Defensive casemated quarters and keeps have formed a prominent feature in the German school of permanent fortifications, but where retained, they will be modified so as to expose no masonry to artillery fire, and will serve only as quarters, and as a last defence and refuge for the garrison when the work is stormed. Some modern forts have been built without keeps. A fulfilment of the conditions requisite to a strong defence, however, requires that the interior of the work be swept by the fire from galleries and casemates into which the garrison may retire when the parapet of the work is carried either by surprise or assault. This last defence may drive out the assailants and preserve the work. It will in any case afford the garrison an opportunity to surrender without the great losses which follow a successful assault upon an open work. Besides, it will add largely to the *morale* of the garrison, and lead them to hold the parapet longer than they would without it.

33. Powder Magazine. Powder magazines, when practicable, should be placed below the surface of the ground, and should never be exposed to the direct fire of the enemy. The structures for this purpose are built with strong, full centre bomb-proof brick arches, supported on heavy stone piers which form the outward walls, and to which interior buttresses are sometimes added. The capping of the arches is covered with from 10 to 16 feet of solidly packed earth. The interior of the magazine, the floors, and the doors and windows are built with a view to security from fire; and to preserve the powder from dampness, by a good system of drainage around the foundations, and of ventilation by means of air-holes made through the piers, and panels of copper pierced with small holes placed in the doors. No iron or steel fastening or sheeting is allowed in any part of the structure; and in arranging the air-holes through the piers they receive a broken direction, and have a copper mesh-work placed across them, to prevent any combustible material, or rats or mice, penetrating to the interior of the magazine.

In large works the magazines are isolated as far as practicable from the enceinte, so as not to endanger it should an accidental explosion take place. The magazine is enclosed by a strong high wall for security, and is provided with lightning-rods. In small works they are placed in the position least exposed to the assailant's fire, and given the greatest amount of cover which can be obtained.

V.

COMMUNICATIONS.

34. General Remarks. The communications form a very important element in the defence of permanent works. The size and disposition of the communications should vary with the character of the work in which they are placed.

In small works, which from the size of their garrisons are calculated to make only a strictly passive defence, communications of just sufficient dimensions for the passage of the troops from point to point will serve every purpose, and can be more easily barricaded and otherwise defended.

But for large works having full garrisons, the communications should be such that sorties of all arms and in large bodies can be quickly made. With communications of this character a besieging force would be constrained to adopt extraordinary measures of safety, keeping large guards in the trenches to secure them from such sorties, to which they would be continually exposed.

35. All communications, to serve properly their ends, should fulfil the following conditions:

1. *They should never, from their position, compromise the safety of the enceinte.*

Frequent instances could be cited of works which have been surprised by an enemy obtaining possession of the gates. Therefore too many precautions cannot be taken to secure the principal outlet from the body of the place from similar attempts.

2. *They should admit of a convenient circulation of the besieged.*

To subserve this purpose, the dimensions, slopes, etc., of the posterns, ramps, and other similar works, should be convenient for the service to which they are applied, and they should be placed in such positions as lead directly to the point to be arrived at.

3. *The position chosen for any communication should be*

ELEMENTS OF PERMANENT FORTIFICATION. 31

such that when an enemy gets possession of it, he may obtain no advantage by it.

To be useless to an enemy, the communication, when in his possession, should not offer a shelter for his works; nor enable him to carry them on with more ease. This end will be obtained by placing the communications in a position to be enfiladed by the fire of the works in their rear, and so arranging them as to preserve the counterscarp wall unbroken.

4. *The communications should be covered from every point where an enemy might establish himself, during the whole period that they can be of service to the besieged; and they should be swept by the fire of the enceinte.*

Without these precautions, an enemy might cut off all communication from the enceinte with the outworks; and in case of retreat, the troops could not derive any assistance from the enceinte, if he attempted to press upon them.

5. *They should be so placed as not to compromise the retreat of the troops.*

This is effected by placing the communication in the reënterings, which are the most secure points; as an enemy to arrive at them will have to brave a powerful column of flank fire. Barriers, gates, and movable bridges of timber should be placed at suitable points, to cut off one communication from another; and thus arrest the progress of a pursuing enemy.

6. *Finally, each work should be independent of every communication, except that one destined for its particular use.*

If this condition be not fulfilled, a work may sometimes be captured by an enemy obtaining possession of a communication passing through it, but designed for the service of some other work.

36. Ramps. The principal communications consist of *ramps, stairs, posterns, gateways, bridges,* and, for wet ditches, *dikes.* The width of ramps at top for the service of the artillery and other vehicles may be from 10 to 15 feet, and their inclination from $\frac{1}{6}$ to $\frac{1}{15}$, or less, depending on the difference of level to be overcome. They are usually placed in positions where they will occupy the least room on the parade, as along the rampart slope of the enceinte. As a general rule, their side slopes are of earth; but where it is desirable to economize room on the parade, the side slopes are replaced on one or both sides by a wall which sustains the earth of the ramp. When ramps serve for infantry alone their width may be reduced to 6 feet, and in some cases to 4 feet.

37. Stairs. Except for temporary purposes, stairs are constructed of stone; each step being a solid block which is 6 feet long in the clear; its breadth at top or the tread 12 inches, and its height or rise 8 inches. Stairs are usually placed along the counterscarp and gorge walls of the outworks, forming a communication, for infantry only, between the ditch and the terre-plein of the work to which they lead. They are also used within the enceinte in positions where there is not sufficient room for ramps, where bomb-proof cover is required, or where, for greater security from surprise, it is desirable to present a narrower and more difficult defile to the assailant. In cases where room is wanting, and the communication not in habitual use, the width of the stair may be reduced to 4 feet.

38. Posterns. Posterns are arched bomb-proof passageways constructed under the terre-pleins and ramparts, forming subterranean communications between the parade and the enceinte ditch, or between the ditches and the interior of the outworks. The width and height of the interior of posterns depend upon the use to which the communication is to be applied. For artillery the width is usually taken at 10 feet, and the height under the crown or key of the arch at least 8 feet. Posterns for infantry may be only from 6 to 4 feet wide, and from 6 feet 6 inches to 8 feet high under the crown of the arch. The thickness of the piers of the arches is generally taken at about half the width of the postern. The arches are from 2 to 3 feet thick. As any injury to the arch from the bursting of a shell over it might obstruct the communication, the arch should be covered with a thickness of earth sufficient to thoroughly protect it. A strong wooden door is placed at each outlet of the postern to secure it against surprise. The doorway in posterns for the service of artillery should be of just sufficient height for the convenient passage of a gun; about 7 feet for each dimension is usually allowed for this purpose.

The most important postern is the one leading from the parade to the enceinte ditch. This generally receives a width of 12 feet and the same height under the crown. For greater security from surprise, its outlet at the enceinte ditch is at least 6 feet above the bottom of the ditch, this difference of level being overcome by means of a temporary wooden ramp which receives an inclination of at least $\frac{1}{6}$. With a like object, besides two strong doors at the two ends of the postern, there is a partition of masonry about midway between the two ends, which is pierced with a doorway of the same size as the doorways of the ends, and closed by a strong door which, as well as the partition wall, is loop-holed for musketry.

In cases where the postern forms the main entrance to the work, an arched chamber is placed on one side of it, at the outlet, which serves as a guard-room for a few men, to secure the outlet from surprise. The wall between this chamber and the postern is loop-holed, so that a fire can be brought to bear on the doorway of the postern; and as a further precaution against surprise a machicoulis defence is sometimes arranged at the top of the scarp wall just above the doorway of the postern.

39. Gateway. In works with large garrisons, where the means of frequent communication with the exterior are requisite, posterns of ordinary dimensions are found not to afford a sufficient convenience for the daily wants. In such cases a passage-way of sufficient width to admit of at least a single carriage-road with narrow foot-paths on each side has to be opened through the rampart, which, whenever it is practicable to do so, should be arched and covered with earth to render it bomb-proof. The passage-way should for security have the bottom of its outlet at least twelve feet above the bottom of the enceinte ditch; and when this difference of level cannot be obtained the main ditch should be deepened sufficiently for the purpose below the outlet. A gateway of sufficient height and width for the passage of the ordinary vehicles for the service of the garrison is made through the scarp-wall. This gateway is arched at top, where a machicoulis defence may also be arranged to guard the outlet on the exterior.

The communication across the enceinte ditch leading from the gateway is usually an ordinary wooden bridge built on piles. The bay of this bridge at the gateway is spanned by a drawbridge of timber, which when drawn up closes and secures the gateway. This drawbridge is manœuvred by some of the usual mechanisms employed for this purpose.

40. Port-Cullis. When the gateway is not preceded by a ditch, and is therefore without a drawbridge, a barrier, termed a *port-cullis*, which can be lowered or raised vertically by machinery, is sometimes added to secure the passage-way from surprise. The ancient port-cullis was a framework of heavy beams, placed vertically, leaving a few inches only between each pair of beams. These vertical beams were either solidly confined between horizontal beams, or clamping-pieces in pairs; or else they were so arranged that they could slide upwards between the clamping-pieces. Each of the vertical beams was shod at the bottom with a strong-pointed iron shoe. The horizontal pieces were framed securely with two heavy vertical beams that formed the sides of the frame. and were fitted into vertical grooves made in the side walls of the passage-way in which the frame could slide when raised or lowered. By arranging the vertical beams to slide upwards between the clamping pieces, it enabled the passage-way to be closed in cases where an obstruction might be designedly placed below the port-cullis to prevent this being done; as the beams which meet the obstruction would be pushed upwards, whilst the others would fall to their ordinary level and close the passage-way on each side of the obstruction.

In the works recently constructed with us the port-cullis, and even the doors preceding them have, been constructed of a strong open lattice-work of wrought-iron bars bolted strongly to the wrought-iron uprights and cross pieces, forming the framework of the lattice. This is a great improvement for these purposes, both as to durability and defence.

Passage-ways of this description should be secured by all the means at an engineer's disposal. A large guard-room, with loop-holes bearing on the passage, should be erected on one side, near the gateway; and if the enceinte is a simple one, without outworks beyond its ditch, a small lunette, or redan, should be constructed beyond the counterscarp, forming a tête-de-pont, for the security of the bridge from surprise. and which in connection with the glacis protects it from artillery and infantry fire.

The drawbridge, which for convenience of manœuvring should not be longer than 12 feet, is constructed in the usual mode.

When passages through the ramparts are provided for railroads, the necessary openings are made, the ditch is crossed by a bridge, usually arched or of iron, with a draw span, and all possible precautions are taken to prevent these openings from becoming weak points in the defence.

VI.

ENCEINTES.

41. The most simple mode of fortifying a position in a permanent manner consists in inclosing it with a rampart surmounted by a parapet, with a ditch the scarp of which when dry is revetted with masonry, and so covered by an earthen mask that it cannot be breached except by batteries placed on the border of the counterscarp.

This line of fortification enclosing the position is termed the *enceinte*, the *body of the place* or the *main inclosure*.

The general outline of the enceinte may be *curvilinear*, or a *polygonal figure* of any character.

42. System of Fortification. Although an infinite diversity of figures may thus be presented in the outline or plan of the enceinte, they may all be classed under four heads, to each of which engineers generally have applied the term *system of fortification*.

These four classes are, 1, the *circular* or *curvilinear system*; 2, the *polygonal* or *caponnière system*; 3, the *tenailled system*; 4, the *bastioned system*.

The term *method of fortification* is now usually applied to the manner of fortifying which is generally prevalent in any country; or to the mode adopted by any individual, as the *German method; Vauban's method*, etc.

Circular System. The circular system consists of an enceinte, the plan of which is circular or curvilinear.

Polygonal System. In the polygonal system the plan is either a polygon with salient angles alone, Pl. 8, Fig. 72, each side of which, A A, is flanked by a casemated caponnière, C, placed in the ditch, D, and midway between the two salients, A; or else each side of the polygon is broken inwards at the centre, so as to form a slight reëntering, Pl. 8, Figs. 73, 74, 75, 76. 77, to procure a casemated flanking arrangement, F F, for the caponnières, C, which occupy these reënterings, and also, in some cases, to flank works in advance of the enceinte.

Tenailled System. The tenailled system, Pl. 8, Fig. 78, consists of a tenailled line, the reëntering angles of which are between 90° and 100°, and the salient angles not less than 60°.

Bastioned System. In the bastioned system, Fig. 79, the bastion usually consists of two faces and two flanks, the scarps of each of which are plane surfaces.

In many of the older fortifications, and in a few of the more recent works in Europe, the flank is broken; the portion of it at the shoulder angle forming a projecting mass which is termed an *orillon*, whilst the portion between the orillon and the enceinte curtain is retired, or brought in towards the interior of the bastion, and is thus partially covered by the orillon from fire, except in the prolongation of the enceinte ditch. In some cases the plan of the orillon as well as that of the retired flank is curvilinear; in others they are both rectilinear.

43. General Remarks. Whatever system may be adopted for the enceinte, there are certain conditions, in addition to those already laid down for all permanent works, which it must satisfy to render it effective:

1. *It should have a steep revetted scarp; unbroken on all sides except for the necessary openings for communications; thoroughly flanked throughout by cannon and small-arms; and of sufficient height to prevent all ordinary attempts at escalade.*

2. *The scarp should be so covered by earthen or other masks that it cannot be reached by the projectiles of an assailant from any position exterior to these masks.*

3. *The parapet and interior covered shelters should be proof against solid and hollow loaded projectiles.*

4. *The parapet should command all the site and outworks exterior to the enceinte and within range of its guns, and sweep them with front, flank, and cross-fires when possible.*

5. *As far as practicable, the principal lines of the parapet should receive such directions, that the assailant cannot take up positions to enfilade them.*

Every enceinte, whatever be the system adopted, will be more or less effective as these conditions are more or less complied with in its arrangement.

VII.

OUTWORKS.

44. A work consisting of an enceinte alone is more or less exposed to surprise, as it must have outlets of some

·description to keep up a communication with the exterior, and a bridge, or other means for crossing the ditch.

But this is not the only defect of a fortification of this simple character; for having no covers beyond the ditch for its garrison, their action must be restricted to what may be termed a passive resistance alone; in any attempt to operate on the exterior, they are exposed to fire as soon as they emerge from the ditch, and in a retreat towards the work, if closely pursued by the assailant, they will not only run the risk of being cut off, but a retreat under such circumstances may lead to the capture of the work itself, by the assailant being enabled to enter it with the retreating force.

To provide against dangers of so grave a character, engineers have devised other defences beyond the ditch, and which they have placed in immediate defensive relations with the enceinte, being under its fire, and in positions where, if assaulted, they can be readily succored by the garrison. To this class of exterior defences the term *outworks* has been applied.

From their position, exterior to the enceinte, and from their angular form, so as to be flanked by it, the outworks, with the enceinte, form salient and reëntering parts, which are very favorable to the security of sortie parties in retiring; and as, if properly arranged, the assailant must take them in succession, they will greatly prolong the defence, by forcing him to a great development of his trenches; through which, in some of the positions he will be obliged to occupy, he will be the enveloped party. Besides this, he will be obliged to establish breach batteries against each work in succession—always a difficult and perilous task.

45. The outworks should satisfy the following conditions to render them effective and secure:

1. *They should have revetted scarps of sufficient height to secure them from any ordinary open assault.*

2. *As far as practicable their scarps should be flanked by the enceinte, and be masked from the positions of the assailant's batteries.*

3. *Their parapets and covered shelters should be shot-proof.*

4. *Those which are most retired should command those in advance; and whenever this cannot be done, the retired work should be defiled from the one in advance by which it is commanded.*

5. *In any combination of outworks the dispositions*

should be such that the more advanced ones shall fall into the hands of the assailant before he will be able to gain possession of the more retired.

6. *The communications should be ample, and satisfy the general conditions for these elements.*

46. The works which come under this head are the *covered-way*, the *tenaille*, the *demi-lune*, the *counterguard*, the *redoubt* or *réduit*, the *tenaillon*, the *horn-work*, and the *crown-work*.

47. Covered-Way. The covered-way, as its name imports, is an open corridor or passage, masked from the assailant's view by an embankment, which borders the ditch of the enceinte alone when there are no other outworks; but, in the contrary case, also envelops the ditches of these, forming thus a continuous covered line of communication around the fortification.

The covering embankment itself is arranged towards the covered-way like an ordinary parapet, and it receives on the exterior a gentle slope or glacis.

By this arrangement the garrison have a covered position beyond the ditch where they can assemble with safety either for the purpose of making a sortie, or to guard the ditches and the communications across them; and which affords them also a secure point of retreat if repulsed in a sortie, as a reserve left in the covered-way will be at hand to check the pursuit by their fire, and enable the retreating party to gain the enceinte.

48. Places-of-Arms. The covered-way from the direction given to the counterscarps of the enceinte and outworks, forms a line of communication with salient and reëntering parts, Pls. 8, 9, Figs. 80 to 85.

The salient portions, s, are termed *salient places-of-arms;* and the reëntering parts the *reëntering places-of-arms*.

The salient places-of-arms, it will be seen, result from the general plan of the covered-way; but the reëntering places-of-arms are formed by changing the directions of the two branches where they form the reënterings, R, so as to make a salient within the reënterings; thus enlarging the covered-way at these points and producing a flanking arrangement, by which the glacis can be swept, and a cross-fire be brought to bear on the ground in advance of the salients.

49. Traverses. The covered-way, from its position, and the usually slight command given to the crest of its glacis, is very much exposed to the effects of an enfilading fire.

With a view to remedy this defect, and also to enable the garrison to dispute foot by foot the possession of this outwork by the assailant, earthen masks, formed like an ordinary parapet and termed *traverses*, are thrown up across it. The traverses usually extend to the counterscarp, the wall of which is built up to sustain them.

At the end, towards the glacis, a passage, or defile, is left between them and the covering embankment, to admit of a free communication throughout the covered-way.

50. Tenaille. The tenaille is a low work placed in the reëntering formed in the enceinte ditch by the curtain and flanks of the bastioned system, being isolated by a ditch between it and these parts of the enceinte. Its chief purpose is to serve as a mask, covering the scarp walls of this reëntering from fire, as well as the outlets to the enceinte ditch, which are usually placed in the centre of the curtains.

The tenaille has received various forms from engineers. In some cases it has been made with two faces or wings, making a reëntering angle opposite the centre of the enceinte curtain. In others the two wings, instead of being prolonged until they meet, are connected by a short curtain parallel to that of the enceinte. In some examples it has the form of a small bastioned front. In others it consists of two flanks connected by a curtain. These flanks in some cases have been casemated for guns and mortars. The tenaille is usually revetted with masonry both in front and rear. In some cases the ends alone, towards the flanks of the enceinte, are revetted, the intermediate portions consisting of an ordinary earthen parapet without either scarp or gorge wall.

51. Demi-lune. The demi-lune. Pl. 9, Figs. 81, 82, 83, 84, is a work in the form of a redan, D, placed in front of the enceinte curtain, which it masks from fire, as well as a portion of each face of the enceinte, at the shoulder angles of the bastions. It is isolated from the enceinte by the main ditch. From its importance the scarp and gorge of the demi-lune are generally revetted, though in some cases the revetment has been omitted.

This work is also called the *ravelin*.

52. Counterguard. The counterguard is an isolated work, c, Fig. 80, in the form of a redan, which envelops the faces of a bastion or other salient. In some cases it consists simply of an earthen mask having the profile of an ordinary parapet; but it is usually revetted both in front and rear.

53. Redoubts. The term redoubt, or *réduit*, is applied to outworks placed within other outworks; their object being to strengthen the defence of the principal work.

A work of this class is usually placed within the demi-lune, and is termed the *demi-lune redoubt*. Small works of this kind are also placed in the salient and reëntering places-of-arms of the covered-way, and are termed the *redoubt of the salient, or reëntering place of-arms*. These redoubts are in some cases simple earthen works; in others they are revetted; and in others casemated both for the service of artillery and small-arms.

54. Tenaillon. The term tenaillon, Pl. 9, Fig. 81, is applied to a kind of face cover, or counterguard, T, of the demi-lune. It is only to be met with in some of the old fortified places of Europe, and was added to give more strength to fronts where the demi-lune was too small.

55. Horn-Work. The horn-work, Pl. 9, Fig. 82, usually consists of a bastioned front, H, with the ordinary outworks, having two long branches, F F, or wings, which rest upon two adjacent bastions, or two adjacent demi-lunes, DD, of the enceinte; its covered-way forming with that of the enceinte a continuous line of communication. The object of this outwork is to strengthen a salient or other weak portion of the enceinte.

56. Crown-Work. The crown-work, Pl. 9, Fig. 83. consists of two or more bastioned fronts, C, with their outworks, placed in front of some portion of the enceinte, to give it additional strength. It is terminated like the horn-work by two wings, FF, which rest either upon the enceinte, or upon two demi-lunes, DD. Its covered-way, like that of the horn-work, forms a continuous communication with that of the enceinte.

VIII.

ADVANCED AND DETACHED WORKS.

57. The term *advanced works* is applied to such works as, placed beyond the outworks, are still in defensive relations with them and the enceinte, by being so brought under the fire of either the enceinte or the outworks that the ground in advance of them will be swept by this fire; their ditches flanked by it; and their interior so exposed to it that. if the work were seized by an open assault, the assailant could be driven from it by this fire.

They are usually in the form of redans or lunettes, and in some cases horn and crown works, depending on the extent of ground that it may be thought necessary to occupy with them.

58. Advanced works are placed in positions which the assailant must necessarily make himself master of before he can approach nearer to the main work; or on points which overlook ground that cannot be swept by the fire of the enceinte; and sometimes on points which, inaccessible to the assailant, give good position from which a flank fire can be brought to bear upon ground over which the assailant will be obliged to make his approaches.

Restricted to these purposes, an advanced work may be of great value in prolonging the defence; and every precaution should be taken to secure the work from a surprise, and to give its garrison a safe means of communication with the outworks upon which they can retire when forced to abandon their work.

In works of great extent, with full and strong garrisons, advanced works, by judicious combination with the works in their rear, may greatly enlarge the field of action of the garrison; keeping the assailant at a distance, and annoying him by frequent sorties in large bodies, made under the protection of the outworks.

In Plate 9, Fig. 84, is an advanced work, L, flanked by the demi-lunes, D, of the enceinte. The plan of this work is a lunette with its covered-way and places-of-arms, R and S.

59. *Detached works* are those which, although having an important bearing on the defence of the main work, are so far from it as to have to depend solely on their own strength in case of assault.

Depending solely on their own strength, they should have a revetted scarp and counterscarp of sufficient height to present great difficulties to an open assault, and have their ditches flanked either from the parapet of the work itself or by caponnières or by counterscarp galleries.

Detached works may be either of a polygonal or bastioned form, depending upon the extent of ground to be occupied; the former being more suitable to small works to which the bastioned form does not lend itself.

They belong to the class of works termed *forts*, as distinguished from fortresses.

They are used to occupy ground like commanding heights, which, although not within good sweep of the fire of the main work, is still within range of the heaviest calibres of the assailant, and which if occupied by him would prove a source of serious annoyance to the work.

The more favorite mode now among engineers for the defensive works of cities is to enclose them with a continuous enceinte of sufficient strength to repel an open assault, or to retain this enceinte if it already exists and to occupy positions in advance of the main work, beyond extreme cannon-range, by a line of forts so strong that they can only be reduced by regular siege, and so placed that one or more must be taken before the assailant can approach the main work. In some cases a second line is established outside the first, and the whole area within the exterior cordon partakes of the nature of an intrenched camp.

IX.

INTERIOR RETRENCHMENTS.

60. Besides the works exterior to the enceinte, the object of which is to retard the assailant in his attempts to enter it by breaching, engineers have placed within it other works which, in some cases, are designed simply to enable the garrison to make an effectual defence of the breach, when the assault upon it is made, and give them a secure point of retreat and safety when driven from it; and in others these interior works are chiefly designed to bring plunging fire to bear on the assailant's siege works exterior to the enceinte. The former class, intended for the defence of the breach alone, are termed *interior retrenchments;* and the latter *cavaliers.*

61. Interior retrenchments in the bastioned system are either placed within the bastions, which are the parts of the enceinte usually breached, or in rear of their gorges. Those which are placed within the bastions extend across them either between the faces or between the flanks. When placed at the gorge they connect the two adjacent curtains.

The plan of these works varies with their position, the size of the bastions, or the more or less openness of their salient angles.

In small bastions with acute salients, when the retrenchment rests upon the faces, it usually receives the form of a tenaille or inverted redan, the angle of the tenaille being about 100°. When the bastions are large and the salient angle quite open or obtuse, the retrenchment may receive the form of a small bastion front, Pl. 9, Fig. 85, resting upon the faces.

Either of these forms may in like manner be used, when the retrenchment rests upon the flanks of the bastion. But as this position enables a retrenchment of the form of an ordinary redan to have its ditches swept by the fire of the flanks of the adjacent bastions, this form is in some cases used in preference.

When placed between two curtains at the gorge of a bastion the plan of the retrenchment is always a bastioned front.

In the polygonal system, until within a few years, the interior retrenchments were high casemated defensive barracks or keeps arranged to fire over the parapet from their upper tiers, and to sweep the terre-pleins and parade from their lower ones. They are now made of less height and their masonry is covered from fire, forming bomb-proof defensive barracks as previously described.

62. Cavaliers are placed either upon the curtains or within the bastions. The latter is the more usual position selected for them. Their plan in this position is usually that of a lunette, the faces and flanks of which are parallel to those of the enveloping bastion. Cavaliers receive a considerable command over the parapet of the enceinte, and, in some cases, they are arranged with a tier of casemated fire, above which is an open battery.

In polygonal works the cavaliers are generally placed at the salients and in the middle of the faces, when they are long, protecting the faces from enfilade and affording cover for magazines and quarters, as well as giving a plunging fire on the ground in front. In some large and important works it is proposed to provide them with iron or steel turrets.

Interior retrenchments and cavaliers are usually constructed with a revetted scarp and counterscarp to secure them from an open assault; and, in some cases, a covered-way, with a small reëntering place-of-arms, R, Pl. 9, Fig. 85, closed by traverses, is arranged in advance of the ditch, to insure the safe retreat of the garrison when driven from the breach.

CHAPTER II.

SYSTEMS OF FORTIFICATION.

In the discussion of the relative merits of different systems of fortification, their capacity to resist the close attack of the besiegers formerly had the greatest weight.

Modern methods have given to the distant attack a value and efficiency much greater than it formerly had; so great that in some cases it alone determines the result of the siege.

The conduct of recent sieges, notably that of Strasburg in 1870, in which the close attack was pushed up to occupying the advanced works, crowning the covered-way, and breaching the main enceinte, have shown, however, that the close attack may not be entirely a thing of the past, and that proper dispositions to meet it must still be made. The relative advantages of the different systems must then be determined, not only by the character of the site and size of the work, but also by the probable nature of the attack and defence, and the other considerations which arise in each particular case.

I.

BASTIONED SYSTEM.

63. A bastioned enceinte consists of a series of bastions which occupy the salient angles of the polygon within which the enceinte is inclosed; the flanks of the bastions being usually connected by straight curtains.

The sides of the polygon which connect the salient angles of the bastions are termed the *exterior sides*, in contradistinction to the sides of an interior polygon which, being parallel to the first and occupying the positions of the curtains, are termed the *interior sides*.

The bastioned enceinte, when its relief and plan are suitably arranged, possesses the advantage of having its ditches thoroughly swept from within the enceinte itself, thus securing the flanking arrangement of the scarp; of bringing a cross and flank fire to bear upon the approaches on the salients of the enceinte, and furnishing a strong direct and cross fire upon the site in advance of the curtains and the faces of the bastions.

64. The principal objections urged against the bastioned system are:

1. That its chief characteristic. a perfect flanking disposition for the entire line of the scarp, is attainable only under certain relations between the requisite relief for a permanent work and the lengths of the exterior side and curtain, which therefore restricts it in its application to fortifications in which these relations exist.

2. That, in order to secure a sufficient length of flank for an effective flanking disposition, the angle between the face of the bastion and the exterior side, termed the *diminished angle* of the polygon, has to be made so great as to decrease considerably the space inclosed within the polygon, whilst the development of the line of the enceinte is greatly increased by it.

3. That the direction necessarily given to the faces from this cause throws their prolongations in positions very favorable to the erection of enfilading batteries against them.

4. That the flanks, upon which the whole system is based, lie in positions in which, like the faces, they can be not only easily enfiladed, but are further exposed to a reverse fire from shot which may pass over the parapet of the faces as well as the opposite flank, or even to being breached by fire intended only to enfilade the face in their front.

5. And that these objections are the stronger as the salient angles of the polygon are smaller or as the number of sides is decreased.

6. That by reason of objections 3 and 4, the artillery of the faces, flanks and demi-lune is not able to withstand the distant enfilade fire of the besieger, and in consequence it has little or no value in retarding his approach until the third parallel is reached, when this distant fire ceases in order to avoid injuring his own men.

That this fact reduces the value of the artillery defence to a minimum, and restricts the size of the fronts to those which can be defended by infantry fire.

Besides these objections, which to a certain extent are well founded, where the defensive arrangements are chiefly open, as is the case in most land fronts, others have been urged against this system, which, being rather of a comparative character, as showing the advantages of other systems over this, will best be examined elsewhere.

II.

VAUBAN'S FIRST METHOD.

65. Vauban, born 1632. died 1707, has left examples of three different methods in the places planned by him. The fortress of New Brisac is fortified after his third method; those of Landau and Belfort after his second; but the greater part of the places fortified by him are planned according to his first or earliest method.

66. Profile of Enceinte. In the profile of this method, Fig. 1, Pl. 10, the scarp wall is 36 feet high, its slope being five perpendicular to one of base; surmounting this is another wall from 4 to 6 feet high, the object of which is to sustain the exterior of the parapet. The parapet is 18 feet thick, the superior slope being $\frac{1}{6}$; the interior crest is 8 feet above the terre-plein, which is 42 feet in width. The mean command of the interior crest above the site is about 26 feet. The bottom of the ditch is about $17\frac{1}{2}$ feet below the site.

67. Plan of Enceinte. Vauban adopted no arbitrary or invariable combination of parts in his methods. His great excellence as an engineer is shown in the skill with which he adapted the fortifications he planned to the defensive requirements of the sites; selecting long, medium, or short exterior sides, and varying the length and directions of the faces and flanks so as to procure the best command over the exterior ground, and to withdraw these parts from the enfilading fire of the assailant.

In his works, however, he has generally taken 360 yards as the greatest limit of the exterior side; the perpendicular of the front $\frac{1}{8}$ when the polygon is a square; $\frac{1}{7}$ for the pentagon; and $\frac{1}{6}$ for all higher polygons.

With these starting-points he procured diminished angles which gave more than 60° to the salient angles of the bastions in all cases, and flanks of suitable length both to flank the main ditch and to encounter with advantage the counter batteries which could be erected against them.

The following constructions both for the enceinte and

outworks are taken from the best French authorities as adopted by him for polygons higher than the pentagon.

68. In the plan of tracè (Fig. 2, Pl. 10), the magistral is taken as the directing line; the exterior side is 360 yards; on the perpendicular of the front a distance of $\frac{1}{8}$ the exterior side is set off; lines drawn through this point and the extremities of the exterior side, determine the directions of the faces, and the lines of defence; from the salients a distance equal to $\frac{2}{7}$ of the exterior side is set off, which gives the lengths of the faces and the positions of the shoulder angles; the flank is drawn by taking the opposite shoulder angle as a centre, and with a radius equal to the distance between the shoulder angles describing an arc to intersect the line of defence; the chord of this arc is the flank; the curtain is drawn by joining the extremities of the flanks. By this construction the flanks will be about 54 yards; the curtain, 146; and the lines of defence, 267; the length of these being determined so that the salients of the bastions can be defended with the *rampart gun*, or *wall-piece*.

69. Tenaille. In many of the places constructed before Vauban's time there was a *fausse-braie*, enveloping the enceinte and connected with it. This work was suppressed by Vauban, who was the first to use the tenaille in its place.

The tenaille is separated from the curtain by a ditch 10 yards wide, and from the flanks by ditches of 6 yards.

The form of the tenaille as used by Vauban was variable. In some cases he made it with a curtain and two small flanks parallel to those of the enceinte; in others it consisted simply of two wings placed on the prolongations of the faces; and finally, he gave it the form in Fig. 2, with a small curtain and two wings, which is the one at present most generally adopted. The relief of the tenaille is so arranged as not to mask the fire of the flanks on the ditch of the enceinte along the faces; for this purpose Vauban places its interior crest on a level with the site, or a little below it.

The tenaille has many valuable properties; it covers the postern under the curtain; masks the masonry of the curtain and flanks, so that a breach cannot be made in them, and in this way prevents retrenchments, resting against those parts, from being turned; a place-of-arms is formed between it and the curtain, where troops can be assembled for sorties in the ditches; finally, its fire sweeps the ditch and counterscarp, and helps to cover the retreat of troops from the other outworks.

70. Main Ditch. Vauban followed no invariable rule in regulating the dimensions of the enceinte ditch; its most usual width at the salients of the bastions, where the counterscarp is an arc of a circle, is about 36 yards; the rest of the counterscarp is tangent to this arc, and directed upon the opposite shoulder angles.

71. Demi-lune and Reduit. Vauban increased the dimensions of the demi-lune, which had been used previous to his time.

The object of this work is to secure the gates of the place from a surprise; to mask from the enemy's batteries the flanks and curtain of the enceinte; to give cross-fires on the salients of the bastions, and to favor sorties.

The plan and dimensions of the demi-lune vary also in Vauban's works. Its magistral is generally laid out by taking a point on the bastion face at 10 yards from the shoulder angle, and drawing a line from this point to the perpendicular of the front, so as to make the face of the demi-lune equal to $\frac{2}{7}$ of the exterior side. The parapet of the demi-lune is the same as that of the enceinte; its command is 3 feet less than that of the enceinte.

All the outworks in this system are commanded by the enceinte; the outworks most advanced being also commanded by those in rear.

The ditch of the demi-lune is generally about 24 yards wide and of the same depth as that of the enceinte; its counterscarp and that of the enceinte forming a continuous wall.

72. To strengthen the demi-lune, and secure for the troops entrusted with its defence a safe retreat when it is carried, Vauban placed in it a small redoubt. This work, in some instances, was only a simple *loop-holed wall* with a ditch in front; sometimes it was made of earth, and after the commencement of the siege.

73. Covered-way. The covered-way envelopes the entire counterscarp. The general width of the covered-way is 12 yards.

To set out the reëntering place-of-arms, two points are taken, at 20 yards from the reëntering angle, made by the interior crests of the covered-ways of the demi-lune and bastion, and upon these crests, and from these points as centres, with radii of 24 yards, arcs are described; the point of their intersection being joined with the centres gives the crests of the reëntering place-of-arms.

The parapet of the covered-way is terminated in a glacis,

the foot of which is from 40 to 50 yards from the interior crests.

74. Traverses. To close the places-of-arms, and enable the troops to defend the covered-way foot by foot, traverses of earth formed into parapets are placed at the places-of-arms. Defiles or passages of 4 feet are left between the traverses and the crest of the covered-way, for the circulation of the troops. The covered-way is palisaded to prevent surprise.

Vauban placed a high value on this work, which, to use his own words, "costs less to the defence and more to the assault than any other work." The covered-way prevents all access to the ditch, by a strong fire of musketry, which sweeps all the exterior ground; it is a secure position where troops can be assembled in safety for sorties; it covers the retreat of troops from the exterior into the other works.

75. Communications. In Vauban's front, ramps are made to ascend from the plane of site to the terre-plein.

A postern is made under the curtain to communicate from the interior with the ditch; another postern is made under the tenaille to lead to the demi-lune. A *double caponnière*, which is a passage covered on each side by a parapet terminated in a glacis towards the ditch, covers the communication through the ditch to the gorge of the demi-lune. Single caponnières are placed in the ditch of the demi-lune, and cover the troops from the enemy's fire through its ditch.

Stairs are placed at the gorges of the tenaille and demi-lune, and along the counterscarp at the places-of-arms, to ascend from the ditch to the terre-pleins of those works.

To communicate with the exterior, narrow openings are made in the faces of the reëntering place-of-arms, to lead from the terre-plein to the glacis; they are termed *sortie-passages or sally-ports;* and are closed by barriers.

76. Analysis. In the *tracé* adopted by Vauban for the enceinte, it may be observed that the length and positions of the lines of the front, resulting from it, are in good defensive relations both for the cannon and small-arms of its day.

1. The foot of the scarp, throughout the length of the curtain and the bastions, is thoroughly swept by the fire of the flanks.

2. The length of the flank is sufficient to contain as many cannon at least as the assailant can place to counterbatter the flank from the glacis crest opposite the flank; and

the flank can also bring an efficient fire of small-arms to bear on this battery of the assailant.

3. The bastions are capacious, and would admit of efficient interior retrenchments being thrown up in them, although Vauban does not indicate this auxiliary in his first method.

4. The tenaille was devised mainly to mask the scarp wall of the curtain and flanks, whilst its relief was so regulated as not to intercept the fire of the flanks on the enceinte ditch before the bastioned faces.

The plan of the earlier tenailles consisted of two flanks connected by a curtain, which were parallel to the same lines of the enceinte. This form was subsequently abandoned, as the flanks were found to be exposed to both an enfilading and reverse fire, from the assailant's positions in front of the enceinte; and the one now in most general use, consisting of either two wings simply, or of two wings connected by a short curtain, adopted in its place.

The tenaille, however, only partially subserves its object, as it does not cover the entire height of the scarp of the enceinte curtain and flanks; and, what is a more serious defect, it leaves the entire height of scarp of that portion of the curtain, opposite to the ditch between the tenaille and the bastion flank, entirely exposed, from the same position, and liable to be breached.

5. From the small size of the demi-lune, it gives but little cover to any portion of the enceinte scarp except the curtain. It is not sufficiently thrown to the front to give a good volume of cross-fire on the glacis in advance of the bastion salients; and the reëntering formed at this point, by the two adjacent demi-lunes, is, from the same cause, shallow and of but little strength. Owing to this last defect the assailant can easily breach and storm the enceinte at the same time as the demi-lune.

Besides these defects the demi-lune is not provided with a permanent réduit, a work necessary to enable the demi-lune to make a vigorous defence, by the support it affords the assailed.

6. From the width given to the demi-lune ditch, the covered-ways are exposed to a slant reverse fire, from which they are but badly screened by the traverses. Their command over the site is rather too little. Their main defect, however, is the small size given to the reëntering place-of-arms, and the failure to secure this important position for assembling troops for sorties by a permanent réduit, by which any open attack of the covered-way could be checked.

7. The dimensions given both to the enceinte and demi-lune ditches present a formidable obstacle to an open assault, and render the assailant's passage of the ditch by the sap also more difficult. The demi-lune ditch, however, offers a wide opening through which the scarp of the bastion-face can be seen down to its foot from the assailant's batteries on the glacis crest in the prolongation of the demi-lune ditch.

8. The communications within the enceinte, and from it to the main ditch, are sufficient and convenient for the character of the defence designed. Those of the outworks are for the most part narrow, inconvenient, and but badly screened from the assailant's fire, and therefore do not furnish a good provision for an active defence beyond the enceinte.

9. The great command over the site, and the high relief given to the enceinte, are very much in favor of the defence both as to the effect of the fire on the assailant's approaches and for security against an escalade. But in attaining these objects Vauban has left exposed to the assailant's distant fire a considerable portion of the scarp wall, which, being destroyed, would lay the enceinte open to a surprise.

III.

CORMONTAIGNE'S METHOD.

77. Cormontaigne, born 1696, died 1752, the immediate successor of Vauban, holds a place only second to this master of the art in the estimation of the engineers of the French school. Cormontaigne, who, to superior abilities united a wide range of experience both in the construction and in the attack of permanent works, studied with great care the results of Vauban's immense labors. In planning the front which has received his name, Cormontaigne seems to have applied himself rather to remedy the defects noticeable in the methods of Vauban, than to produce any radical change in the combinations which had thus far received the sanction of engineers generally. He was thus led to reject the 2d and 3d methods of Vauban, and to take the first method as the basis of his own changes.

78. Cormontaigne was the first to develop clearly the influence of large demi-lunes on the progress of the attack, by their forming deep reënterings between them in front of the bastion salients; and also the increased strength gained by fortifying on a right line, or on polygons with a great number of sides, as in both of these cases the fronts assailed cannot be enveloped by the assailant's works, and the demi-lunes from their salient position intercept the prolongations of the bastion-faces, and thus mask them from the positions from which alone an enfilading fire could be brought upon them.

79. He likewise lays down as a principle that *no masonry should be exposed to the distant batteries of the assailant*, and to obtain this point he has so arranged the height of his principal scarps, and the command given to the glacis crest in front of them, that the top of the scarp shall not lie above the level of the crest, thus masking from view the entire scarp, by the earth forming the glacis, from all positions in advance of the glacis crest.

His modifications of the plan and profile of Vauban's 1st method chiefly result from the above as a basis.

80. Enceinte. The modifications of Vauban's tracé (Fig. 4, Pl. 10) are different in the various works of Cormontaigne; but the following he indicates in his memoirs as the one preferred by him.

The exterior side is 360 yards; the perpendicular $\frac{1}{6}$; the faces of the bastions $\frac{1}{3}$ of the exterior side; the flanks are 40 yards, and are so placed that the curtain shall be 120 yards. This combination makes the lines of defence somewhat less, and the bastions larger than in Vauban's method.

The dimensions of the enceinte ditch are so regulated by Cormontaigne as to furnish earth sufficient for the embankments. It is 28 yards wide at the salient and from 2 to 4 yards wider opposite the tenaille; this admits the entire fire of the flanks to sweep the ditch.

81. Tenaille. The tenaille is made with a curtain and wings; a ditch 10 yards wide being left between it, the curtain, and the flanks.

82. Demi-lune. Cormontaigne placed little value on small demi-lunes, as they form but slight and therefore weak reënterings before the bastions, and consequently retard but little the enemy's attack upon them; besides this, a small demi-lune covers but very imperfectly the shoulder angles of the bastions.

To remedy these defects, his demi-lune is so laid out that the prolongations of the magistrals of its faces will intersect the bastion-faces at 30 yards from the shoulder angles; the lengths of its faces being 120 yards.

The ditch of the demi-lune is 20 yards wide; its depth is the same as that of the enceinte. By thus enlarging the demi-lune, sufficient space is gained to place a strong réduit in its interior. The defence of the demi-lune may be made with more obstinacy from the support it receives from the réduit; and the enemy will be obliged to carry it before he can assault the breach he may have made in the bastion face, as this breach is seen in reverse by the fire of the flanks of this work.

83. Demi-lune Reduit. To circumscribe as much as practicable the space in the demi-lune which the enemy, after he gains it, requires for his works, the extremity of the demi-lune terre-plein, which is also the top of the counterscarp of the réduit, is drawn at 20 yards from the magistral of the face; the ditch of the réduit is 10 yards wide, and the magistral of its face is parallel with the counterscarp. By this arrangement the ditch is well flanked by the face of the bastion near the shoulder angle.

To lay out its flanks, the counterscarps of the enceinte are prolonged to intersect the perpendicular of the front; from this point of intersection a distance of 20 yards is set off along each counterscarp; the two points thus obtained are joined by a right line, which is the gorge of the work: from the extremities of the gorge two lines are drawn parallel to the capital of the demi-lune, these lines limit the terre-plein of the flanks; the magistrals of the flanks are drawn parallel to and at 16 yards from the last lines.

84. Covered-way, etc. The general width of the covered-way is 10 yards. Cormontaigne enlarged considerably the reëntering place-of-arms, to which he added a réduit with a revetted scarp and counterscarp. The addition of this work is a great improvement upon the covered-way of Vauban, who indicates in his works small réduits of earth, or tambours of wood, for the same purpose.

Cormontaigne's réduit increases the strength of the covered way; the troops assembled in the covered-way for sorties are secure under its fire; it sees in reverse, and protects any breach made in the face of the demi-lune; finally, it serves, in connection with the extremity of the demi-lune, to cover the opening left between the flanks of the bastion and the wings of the tenaille, through which, if a breach was made in the curtain, the interior retrenchments, resting upon either the flank, or faces of the bastion, could be turned.

To lay out the interior crests of the reëntering place-of-arms, two points are taken on the counterscarps of the bastion and demi-lune at 54 yards from their point of intersection; from these points as centres, with radii of 60 yards, arcs are described, whose intersection joined with the centres gives the direction of the faces.

The magistral of its réduit is found by a similar construction; distances of 40 yards being set off along the counterscarps, and the faces being drawn from these points so as to be 36 yards long. The ditch of the réduit is 5 yards wide and $2\frac{1}{2}$ yards deep.

Traverses are placed along the covered-way, to close the places-of-arms, defend the covered-way, and intercept projectiles fired in ricochet.

The crest of the glacis is broken into a cremaillère line to allow room for the defiles of the traverses. The short branches of the cremaillère throw a fire on the salients of the covered-way; the positions of the long branches are so taken that the defiles may be seen and swept by the fire of the works in their rear.

85. Profiles. Cormontaigne, after a series of trials, whose object was to give the ditches such dimensions that they should furnish the earth required for the embankments, regulated the command of the different works as follows:

The lowest work, which is the demi-lune covered-way, he lays down as a rule, shall command the exterior ground by not less than $7\frac{1}{2}$ feet; and the works most advanced shall be commanded by those in the rear.

It was found that, for the purpose of equalizing the excavations and embankments of the front, the crest of the demi-lune covered-way should have a command of $10\frac{1}{2}$ feet above the natural ground.

The crest of the bastion covered-way and of the reëntering place-of-arms commands the crest of the demi-lune covered-way by 2 feet.

The magistral of the enceinte is horizontal, its elevation being the same as the mean elevation of the crest of the bastion covered-way.

The scarp wall is 30 feet high. This dimension has until recently been generally adopted by engineers, a wall of this height opposing a sufficient obstacle to an attempt at escalade.

The salient of the bastion commands its covered-way by 8 feet. The absolute relief of the flanks is $38\frac{1}{2}$ feet. With this relief a piece, firing under a depression of $\frac{1}{6}$ through an embrasure in the flank, and in the direction of the curtain, will strike the bottom of the ditch at the middle point of the curtain; so that were the relief increased, the length of curtain remaining the same, the ditch would no longer be thoroughly flanked.

The relief of the tenaille is determined as in Vauban's method, so as not to mask the fire of the flanks upon the ditch opposite the extremity of the demi-lune; as it is here that a breach may be made in the bastion face, through the ditch of the demi-lune.

The demi-lune is commanded by the enceinte 3 feet, and by its own réduit $1\frac{1}{2}$ feet. The demi-lune, therefore, commands its covered-way 7 feet, which is more than is indispensably requisite; for an enemy standing on the crest of the covered-way cannot have a plunging fire into a work in the rear of it, if the latter commands its crest by 5 feet.

The réduit of the reëntering place-of-arms commands the crest of the glacis only 4^1 feet; its interior crest is so placed as not to mask the fire of the bastion faces on the glacis in advance of it.

The interior crests of all the works are $7\frac{1}{2}$ feet above their terre-pleins, except that of the tenaille, which is $6\frac{1}{2}$ feet; and of the réduit of the reëntering-place-of-arms, which is 9 feet.

The interior crests of the faces of all the works exposed to enfilading fires are one foot higher at the salients than at the extremities.

The profile of the parapet of the principal outworks is the same as that of the enceinte.

86. Communications. The communications are generally of the same nature, and placed about in the same positions as in Vauban's method.

87. Glacis. The planes of the glacis are so determined that they may be swept by the fire of the works in the rear; their inclination is usually about twenty-four base to one altitude.

Interior Retrenchments. Cormontaigne indicates the gorge and shoulders of the bastion as the position for an interior retrenchment, when this addition to the front is made solely with a view of disputing the breach in the bastion and its interior with the assailant. In this case he gives the retrenchment the form of a tenaille, or a bastioned front, resting it either upon the shoulder angles of the bastion, or upon the two adjacent curtains on the points beyond the prolongation of the ditch between the tenailles and the flanks, and in this position he gives it the form of a bastioned front.

In the former case, the portion of the interior of the bastions between the flanks is preserved for the defence, but the retrenchment is liable to be turned, by a breach made in the flank, or in the portion of the curtain where it joins the flank. In the latter case a breach in the bastion places the whole of the interior within view of the assailant, but the retrenchment itself is secure, from its position, from being turned, as a breach in the curtain cannot be made in rear of it.

88. Cavalier. When a greater command of the site than that afforded by the enceinte is requisite on any front, Cormontaigne places a cavalier within the bastion. To this work he gives the same form as that of the bastion; placing the faces and flanks of the two parallel to each other. The faces of the cavalier are alone revetted, as well as the counterscarp of their ditch, which is cut within the bastion. This ditch is broken off at the shoulder angles of the cavalier, and directed upon the faces; these portions also having a revetted scarp and counterscarp. A parapet is thrown up behind the scarp and between the flank of the cavalier and the bastion faces; thus isolating the anterior portion of the bastion, and furnishing an interior retrenchment which, when the shoulders and flanks of the bastions are masked from the assailant's view, can only be carried by a breach made either in the cavalier face, or in the portions resting on the cavalier and bastion faces.

89. Analysis. From the preceding description, it appears that the most important modifications made by Cormontaigne in Vauban's first method, consist:

1. In the means taken to cover the *masonry* from distant batteries.

2. In more capacious bastions susceptible of receiving efficient permanent interior retrenchments.

3. In an enlarged demi-lune, which places the bastions in strong reënterings, covers the shoulder angles, and admits of a réduit in its interior, which work strengthens the demi-lune, and sees in reverse the breach made in the bastion face.

4. In an enlarged reëntering place-of-arms, containing a réduit which strengthens the entire covered-way, and covers the movement of the troops in sorties.

These modifications, although of great value, and constituting an important step in the art, still leave much to be desired; and engineers since Cormontaigne's time have sought to remedy the defects of his method, of which the following are the principal:

1. The enceinte has rather too slight a command, and is without any bomb-proof shelters.
2. The inclination of the superior slope of its parapet, which is ⅙, is too small to have the ditches well flanked.
3. A breach can be made in the bastion face through the ditch of the demi-lune.
4. There are dead spaces in the ditch of the demi-lune, near the extremities of its faces.
5. The réduit of the reëntering place-of-arms is not tenable after the demi-lune is taken.
6. The traverses of the covered-way do not afford the requisite protection to that work.
7. Finally, the communications are mostly inconvenient, and not well covered from the assailant's fires.

90. Counterguard. Vauban, in his third method, forms his enceinte with a high scarp wall, of the same dimensions and form as in his first method; and he procures his flanking arrangements for the enceinte by small bastioned towers of masonry, which are casemated in the lower story, and have an open battery in the upper, covered by a masonry parapet.

This enceinte he covers with spacious counterguards of the form of lunettes; the faces, flanks, and gorges of which are revetted, and which cover the bastioned towers of the enceinte; and between the flanks of these counterguards, and covering the curtain of the enceinte between the bastioned towers, he places a tenaille.

A demi-lune, in the form of a lunette, is placed in front of the counterguards and tenaille; within which he has placed a réduit with a revetted scarp and counterscarp. The whole of this combination of outworks he incloses with a covered-way arranged in the usual manner.

91. Cormontaigne uses the counterguard only as an exceptional outwork; and has applied it, in some of the works constructed by him, to strengthen a point that would otherwise have been too weak; but not like Vauban, as a constituent part of his method.

92. Two of the most eminent modern engineers, Coehoorn, born 1641, died 1704, and Carnot, born 1753, died 1823, in their methods, use earthen counterguards to cover their enceintes, giving them only sufficient thickness at the top for a parapet and a banquette for infantry; so that, being taken by the assailant, he will not find sufficient room to place a breaching battery upon their terre pleins against the enceinte. In this way they serve chiefly as masks or face covers to the enceinte faces.

93. Haxo, born 1774, died 1838, forms of the counterguard a constituent element of his method, giving it, like Vauban, the form of a lunette.

94. Noizet, born 1792, died 1885, although adopting the features of Cormontaigne's method as the basis of his, speaks of the counterguard as a valuable, and sometimes a necessary, element of a front; preferring it in some cases to the demi-lune.

Like all other outworks, when used, it should be flanked by the enceinte flanks; be swept on the interior by the fire of its faces; and not intercept their fire on the ground in advance of it.

IV.

METHODS OF THE SCHOOLS OF MÉZIÈRES AND METZ.

95. The schools of application for engineer and artillery officers, first established at Mézières and subsequently at Metz, now at Fontainebleau, has given to France, from about the period of the French Revolution down to the present day, the far greater portion of the many able officers who have gained such universal and deserved celebrity for these two corps.

In these schools the precepts of Vauban and Cormontaigne have been jealously regarded as the highest authority, and their manuscripts and published works have formed the basis of the instruction given in them.

96. Some slight modifications were proposed in the front of Cormontaigne by two engineers, *Chatillon* and *Duvigneau*, and taught by them in the course of permanent fortification given in the school. These changes chiefly consisted in enlarging the demi-lune and making it more salient; and in placing in the flanks of its réduit casemates for cannon with reverse views on the breaches that might be made in the bastion faces.

97. The teaching of the school of Metz received its principal impress from General Noizet, himself a pupil of General Haxo, regarded as the first among the successors of Vauban and Cormontaigne, who for several years, while a captain of engineers, performed the functions of professor of fortification, and who subsequently gave to the public the results of his lectures delivered in the school.

98. The front which, until a few years back, has been taught in this school, goes by the appellation of *Noizet's Method*. In it there is no sensible departure from the views and methods of Vauban and Cormontaigne; the object being to introduce such modifications into the front of the latter as would remedy some of its acknowledged defects.

In doing this, another object was kept in view which was to present, in the combinations of this front, a problem, in the solution of which the pupil would be called upon to apply both the elementary principles of fortifications and the geometrical methods that the engineer has to use as his principal tool in such problems, to a special case, that of a front adapted to a *horizontal site*. It was in this point of view that the analysis and construction of this front were for many years adopted as the basis for the elementary instruction given in permanent fortification in this Institution.

V.

NOIZET'S METHOD.

99. General Requirements. Noizet in his front takes as the basis of the construction of the enceinte the length of the exterior side, and the command, assuming these within the limits laid down by Vauban and Cormontaigne, and in the combinations of outworks with the enceinte, following the latter engineer; introducing only such modifications as seem to best fulfil the general conditions of the problem.

100. General data of the Enceinte. In the following description of the front of Noizet, (Plate 11a, Fig. 1,) the plane of comparison is assumed at 60 feet below the horizontal plane of site, the reference of which will be, therefore, (60.0). The yard is taken as the unit for the horizontal dimensions of the plan; and the foot as the unit for the references and vertical dimensions.

Converting the French measures into their equivalent English units, the exterior side of the front is 380 yards; the height of the scarp wall 33 feet; the command of the interior crest of the curtain over the plane of site 21 feet; and its height above the magistral 13 feet.

The dimensions of the exterior side and of the relief, as here given, are so taken as to secure an efficient flanking arrangement of the curtain; and of the outworks by the bastion faces.

101. Profile of Enceinte. The profile of the enceinte here given is similar to that of Cormontaigne, and was adopted by subsequent engineers until the more recently modified one already described.

Its slopes and dimensions are as follows:—The scarp and counterscarp slopes $\frac{2}{1}$, or one base to twenty altitude. Exterior slopes $\frac{1}{1}$, or 45°. Superior slope $\frac{1}{6}$. Interior slope $\frac{3}{1}$. Banquette slope $\frac{1}{2}$. Rampart slope $\frac{2}{3}$. Terre-pleins 8 feet below the interior crests. Berm 2 feet. Distance between the magistral and foot of the exterior slope 1.5 feet. Thickness of parapet 20 feet. Height of interior crest above the banquette tread 4.5 feet. General width of terre-plein estimated from the vertical through the interior crest 48 feet.

102. Magistral of the Curtain. The length of this is a minimum consistent with the artillery fire of the flanks passing $1\frac{1}{2}$ feet above the bottom of the ditch at the centre; this fixes it between 139 and 140 yards.

103. Magistral of the Enceinte. The perpendicular to the front is $\frac{1}{6}$ the exterior side, the lines of defence are drawn as usual. the flanks make an angle of $\frac{1}{8}$ with the perpendicular to the front; the faces are determined by the curtain and flanks.

A limited amount of protection from enfilade is given to the long lines by giving greater command to the bastion and demi-lune salients, but the scarp walls are not correspondingly raised

104. The Outworks. These satisfy the general conditions of defence, and are carefully designed to fulfil the requirements of a problem in fortification-drawing, in which the details are thoroughly worked out, and the determination of whose relations involve most of the geometrical problems met with in such work.

105. Remarks. The principal points of difference from Cormontaigne's method consist in a change in the directions and lengths of the faces of the redoubt of the reëntering place-of-arms, without, however, destroying its usefulness in connection with the ravelin as a mask to the curtain; in making a cut or *coupure* in the ravelin face in front of the redoubt of the reëntering place-of-arms, to prevent the redoubt being turned when the besiegers get possession of the ravelin; in prolonging the bastion counterscarp across the ditch of the demi-lune and its redoubt, and constructing in the first a face-cover for the bastion, and a covered communication and single caponier for sweeping the ditch; and in the second, a mask to cover the shoulder angle from fire coming through the redoubt ditch; and in placing four traverses in the demi-lune covered-way, which is made wider toward the reëntering place-of-arms to give better cover to the defiles of the traverses.

A complicated system of glacis planes was designed, adding to the value of the front as a problem in construction.

106. General Remarks. In the combination and arrangement of the outworks, Noizet has followed closely the methods of Cormontaigne, and of the school of Mézières.

The principal objections to these combinations are:

1. That from the command given to these works, a considerable portion of the fire of the enceinte, on the site exterior to these works, is obstructed by them. And that some of these works, like the réduit of the demi-lune, and the parapet behind the cut in the demi-lune face, mask the interior of the demi-lune from a portion of this fire.

2. That from the revetted gorges of these works, and the kind of communication between them and the enceinte ditch, sorties on the assailants' works in them, can only be made in small and feeble parties.

3. That the traverses of the covered-ways obstruct the free movement of troops along them, and also obstruct the fire of the enceinte on their terre-pleins.

4. The plunging fire of modern artillery searches out the masonry scarps over the glacis and through the ditches of the outworks, making it practicable to breach the enceinte by the distant fire.

107. For these defects various changes have been suggested, and some of them have been adopted in some of the more recent European fortifications.

These consist—

1. In giving a greater command to the enceinte than that usually found in the methods described.

2. In suppressing the réduit of the demi-lune, as usually constructed, in decreasing its command, and replacing it by a casemated réduit placed at the gorge of the demi-lune.

3. In suppressing the traverses of the covered-ways except those enclosing the reëntering place-of-arms; depending on the short branches of the crèmaillères into which the interior crest of the covered-way is broken to limit the effects of enfilade fire, and in reducing its width, to bring its

crest nearer the scarp wall; using it as a *chemin de ronde* only.

4. To replace the narrow stairs used by Vauban for communicating with the terre-pleins of the outworks, by wide ramps to facilitate sorties in large bodies.

5. To flank both the covered-way and the demi-lune ditch by a casemated réduit placed within the reëntering place-of-arms.

6. To make the communications more ample and direct.

7. To simplify the outworks, suppressing some, and making the others more subservient to the artillery fire of the enceinte.

Most of these modifications have been introduced into the front now taught at the school of Fontainebleau.

Plate 1, Figs. 4 and 6, show the latest and simplest form of the bastioned system without outworks.

108. In every combination the engineer must be guided by the exigencies of the sites that he is called upon to fortify, the character of the defence that it is proposed that the work shall make, and the relative pecuniary cost of different combinations. In taking this last consideration, however, into account, he should not forget that the pecuniary outlay for a work that will protract the defence only a few days longer may often bear no comparison to the benefits arising from it.

NOTE.—A full description of Noizet's method, with the analysis of the different parts, will be found in the unrevised edition of this work.

VI.

CHOUMARA'S METHOD.

109. Choumara, born 1787, died 1870, a French officer of engineers, of distinguished abilities, is the author of several remarkable memoirs on the defects of the bastioned system, and the means by which they may be removed and much additional strength be thereby given to the defences. His propositions for this purpose may be briefly stated as follows:

1. That part of a permanent work which can undergo no modification during the progress of a siege is the masonry, and it may therefore be regarded as the really permanent feature; all the parts of earth, as the parapets, etc., being susceptible of such modifications as circumstances may demand.

This Choumara terms *the independence of the parapets as respects the scarps.*

The latter, upon which the security of the work against an open assault or a surprise depends, must necessarily receive a direction, such that it can be swept by the flanking arrangements, a necessity that does not exist for the parapets, which may receive any direction compatible with the interior space.

The parapets may therefore be thrown back from the salients, as in the bastion, (Pl. 12. Fig. 1,) and receive a curvilinear form to throw a greater volume of fire in the direction of the capital.

Or they can be retired from the faces, as in the bastion (Fig. A), for the purpose of giving them such directions that their prolongations shall cut the adjacent demi-lunes, and thus be masked from enfilading views.

Or they may be prolonged so as to afford a greater column of flank fire, as in the flanks 1, (Fig. 1,) or they may be broken into any direction for the same purpose, or to give a more effective direction to their fire.

Or, finally, they may be thrown back from the scarp walls instead of resting immediately upon them, and thus render a breach less practicable, since the whole, or a portion, of the parapet will still retain its place after the breach has been made in the scarp. depending on the distance at which the parapet has been moved back.

In all of these cases of the application of the independence of the parapets, Choumara proposes to convert the space left between the foot of the parapet and the scarp wall into a *chemin de ronde*, or corridor, which is covered in front by a slight parapet, and from enfilading fire by giving an increased height to the portion of the parapet adjacent to the salients, forming a *bonnet*, as in Figs. 1, A, B, etc. This corridor is occupied by sharpshooters to annoy the besieger's trenches. Furthermore, Choumara regards the corridor as an additional security against surprise and escalade.

2. Choumara proposes to place high traverses in the bastion salients, to cover the faces from enfilade and the flanks from reverse views, and similar traverses at the shoulder angles with the same object. These he also proposes to casemate, or else construct with blindages for artillery to obtain a fire in the directions of the capitals, and reverse views on the demi-lune glacis and the breach in the bastion face. As these traverses, from their height, might give the besiegers in possession of them a plunging fire on the bastion

retrenchments, he proposes so to arrange them that they can be readily destroyed at any moment by mines, or, if of timber, be burned.

3. To mask the masonry of the enceinte and demi-lune from breaching batteries, erected in their usual positions along the crests of the glacis, Choumara proposes to form what he terms an *interior glacis*, or covering mass of earth, in the ditches, the crests of which shall mask the masonry of the scarps from the positions in question; and the upper surface of which, forming a glacis, shall be swept by the fire of the works in its rear. In this manner he expects to force the besiegers to the difficult operation of making lodgments in this glacis to obtain suitable positions for their breaching batteries.

4. By selecting for some of his outworks those points on the exterior which are most favorable to the action of the assailant's sharpshooters, he proposes in this way to cripple this important means of attack.

5. By giving greater extent to the exterior side, and a more retired position to the curtain, which is also to be made as short as possible, Choumara obtains bastions of ample size, not only to admit of the modifications he proposes for the parapets, traverses, and *chemins de ronde*, but for strong interior retrenchments, so organized with bombproof shelters, and arranged defensively towards the interior, that each bastion will admit of a defence to the rear at its gorge, after the besiegers may have effected a breach at other points and penetrated within the enceinte.

110. Plan. In adapting these propositions for a bastioned front, Choumara proposes, in order to obtain the requisite room in the interior of the bastions and a large increase of flank fire, to take the exterior side from 400 to 600 metres, French. In the front (Fig. 1, Pl. 12), for example, the exterior side is 440 metres; the lines of defence are drawn through a point on the perpendicular of the front at 74 metres, or one-sixth of 440 metres within the exterior side; the faces are 150 metres, and the flanks, drawn perpendicular to the lines of defence, are 85 metres, a length which prolongs them 35 metres within their intersections with the lines of defence.

By this construction the curtain, which will be 115 metres long, will be well swept, and the gun at the curtain angle can be brought to bear on the one of the besieger's counter-battery against the flanks which is furthest out, thus giving a very great preponderance in fire to the flank over the counter-battery.

The deep reëntering thus formed between the flanks and curtains gives ample room for a tenaille with flanks for four guns; these guns are covered in flank by a traverse. The tenaille is not revetted in front of its curtain and flanks, or at its gorge. It masks sufficiently the scarp of the flanks, and curtain of the enceinte, to prevent any danger to the latter from the destruction of the portion of the scarp wall that can be seen over the tenaille.

111. The salient of the demi-lune is the vertex of an equilateral triangle, the base of which is drawn between two points on the bastion faces, at 18 metres from the shoulder angles. The faces of the demi-lune, D, are 144 metres, and revetted. The parapet of the demi-lune is thrown back from the revetment, leaving a corridor covered by a parapet at the foot of its exterior slope. The parapet is broken near the gorge, so as to give two short flanks of 13 metres perpendicular to the exterior side. The salient is occupied by a casemated traverse with flanks for three guns. This traverse masks the interior of the demi-lune and the corridor from enfilading views. A disposition is shown for cuts across the demi-lune faces, the parapets of which are to be thrown up after the siege commences. The demi lune ditch is 17 metres wide. The portion of this ditch towards the gorge slopes upward as a glacis, and is swept by the fire of the enceinte.

112. The interior glacis of the demi-lune commences at the counterscarp of this work and has a glacis slope outwards, its width being 45 metres. Here commences the revetted gorge of the covered-way. The width of the covered-way is 10 metres. Its interior crest is an indented line. There are no traverses in this work unless required for its defilement.

113. A spacious and strong réduit is placed in the demi-lune salient place-of-arms. Its faces are 132 metres long, and revetted. Its parapet is thrown back, leaving a corridor in front of it, and is curved at the salient for five guns, sweeping along the capital. A bonnet is placed in its salient to cover the corridor from enfilade, and two traverses for the same object on its terre-plein. This réduit forms a mask for the portion of the demi lune occupied by the traverse.

114. Choumara places strong réduits, M, with revetted scarps and gorges in the reëntering place-of-arms. The parapets of these works are curved at the salients for batteries to sweep the approaches on the bastion capitals and the demi-lune glacis, and they are thrown back from the scarp walls to give a corridor for sharpshooters. As these réduits are necessarily contracted, Choumara prefers to them a strong réduit of larger dimensions, placed in the bastion salient place-of-arms and organized like the preceding.

115. One of the most striking features of Choumara's modifications is the mode in which he proposes to organize the large bastions, with defences which shall serve as an interior retrenchment, in case the bastion is one of the points of attack; or convert the bastion into an isolated fort or citadel for the garrison, in case the besieger gains possession of the interior of the enceinte through an assault at some other point. This he proposes to accomplish by increasing the lengths of the exterior side, and also of the bastion flanks.

116. With this object Choumara places a row of casemates within the bastions, on a line perpendicular to their capitals. Each casemate is from 60 to 80 feet long, from 12 to 20 feet wide, and 12 feet high. This row of casemates serves as a curtain both for the retrenchment of the bastion and for the defence of the gorge against an interior attack. For the defence of the salient portion of the bastion a cut is made across each face and extended to the capital. The scarp of this cut is made into the form of a bastion front with orillons at the shoulder angles; the casemates forming the curtain of this front. The counterscarp of the cut may be either revetted, or have a simple slope of earth. In the latter case the bottom of the ditch of the front at the foot of the scarp wall is at a suitable level to admit of an efficient height of scarp wall to secure it from escalade. A broad ramp leads from the centre casemate, along the capital, towards the bastion salient, to the counterscarp of the cut, and there branches into two other ramps leading up to the bastion terre-plein on the right and left. Until the besiegers are about to breach the bastion faces their parapets are left intact; and the portions of the cut along which the parapets run are filled up, as in the bastion on the right, thus leaving a free communication throughout the interior of the bastion. So soon as it is thought necessary to cut off this communication and to get the retrenched portion in a state of defence, that part of the parapet across the cuts is demolished; the cut excavated and suitably arranged; and the parapet of the retrenchment formed in part of the earth arising from these changes. The parapet of the front of the retrenchment is thrown back, leaving a corridor for sharpshooters covered by a slight parapet; that portion of this corridor along the retired flank being covered by the earthen mask of the orillon. Choumara further proposes, where there is a probability of the scarp of the bastion-face, which closes the cut on the exterior, being opened, so that a breach might be made by firing through it on the flank of the retrenchment, to run the scarp wall of the retrenchment at right angles across the cut, as shown on the right face of the left bastion, and to arrange the bastionnet, which this modification would give at the shoulder angle, for sharpshooters.

117. To expose the interior of the retrenchment to the fire of the flanks of the adjacent bastions, and to the parapet of a second retired interior retrenchment resting on the two curtains adjacent to the bastion of attack, a portion of the parapet of the bastion flanks, near the curtain, is demolished, and a slope is given to the portion of the terre-plein on which it rested. The retired interior retrenchment Choumara proposes to make of earth in the form of a bastioned front, breaking the faces in the most suitable manner to sweep the rear of the retrenchment in its front.

118. The dispositions for converting the bastion into a citadel are similar to the preceding, consisting of a small front, the faces of which are nearly in the prolongations of the adjacent curtains, with orillons to cover the corridor of the retired flank. This front has a covered-way and glacis in advance of it, the crest of which masks the scarp.

119. Choumara has made an ample provision for easy communications between all points of the enceinte and the outworks, so placing them as to be well covered from the besieger's fire and well swept by that of the garrison; preferring wide ramps for this purpose. The communication from the enceinte with the main ditch is through gateways in the scarp wall of the curtain, at its extremities. The rampart at these points is removed to the level of the main ditch; the portion of it between them, along the centre of the curtain, being sustained at the ends by revetment walls run back perpendicularly to the scarp wall of the curtain; Ramps lead from the gorges of the bastions down to these outlets into the main ditch. From these outlets the communications to the outworks are around the flanks of the tenaille, and through the enceinte ditch, to ramps placed along the enceinte counterscarp leading into the demi-lune, the demi-lune ditch, the enceinte covered-way, and its redoubts in the places-of-arms; and from the demi-lune ditch to the redoubt of the demi-lune salient place of-arms. Posterns on the faces and flanks of the bastions, near the shoulder angles, lead to the corridors of the enceinte. Passages are left at the ends of the faces of the outworks leading from their corridors to the interior of the works. To keep open the communication between the bastions, a gallery between their gorges is made along the curtain wall.

For the security of the casemates, barricades can be made in their doors and windows, by means of timber let in grooves made in the walls; the space between the exterior and interior timber facing being filled with sand-bags.

120. Remarks. The memoirs in which Choumara brought his propositions before the public naturally attracted attention, as much, perhaps, from their polemical character and piquancy of style as their professional interest. They contain but few things the germs of which are not to be found in writers who preceded him.

His modifications respecting the parapets, throwing them back from the scarps and breaking them into directions best suited for defence, are to be met with in *Chasseloupe's* propositions.

His proposals for lengthening the bastion flanks and occupying the salient places-of-arms by redoubts with considerable command, are to be found in the method of *de la Chiche.*

To *Virgin* he seems to be indebted for his organization of interior retrenchments, which are to convert each bastion into an independent work, equally provided for defence against approaches both from the interior and exterior of the enceinte.

Like disputants, usually, of an ardent temperament, he over-estimates the value of many of his propositions and loses sight of their countervailing defects. By laying down as a principle what may be exceptionally good in practice, he has rather weakened his own positions. This is the case, particularly, with his rule of independence of the parapets on the scarps, which, if adopted in all cases, might demand a greatly increased and hurtful command, and cut up to great disadvantage the interior spaces of the bastions.

His introduction of the *chemins de ronde* on the faces of the bastion and the demi-lune adds really very little, if at all, to the exterior defence; whilst they contract the interior space of these works, break in upon the unity of the defence, and place the troops in them in a very exposed position to the means of annoyance possessed by the besieger.

His expectations with respect to the effect of his fire in the direction of the capitals, in delaying the besieger's approach to the 3d parallel, were hardly warranted by the experience gained in artillery and small arms, even at the time the last edition of his memoirs appeared. It is hardly to be questioned, now that these weapons have been so greatly improved, both in range and accuracy of fire, that, considering the increased development of the besieger's parallels, which gives him a choice of positions for his batteries on so extended a line, the concentrated fire he could bring to bear on the batteries in question would not only soon ruin their casemates, but would greatly damage the adjacent faces and also the flanks of the bastions, although covered from enfilading views, either by the direction of the parapets of the faces, or the high traverses raised with the same object.

These advantages in the position of the besieger, it is thought, would prevent any delay in pushing forward his approaches up to the 3d parallel. After this the approaches would probably be retarded beyond the usual time in the attack on Cormontaigne's front, owing chiefly to the réduits in the bastion and demi lune salient places of-arms, and the arrangement of the face-cover in the enceinte ditch.

121. Supposing an enceinte organized according to his method, and containing interior retrenchments to oppose the besieger's approaches both from without and within the enceinte, Choumara estimates at least six separate epochs of breaching batteries, as follows:

1st, against the réduit of the demi-lune salient place of-arms.

2d, against the demi-lune and the réduit of the bastion salient places-of-arms.

3d, against the bastions.

4th, against the bastion retrenchment; 5th, against the retired retrenchment.

6th, and finally, against the bastions converted into citadels by the fronts with which their gorges are closed.

According to the estimate of the time made by Choumara, the time between opening the trenches and the final assault would be nearly three times as great as it would be in Cormontaigne's method.

122. The complications of this method unfitted it for practical application, even at the time of its design, and render it useless as a fortification to oppose modern arms. It combines, however, many of the features introduced into permanent works by the best engineers who had lived previous to the date of its design, and a large number which, with changes in dimensions only, are to be found in the most recently constructed outworks and detached forts. While as a system it is obsolete, its details are well worth study.

CHAPTER III.

TENAILLED SYSTEM.

123. Several engineers of professional eminence have proposed tenailled enceintes, as offering defensive properties superior to bastioned enceintes. This system has found but few advocates, and, except in particular localities, where the natural features of the site demanded it, and for small works, it has met with no practical applications.

Requiring that the salient angles shall not be less than 60°, and the reëntering angles between 90° and 100°, the tenailled system is only adapted to regular polygons of a sufficient number of sides to admit of these conditions being satisfied.

If the exterior sides are kept within the limits usually admitted by engineers for bastioned enceintes, the faces of the tenailles become very long, and the reënterings very deep; thus presenting two serious defects—long lines which are very much exposed to enfilade, and a great diminution of the interior space, as compared with the bastioned enceinte.

The ditches when dry can only be swept by casemated defences in the reëntering angles; and even then but partially, unless the casemated embrasures are placed very near the level of the bottom of the ditch, in which case the enceinte would be exposed to a surprise through the embrasures; and, in the contrary case, liable to a like attempt from the dead space at the reënterings below the embrasures. In wet ditches this exposure to surprise would be much less if the ditches could not be forded. In either case the defect arising from embrasure casemates placed in a reëntering angle would be a serious objection to using the guns of each side simultaneously.

When the salient angles of the tenailles are acute, the effect of the enfilading fire would not be felt alone on the face enfiladed, but on the adjacent face or front, and shot passing over would damage the adjacent tenailles.

The foregoing are the chief objections to this system. It presents no advantage but the very illusory one, considering the consequences arising from it, of long faces presenting a mutual flanking and cross fire of considerable extent.

CHAPTER IV.

POLYGONAL SYSTEM.

I.

POLYGONAL SYSTEM.

124. The polygonal system had previously been proposed by several engineers of distinction, but its most ardent advocate was the celebrated Montalembert, born 1714, died 1800, whose views have been more or less carried out in many of the constructions of Germany since his time.

Consisting of either a simple polygonal enceinte without reënterings, the sides of which are flanked by casemated caponnières, placed at the middle point of the fronts, or of fronts either slightly tenailled or of a bastion form, with short casemated flanks to flank the faces of the central caponnières, this system affords more interior space, and from the mode adopted of flanking the enceinte, will admit of much larger fronts than either the bastioned or the tenailled systems. The salient angles moreover will be more open in this than in the other two systems.

From these peculiarities of this system the positions suitable for the erection of batteries to enfilade the faces of the enceinte are less advantageous, from their being thrown in nearer to the adjacent fronts than in either of the other systems; whilst a greater development of trenches will also be requisite to envelop the fronts of attack.

These obvious advantages for the distant defence, however, are counterbalanced to some extent for the close defence by the want of the concentrated cross-fires which are afforded by the enceinte itself, in both the bastioned and tenailled systems, in advance of the salients, and upon the ground generally in advance of the fronts.

Each front of the polygonal system when its angles are acute offers moreover a long line to enfilading and slant fire which takes the adjacent front in reverse.

But the chief objection to this system lies in the mode adopted for flanking the enceinte. The casemated caponnières for this purpose being exterior to the enceinte, it will be exposed to escalade as soon as the fire of the caponnières is silenced, which, considering the structure formerly adopted for them and the exposure of their embrasures to the enfilading batteries, would, in all probability, take place at an early period after this fire is opened.

These defects in masonry caponnières have been removed in some degree as previously described, and those of iron and steel, constructed and proposed, will probably resist the most vigorous attack of the assailant. The advantages of this system in its modern methods have led to its almost universal adoption. The new forts around Paris are polygonal in their tracé.

II.

MONTALEMBERT'S POLYGONAL METHOD.

125. Among the writers on permanent fortification whose works have had an important bearing on the progress of the art, Montalembert holds a conspicuous place, although not educated as an engineer. Struck by the evident defects of the methods of his predecessors, particularly the want of casemates, both for defensive dispositions for artillery and musketry, and the shelter of the garrison and munitions, Montalembert devoted his time, talents, and fortune to bringing about a change in the direction in which it seemed to him called for. His efforts, however, led to no modifications of consequence during his life, which was principally spent in angry controversies with his opponents, except the extension of casemated defences for sea-coast works; but after the termination of Napoleon's wars a new school of engineers grew up in Germany, based mainly upon the views put forth by Montalembert, which views met favor in other parts, although still opposed by many able engineers in all countries who contested their soundness.

The principal propositions of Montalembert consist:

1. In the entire rejection of the bastioned system, as, according to his views, unsuitable to a good defensive disposition; and in its stead he proposed to use either the *tenailled system*, or else the *polygonal system*.

2. In basing the strength of these last systems upon an overwhelming force of artillery fire in defensive casemates.

3. In organizing strong permanent works within, and independent of the body of the place, which are to serve as a secure retreat for the garrison when forced to give up its defence.

Most of the objections urged against the bastioned system and its outworks having already been adverted to in the analysis of the front, it will be unnecessary to recapitulate them here; and as the tenailled system, composed of faces of equal lengths with reëntering angles of 90°, and salient angles of 60°, and termed by Montalembert *perpendicular fortification*, from the position of the faces at the reënterings, has many obvious and more serious defects than either of the other two, it is proposed to give here a description of the polygonal system alone, and that in its most simple form—the one in which Montalembert presented it for the fortifications at Cherbourg, one of the most important naval stations in France.

126. Montalembert first gave the name polygonal system to a tracé of the enceinte in which all of the angles are either salient, or where the reëntering are very slight.

Plan. In the tracé proposed for this place, x, y, (Fig. 1, Pl. 13,) is the exterior side, or magistral of the scarp. The body of the place consists of the scarp wall, D, Fig. 1 and section on P Q, arranged with casemates for artillery and musketry; of a corridor, C, between these casemates and the earthen rampart and parapet, B. In rear of the rampart is a high wall, A, arranged with loop-holes, within which the garrison retires when driven from the defence of the rampart.

Casemated caponnières, M, which are secured from a *coup-de-main*, are placed along the rampart, and so arranged that a fire can be thrown from them over the parapet and also along the terre-plein. The corridor, C, is also swept by a casemated caponnière, G, for musketry; and the front of the wall, A, by a like arrangement.

The principal caponnière for flanking the main ditch is in the form of a lunette, and placed at the middle of the exterior side, its flanks joining the casemated gallery, D, of the enceinte. The flanks, H, and the faces, K, of this work, are arranged with two tiers of artillery and musketry fire; each flank carrying ten guns and each face twelve guns. A wet ditch, I, separates the faces and flanks; a loop-holed wall encloses the portion between the flanks, from which the opposite portion between the faces is swept by musketry.

The caponnière is covered in front by a face cover, N, of earth, in the shape of a redan. The scarp of the enceinte is covered in like manner by the continuous face-cover, o, of earth, in the reëntering angles of which casemated batteries of two stories, for artillery and musketry, are placed to flank the ditches and sweep the positions for counter-batteries around the salients of the covered-way. These batteries are masked in front by the earthen works, s and Q. The whole is covered by the glacis of the covered-way, arranged in the usual manner.

The better to flank the main caponnière, the portion of the casemated gallery joining it is arranged with two tiers of artillery fire, the remaining portion having but one tier of guns.

127. Profiles. The sections along P Q, R S, and T U, show the relative command of the different works and the width of the ditches and earthen ramparts.

The communications between the different works are by bridges across the wet ditches.

128. It is now generally admitted that although Montalembert has rendered important services to the progress of fortification, particularly as regards the more extensive employment of casemated defences, still many of his projects were visionary.

Many of the details of his system in the state of development in which he left it may be said to have become obsolete without being subjected to trial by the guns which it was designed to resist.

The improvement in artillery having rendered the complete masking of masonry obligatory, compelled the advocates of the polygonal system to introduce many modifications to accomplish this object.

129. Among these advocates, General Brialmont of the Belgian engineers, born 1821, has in his writings and long experience in the construction of fortifications, particularly those of Antwerp, continued the development and improvement of the system up to the present time. He proposes in his latest works the extensive use of iron and steel casemates and turrets at important points, and in his earlier constructions displayed great skill in masking masonry from the besiegers' fire.

130. The defences of Antwerp planned and carried on under his direction since 1859 exemplify, better than any other large work, the latest applications of the polygonal system with its outworks. Plate 11, Figs. 2, 3, 4, 5, 6 and

7, show a half of one of these fronts of which the exterior side is 1000 metres. The references and dimensions are in metres.

The ditches, which are wet, are from 50 to 80 metres wide and from 2 to 3 deep. They are flanked by a central caponnière which is itself defended by the first and second flanks of the enceinte. These are protected from front fire by being broken back and covered by orillons.

At the middle of the curtain is a defensible barrack, which serves as a cavalier and retrenchment, and whose front is masked by the caponnière and its wings.

The caponnière is covered by the counterguard, in front of whose ditch, which is dry, and 15 metres wide, is a ravelin with a ditch and covered-way.

The ravelin ditch is flanked by casemated low batteries, serving as keeps for the reëntering place-of-arms.

The salient of the caponnière, the salient angle being about 60°, is 95 metres from the exterior side. The curtain is 65 metres within the exterior side and is 330 metres in length.

The first and second flanks have a length of $31\frac{1}{2}$ and 11 metres respectively. They are designed to flank the faces and gorge of the caponnière, its flanks being swept by the fire of its wings.

The curtain is made up of two half curtains and a defensible barrack separated from each other by roadways leading by bridges to the low terre-plein in rear of the caponnière.

The flanks of the caponnière, which have two tiers of casemates, are separated by a court 70 metres long, 10 metres wide at its outer extremity, and 16 metres at the exterior side.

Its wings are broken back and provided with a traverse as shown.

The defensible barrack is of the form shown in the figure. The length of its head is such that it is masked by the wing of the caponnière and the orillon. Its flanks make an angle of about 100° with the head, and are 75 metres long. The gorge is closed by masonry, forming a keep for the front.

The salient of the counterguard is 165 metres from the exterior side, and that of the ravelin 270 metres. The distance, K D, is 175 metres, and K B, 225.

The magistral of the low battery flanking the ravelin

ditch has a length of 50 metres, and makes an angle of 120° with that of the ravelin.

The covered-way of the main work is 20 metres wide, that of the ravelin from 8 to 14 metres, and arranged as shown.

The parapet of the ravelin is broken as shown, to prevent enfilade and is provided with a traverse and a "reverse battery" near the salient, sweeping the ground in front of the salient of the main work, which salient usually contains a cavalier.

The communications, which are shown in the plan, are direct, broad, and well protected.

The sections give the profiles of the enceinte and its outworks. Fig. 5, section on $e\ f$, shows a modification of the defensible barrack proposed by Brialmont, to give better protection to the masonry.

The parapets are generally 8 metres thick. The casemated quarters will accommodate 2000 men.

This enceinte is strengthened by a belt of polygonal detached forts placed in defensive relations with each other at a distance of about $1\frac{1}{4}$ miles apart, and from 2 to 3 miles from the enceinte.

NOTE.—Full descriptions of the details of this front, with an analysis of its different parts and some proposed modifications, will be found in Brialmont, "Traité de Fortification Polygonale," Paris, 1869.

CHAPTER V.

EXISTING GERMAN FORTIFICATIONS.

I.

RECENT GERMAN FORTIFICATIONS.

131. In the large additions made to the fortifications of the German States, between the general peace in Europe in 1815, and the close of the Franco-Prussian war in 1871, the German engineers for the most part of these structures embraced the ideas put forth in the works of Montalembert and Carnot, adopting for the plan of their enceintes the polygonal system with flanking caponnières, combining with these numerous casemates for defence, for bomb-proof shelters, for quartering the troops and preserving the munitions and other stores.

132. From what has been published on this subject by the German engineers themselves and other European writers, the following appear to be the leading features upon which these works are based:

1. To occupy the principal assailable points of the position to be fortified by works which shall contain within themselves all the resources for a vigorous defence by their garrisons; these works being placed in reciprocal defensive relations with each other, but so arranged that the falling of one of them into the besieger's hands will neither compel the loss of the others nor the surrender of the position.

2. To cover the space to the rear of these independent works either by a continuous enceinte, usually of the polygonal system, with a revetted scarp of sufficient height to secure it from escalade; the parts of this enceinte being so combined with the independent works in advance that all the approaches of the besiegers upon each, both during the near and distant defence, shall be swept in the most

effective manner by their fire; or else to connect these works by long curtains; or, finally, to employ them, as in a system of detached works, either to occupy important points in advance of the main work, or for forming capacious intrenched camps with a view to the eventualities of a war.

3. To provide the most ample means for an active defence by covered-ways strongly organized with casemated redoubts, and with spacious communications between them and the interior for sorties in large bodies.

4. So to organize the artillery for the near defence that it shall be superior to that of the besiegers at the same epoch, and be placed in positions where it will be sheltered from the besieger's guns up to the time that it is to be brought into play.

133. The plan of the independent works may be of any polygonal figure which is best adapted to the part assigned them in the defence of the position; but they are generally in the form of lunettes, (Pl. 15, Fig. 2,) having a revetted scarp and counterscarp to secure them from escalade.

In the gorge of the work a casemated defensive barrack is placed, which serves as a réduit or keep; a simple loop-holed wall which is flanked by the barrack closing the space between it and the flanks of the work, and securing the latter from an assault in the rear. The ditches of the work are either flanked from the enceinte in the rear; or, when the work is a detached one, by caponnières, or counterscarp galleries. The work is usually organized with a covered-way having one or more casemated redoubts, and a system of mines both for the exterior and interior defence.

134. The defensive barrack is usually arranged for two or three tiers of covered fire, and an upper one with an ordinary parapet and terre-plein on which the guns are uncovered and destined for the distant defence. The two upper tiers of covered fire are for artillery, to sweep the interior of the work, and to reach by curvated fires the approaches on the exterior. The lower tier is loop-holed for musketry to sweep the interior. The barrack is surrounded by a narrow ditch on the interior, and this, when necessary, is flanked by small caponnières placed in it, which are entered from the lowest story. The barrack communicates with the interior by a door at some suitable point; and the communication between the interior of the work and the exterior is through doors in the wall enclosing the gorge.

135. Considerable diversity is shown in the profiles of these works. They usually consist of a parapet and rampart of ordinary dimensions for the uncovered defence; of scarps either partly detached and loop-holed, with a corridor between them and the parapet; or of scarps with relieving arches arranged with loop-holes for musketry; or of a combination of these two. The height of the barrack, and the command of the parapet of the exterior work, are so determined that the masonry of the former shall be perfectly covered from the direct fire of artillery, and the exterior be perfectly swept by the artillery of the work. The portions of the counterscarps at the salients are also arranged with defensive galleries to sweep the ditches; usually with musketry, but in some cases with artillery.

136. Casemates are arranged for mortars in the salient angles of the work, to fire in the direction of the capitals; and one or more casemated traverses are placed on the terreplein, to obtain a fire on the exterior and to cover the terreplein from ricochet. The masonry of these traverses is masked by the parapet.

137. Posterns lead from the interior of the work to the scarp galleries, the corridors, the ditch caponnières, and the casemated mortar battery in the salient.

138. The system of mines for the exterior defence consists simply of listening galleries leading outwards from the counterscarp galleries. That for interior defence is similarly arranged; the communications with it being either from the barrack caponnières, or from the counterscarp of its ditch.

139. The work is provided with powder magazines which are placed at the points of the interior least exposed to the enemy's fire; and covered guard-rooms, store-rooms for mining tools, etc., are made in connection with the posterns.

140. In the profiles of their works, the German engineers follow nearly the same rules for the forms and dimensions of their parapets as those in general use in other services. They employ three kinds of scarp revetments.

1. The ordinary full revetment, or sustaining wall, with counterforts.

2. Revetments with relieving arches, either with or without defensive dispositions, as circumstances may demand.

3. Scarp walls either partly or wholly detached from the rampart and parapet.

In all these cases, they give to their scarp walls a height

from 27 to 30 feet for important works; and about 15 feet for those less so. The batter of these walls is usually one base to twelve perpendicular. For the full revetment with counterforts, they regulate the dimensions of both so as to afford the same stability as in the revetments of Vauban.

In their revetments with simple relieving arches, they use either one or two tiers of arches; placing the single tier either near the top, or towards the middle of the wall, according to the nature of the soil and the pressure to be sustained.

Revetments with relieving arches for defence, or scarp galleries, are arranged for one or two tiers of fire. The back of the gallery is sometimes left open, the earth falling in the natural slope in the rear; or it is enclosed either with a plane or a cylindrical wall, according to the pressure to be sustained.

When the upper part of the wall is detached, to form a corridor between it and the parapet in its rear, the top portion alone is, in some cases, arranged with loop-holes and arcades, or with recesses to their rear, to cover the men from shells; in others, a scarp gallery is made below the floor of the corridor to give two tiers of fire. The corridors are from 8 to 20 feet in width; and when deemed requisite, they are divided, from distance to distance, by transverse loop-holed traverse walls for defence.

When the scarp walls are entirely detached, they are arranged for either one or two tiers of fire, with arcades to cover the men; the banquette tread of the upper tier of loop-holes resting on the arches of the lower tier of arcades.

The counterscarps are revetted either with the ordinary wall, or arranged with a defensive gallery with a full centre arch, parallel to the face of the counterscarp wall.

141. The German engineers make a liberal use of bomb-proof casemates for mortar and gun batteries. The former are either placed in the rear of the parapet, or of the rampart and along the faces; or else in a salient angle.

In the former case, they are covered in front by the parapet; in the latter, either by the scarp wall alone, or by a casemated defensive mask, placed in front of the battery.

When placed along the face (Pl. 6, Fig. 50), they are arranged for one or several mortars, and frequently with two tiers of arches, the upper one for the service of the mortar, and the lower one for a bomb-proof shelter for troops, or munitions. The chamber occupied by each mortar is a rectangle 12 feet wide and about 20 feet in depth;

this is covered by a full centre rampant arch, the height of the piers at the back of the chamber being 4 feet and in front from 6 to 9 feet above the level of the mortar-platform. This enables the shell to clear the top of the parapet in front, which is about 12 feet above the level of the platform, and 21 feet in front of the battery.

The chamber is, in some cases, left open both in front and rear, to allow the smoke to escape readily, and to diminish the effect of the concussion of the discharge on the masonry; in other cases it is closed by a wall in the rear; an opening being left in this wall immediately under the arch for the same purpose.

A small ditch is placed in front of the battery; and the wall in front is extended about three feet above the platform, to shelter the men from the explosion of shells that may fall into the ditch.

The abutments of the arches are 7 feet thick and the piers 4 feet. The arches are two feet 6 inches thick; they are covered on top by from 4 to 6 feet in thickness of earth; and, in like manner, the arch and abutment are secured on the side exposed to an enfilading fire.

An ordinary traverse is placed on the same side, to cover the masonry and communication between the front of the battery and the parapet; the chambers of the mortars are entered from the front, or from the sheltered side, by a door in the abutment.

When placed in an obtuse salient, behind a scarp with a corridor, a space of 10 or 12 feet is left between the back of the scarp wall and the front of the battery. The platforms of the mortars are about the same distance below the top of the scarp. The arches are covered by the earth of the parapet to the depth of 5 or 6 feet. The dimensions and arrangement of the chambers and arches are the same in this as in the preceding case.

The communication from the interior of the work to the battery is by a postern 6 feet in width. A casemated guard-room is made in connection with the postern; and when the scarp is arranged with relieving arches, either for defence or for other purposes, an arched stairway is in some cases made as a communication from the postern to the casemates. A transversal wall with a doorway serves to cut off the court in front of the battery from the corridor to the rear of the wall.

In the less obtuse salients, the front of the battery is

made circular; the chambers being so placed that the fire of the mortars can be thrown in the direction of the capital. A casemated defensive traverse, placed in the salient, masks the battery in front; and it is covered on the flanks by the earth on the top of the arches. The details otherwise are the same as in the preceding case.

142. In the arrangement of casemated traverses for guns (Pl. 6, Figs. 48, 49), the chamber for each gun is a rectangle 24 feet in depth, estimated from the interior crest of the parapet, and 12 feet wide. The chamber is covered by a full centre arch, the height from the level of the platform to the crown of the arch being $8\frac{1}{2}$ feet. The arch is 2 feet thick, the piers between the arches 3 feet, and the abutments $3\frac{1}{2}$ feet. The mask wall in front of the chambers is 3 feet thick. This wall is covered in front by the parapet, and by several layers of fascines, or of heavy timber laid across the embrasure in the parapet and above the one through the mask wall. The cheeks of the embrasure in the parapet are likewise revetted with heavy timber at some distance in front of the mask wall. The masonry is covered on top and on the sides with 5 or 6 feet thickness of earth, to secure it from shells and enfilading shot. The casemates are left open to the rear.

In some cases, a blinded battery for a single gun (Pl. 6, Fig. 49), is arranged by enclosing the sides and front of the chamber with walls, and covering it with a layer of heavy timber, supporting two thicknesses of large fascines, covered with a thickness of 5 or 6 feet of earth; the dimensions of the chamber are the same as in the preceding case.

143. The caponnières (Pl. 5, Figs. 37, 38), for flanking the main ditch, usually consist of two faces and two casemated flank batteries of two stories each; the lower story being loop-holed tor musketry, and the upper pierced for artillery. Each battery consists of several rectangular chambers; each chamber for a single gun being 12 feet wide and 24 feet deep; or of smaller dimensions, according to the calibre of the gun and the kind of carriage on which it is mounted. The upper chambers are covered with bomb-proof arches, the lower one by arches of sufficient strength for the weight thrown upon them. The front mask wall of the casemates is 6 feet thick; the wall in the rear is 3 feet thick and is pierced with windows for light and ventilation. Openings for the escape of the smoke are also made in the front mask wall immediately below the crowns of the arches.

An interior court 30 feet in width is left between the two flank batteries, and when the batteries are detached from the scarp wall the space between is enclosed by a loop-holed wall built on each side in the prolongation of the front mask wall.

The faces of the caponnière form a salient of 60°. They are separated from the flanks by two stories of arched corridors, in front of which are two arched chambers of two stories; the upper chamber being arranged for mortars. An open triangular court is left between the front walls of these chambers and the faces of the caponnière. The upper part of the walls of the faces along this court are arranged with arcades and loop-holed for musketry, and have an open corridor in their rear on the same level as the chambers of the second story.

The caponnière is provided with a powder magazine and other necessary conveniencies for the defence.

The flanks of the caponnière and its interior are swept by the musketry of the scarp galleries in its rear. The faces in like manner are swept by artillery and musketry in casemates behind the scarp.

The arched chambers of the upper story are covered by a thickness of 5 or 6 feet of earth.

144. Caponnières of smaller dimensions, termed *bastionnets* (Pl. 5, Fig. 39), placed at the angles of redoubts to flank the ditches, are usually arranged for musketry, but sometimes receive artillery. Those for flanking the ditches of the independent works in advance of the enceinte, are sometimes placed in the ditches of these works; sometimes behind the scarp wall of the enceinte; and sometimes in casemates in the main ditch, detached from the scarp wall.

The communications from the interior with the caponnières are by posterns.

145. The defensive barracks, forms one of the most distinctive features in the organization of the German fortifications. The plan of these works may be of any figure to suit the object to be subserved by them. When placed in the gorge of an independent work and serving as a keep to it, their plan is usually semicircular. (Pl. 15, Fig. 2.)

The barrack consists of one or two stories of arched chambers for covered fire, and an open battery on top with an earthen parapet and terre-plein.

The arched chambers are formed by connecting the front and rear walls of the barrack by transversal walls which serve as piers for the arches of the ceiling, the soffits of which are either cylindrical or conoidal, according as the piers are parallel or otherwise. The chambers are about 18 to 20 feet wide, and 60 feet in depth; their height, under the crown of the arch, from 9 to 11 feet. The arch of the highest chamber is $2\frac{1}{2}$ feet thick, and being covered with a capping and the earth of the open battery on top, is bomb-proof. The arches of the lower stories are $1\frac{1}{2}$ feet thick. The front wall of the barrack is usually 6 feet, and is pierced in each chamber with one embrasure and two loop-holes. The rear wall is 3 feet thick, and has a window in each chamber for light and ventilation. Openings for ventilation are also made in the front wall just beneath the crowns of the arches. Doorways are made through the transversal walls to form a communication between all the chambers. These are sometimes placed along the centre of the piers, at others near their extremities, so that the chambers being divided by slight partitions into two compartments for the quartering of the troops, there will be a continuous hall either along the centre, or near the rear wall, upon which all the apartments open. The barracks are, otherwise, arranged with all the requisites for lodging the troops comfortably and healthfully. The lower story of the barrack is surrounded by a narrow ditch. A drawbridge across this ditch secures the entrance to the barrack at the gorge.

In some cases where the front wall of the barrack is much exposed to the besieger's fire, the piers are made thicker nearer the front wall; and they each have two vertical grooves to receive timber, laid horizontally, between which sand-bags can be packed in to afford shelter when the front wall has become much damaged by the besieger's artillery.

146. Remarks. The foregoing summary description, with the plates, will give a good general idea of the principal defensive arrangements constructed of masonry which enter so largely into the existing German fortifications, and upon the details of which the German engineers have bestowed great attention.

The adoption of the polygonal system, with caponnière defences for the main ditch, has enabled the German engineers to give, in their fortifications, a greater exterior side than in the bastioned system generally, and still admit of lines of defence, in which grape, canister and small-arms, particularly the later improved musket, will tell with efficacy upon the besieger's works on the glacis around the salients of the enceinte. With a few exceptions, nothing of a very reliable character has been published as to the plan of these works, further than the general defensive dispositions. From these it appears that, keeping in view the cardinal point in all fortification, the adaptation of the various fronts to the site of the work, so that all the approaches upon them shall be commanded and swept by their fires, whilst the principal lines of the enceinte receive the best direction to place them as little as possible within the range of enfilading positions, the exterior side is usually kept somewhere between 500 and 600 French metres, or between 550 and 700 yards.

147. This system of fortifications being in existence before the recent improvements in arms and the works being located in accordance with correct principles, the changes required in them are of detail and dimensions rather than of principle. The principal changes of a general character are: 1st, in reducing the number of strong places, retaining those guarding the frontier, and those covering strategic points, large depots of supplies and centres of production. These include generally centres of communication and some of the large cities. 2d, in enlarging the detached forts, placing them further from the centre of defence (from 4 to 8 miles) and making them much stronger, placing in the intervals between them, when necessary, smaller redoubts or batteries, thus making an exterior line of defence of great development and within which large armies can be assembled and manœuvred.

The existing enceintes enclosing cities thus fortified will in general be retained, or, as at Cologne, replaced by a continuous enclosure, without outworks, generally polygonal, with flanking bastionettes, provided with revetted scarps and counterscarps; the parapet being arranged for infantry, and field or garrison guns of moderate calibre, the whole being designed for security against attack or escalade by any force breaking through the outer lines, but owing to its proximity to the city not intended to withstand regular approaches.

The detached works already built may be used as a second line, or in many cases destroyed.

The fortifications of those cities which are not strengthened, and the small forts not included in the classes named, may be either retained unaltered or torn down.

The principal changes required in the details of the works described in order to fit them for defence are as follows, viz.:

The covered-ways should be reduced in width, to draw their crests nearer the scarp wall. The defensive barracks, keeps, bastionettes, and caponnières, should be cut down to one tier of fire, their face-walls masked and their arches covered with a sufficient thickness of earth to render them bomb-proof. All casemates exposed to direct fire must be thoroughly masked or shielded with armor.

The scarp walls may be reduced to a height of from 13 to 23 feet, according to the importance of the work, and covered against a plunging fire by the glacis. Wing batteries for flanking and ditch defence may be built outside the work in the continuation of the gorge, and other changes made to bring them so far as practicable into conformity with the most recent constructions.

II.

FRONTS OF POSEN.

148. The following is an outline of the plan and defensive dispositions of a front of the fortifications of Posen, one of the most noted of these structures.

The exterior side, AB, (Pl. 14, Fig. 2), is 600 yards; a distance, $CD = \frac{1}{15} AB$, is set off on the perpendicular to the front and without it; and on the line joining the salients A, B with D, distances, AH, BM, equal $\frac{1}{4}$ AB, being set off, give the faces of the front.

The salient, E, of the independent work is on the perpendicular of the front, and at a distance from C equal to $\frac{1}{8}$ AB. Describing from E an arc with a radius of 20 yards, and drawing tangents to it from the points H and M, gives the counterscarps of the independent work; the faces, EF, EF′, are parallel to the counterscarp and equal $\frac{1}{4}$ AB.

The ditches of this work are flanked by casemated caponnières, HI, MN, which are 35 yards in length, or sufficient for four guns; the directions of these flanking casemates being nearly perpendicular to the direction of the faces EF′. The flanks, FG, F′G′, receive the most suitable directions for sweeping the approaches in advance of the salients of the front.

The main ditch is about 30 yards wide, its counterscarp being parallel to the faces of the enceinte; and the gorge of the independent work is on the prolongation of this counterscarp.

The curtains of the enceinte are directed from the points

I, N on the point c, and are thus nearly parallel to the exterior side.

The main ditch is flanked by a large, casemated, defensive barrack, having three stories of covered fire, the lower for musketry and the upper for artillery, and an open battery on top. The plan of this work is that of the letter U; the circular part projects within the independent work, and serves as its keep; the sides are nearly perpendicular to the faces of the enceinte, and are prolonged within the enceinte, serving as a defensive caponnière to flank the main ditch, to sweep the terre-pleins of the enceinte curtains, and also the interior within the range of the guns of two round towers with which the sides are terminated. The sides of the barrack are separated from the rampart of the curtain by lateral ditches 10 yards wide, which give access to the main ditch from the interior for troops in large bodies for sorties.

The parapet of the enceinte (Fig. 4) is thrown back from the scarp, leaving a corridor between the foot of its exterior slope and the scarp wall, the floor of which is 12 feet above the bottom of the main ditch.

The scarp wall rises 16 feet above the level of the floor, thus giving it a total height of 28 feet above the bottom of the main ditch. This wall is loop-holed for small arms.

The counterscarp wall of the main ditch is 24 feet in height.

The faces and flanks of the enceinte have a relief of 44 feet; the relief of the curtain being only 40 feet.

The corridors of the curtain terminate at the court or open space behind the flanking casemates, HI, MN.

Posterns lead from the interior to the corridors of the faces and flanks, and from the lateral ditches to the corridors of the curtain.

The interior open space between the sides of the defensive barrack is closed by a loop-holed wall between the end towers. A ditch surrounds the towers and the gorge between them, across which a bridge, terminated at the wall by a draw, gives access to the interior open space and the barracks.

149. The scarp, rampart and parapet (Fig. 5), of the independent work are arranged with a profile similar to that of the enceinte. The circular portion of the defensive barrack which serves as the keep is surrounded by a ditch, which is swept by small caponnières attached to the keep. A circular mortar battery, covered in front by a casemated traverse, is placed in the angle of the independent work and behind this a casemated battery for howitzers is placed on its terre-plein, in the direction of its capital, to give reverse fire on the glacis of the collateral independent works. The gorge of this work is closed by a loop-holed wall which extends between the keep and the scarp wall of the flanks.

The communication between the main ditch and the interior is through a gateway in this wall. Posterns lead from the interior to the corridors of the faces and flanks, and to the mortar battery in the salient.

150. The counterscarp of the independent work is arranged with a defensive gallery, with which a system of mines for the exterior defence is connected. An interior system of mines is connected with the small caponnières in the ditch of the keep.

151. The covered-way is without the usual traverses, its interior crest being broken into a crémaillière line. Its salient and reëntering places-of-arms are occupied by casemated redoubts. The communications from the main ditch to the covered-way are by wide ramps which are at the gorges of the reëntering places-of-arms and under the fire of their redoubts.

III.

FORT ALEXANDER.

Among the most reliable of the published plans of German fortification is that of the main front of Fort Alexander, a detached quadrilateral work of the fortifications of Coblentz, given by Colonel Humphrey of the British Army.

152. Plan. The exterior sides of the enceinte of this fort (Pl. 14, Fig. 6) form a parallelogram, the acute angles of which are 85°. The main and rear fronts are each 500 yards, and the other two 420 yards each. The main front is of the polygonal system, with a strong defensive caponnière to flank the main ditch.

The caponnière is covered by a demi-lune, and the salients of the enceinte by counterguards; the ditches of these works being flanked by casemated batteries at the reëntering formed between them.

There is no covered-way in front of these outworks, their counterscarps being of earth with a gentle slope. A small earthen work, containing a casemated redoubt, is thrown up at the salients of the counterguard counterscarp.

To construct the tracé, take $ab = 500$ yards for the exterior side of the enceinte, which divide into three equal parts, ad = de = eb. Bisect ab by a perpendicular on which set off hH = hd = he = $\frac{1}{6}$ ab. Through H drawing a parallel to ab and setting off along it the distances HA = HB = 320 yards, the points A and B will be the salients of the counterguards.

From H, as a centre, with the radii Hd = He, describe two arcs, on which set off from d and e the chords di = ek = 33 yards, these will be the lengths of the casemated flanks; ik being joined gives the enceinte curtain.

The salient angle of the main caponnière is constructed by drawing from a point, m, on the capital, at a distance of 20 yards from the lines Hd, He, lines to the extremities i and k of the casemated flanks. The flanks of the caponnière, tn = vo, extend back to the exterior side, and are 33 yards in length and 33 yards apart; or each $16\frac{1}{2}$ yards on each side of the capital.

The faces of the counterguards are directed on the point c = $\frac{1}{12}$ AB = $53\frac{1}{2}$ yards on the capital from H.

The salient F, of the demi-lune is $\frac{1}{4}$ AB = 106 yards from the point c; its faces FD, FE, are parallel to the lines Hd, He, which last, joined by an arc of a circle described from m as a centre, with a radius of 20 yards, and terminated at the counterscarp of the enceinte ditch, which is 28 yards from ab, will give the demi-lune gorge.

A casemated battery for 3 guns, behind the demi-lune scarp wall, flanks the counterguard ditch; and one for 3 guns flanks the demi-lune ditch, and closes the opening between the demi-lune and counterguard at this point. A narrow ditch 10 feet wide is left between the flank of this battery and the extremity of the counterguard, as a communication between the main ditch and the ditches of the outworks. This opening is masked by an overlap of the counterguard.

Casemated, or blinded, batteries are made in the salients of the enceinte and of the demi-lune.

153. The main caponnière (Fig. 8) has two tiers of covered artillery fire on the flanks, of 5 guns each; the lower to sweep the main ditch, the upper the terre-pleins of the counterguards; its faces have two tiers of loop-holes. It has no uncovered fire, but a simple covering of earth as a bomb-proof.

154. Casemates for five mortars each, are placed in the salients of the enceinte at the foot of the rampart slope.

155. A narrow corridor (Fig. 7), the floor of which is $4\frac{1}{2}$ feet above the bottom of the main ditch, is left behind the scarp wall of the enceinte; the faces and curtains of this wall are loop-holed and arranged with arcades to shelter the men, like the detached scarp walls of Carnot. These scarps are 21 feet high. The height of the enceinte above the parade is 26 feet.

156. The scarp walls of the demi-lune and counterguards (Fig. 7,) are arranged like those of the enceinte. The command of these works is 16 feet. Their counterscarps are arranged at the salients with loop-holed galleries, from which communications lead to a system of mines for exterior and interior defence.

157. The rear side of this fort, not being exposed to artillery, is simply closed by a loop-holed wall and ditch. A large, circular, defensive barrack occupies the centre of this rear front, serving as a keep to the fort, and to sweep by its fire the ground on the rear and flanks of the front.

158. Up to 1883 no changes had been made in this or the other works about Coblentz, but additional detached works had been built further from the city.

159. Remarks. It will be seen that in the arrangement of the plan of this work, the polygonal system, with caponnière defences, of Montalembert, has been adopted as the basis, with such modifications as the features of the site afforded to withdraw the principal lines from the range of enfilading views.

The German engineers apply the preceding dispositions to every class of detached works, whether within reach of the artillery of the main work or beyond it.

In the former case the work is either in the form of a lunette or a redan, according to the requirements of the site; the gorge of the work being secured by a slight loop-holed wall that can be readily destroyed by the artillery of the place; and thus open its interior to view when occupied by the besieger.

In the latter, the plan is that of polygonal redoubt enclosed on all sides by a parapet.

The ditches in all such cases are flanked by small caponnières, placed at the angles of the work, and arranged both for musketry and artillery; besides having a counterscarp gallery which serves as the point of departure for the galleries of the exterior system of mines.

The apparently wide divergence between the German fortification of the present day and the bastioned system, which last had been adopted as the normal one throughout the world until these innovations were practically introduced, has given rise to active discussions among engineers in Europe, in which, as in all cases, very ultra ground has been taken by both parties to the dispute.

160. In each system the points admitted as essential in all fortification of a permanent character are sought for, viz.:

1. An enceinte secure from escalade and thoroughly flanked by artillery and small-arms.

2. Such an adaptation of the plan of the enceinte to the site as shall secure, as far as practicable, the principal lines from enfilading views.

3. Outworks and detached works of sufficient strength in themselves, and of such defensive relations to the enceinte, as to force the besieger to carry them by regular approaches before being able to assault the enceinte.

4. Interior defensive works, or keeps within the assailable points of the enceinte; and also in the outworks first subject to an attack, to give confidence to their garrisons in holding out to the last extremity.

5. The means necessary for an active defence.

6. The use of mines as an auxiliary.

7. The protection of all masonry by earthen masks from the distant batteries of the besieger.

The only question then is by which of these two systems the object in view is best attained.

161. The polygonal tracé which obtains in most of the recent German works has certain prominent advantages and defects which may be seen by a slight comparison with the bastioned system.

As the exterior sides are longer and the reëntering of the enceinte less deep than in the bastioned systems, it follows:

1. That the interior space enclosed by the enceinte is greater in the polygonal tracé.

2. That the faces of the enceinte are less exposed to ricochet from the greater obtuseness of the salient angles.

3. That the fire of the faces has thus a better bearing on the distant defence.

4. That, requiring fewer fronts on a given extent of line to be fortified, there will be fewer flanks and more artillery therefore disposable for the faces and curtains.

5. That, in the usual mode of attack, the besiegers will be forced into a greater development of trenches for the same number of fronts.

162. Its defects are:

1. That the enceinte, having no other flanking defence

than the main caponnière, will be exposed to an escalade so soon as the fire of this defence is silenced.

2. That the progress of the besiegers during the last and most important period of the siege is but little delayed, owing to the slighter reënterings formed by the independent works in front of the enceinte salients.

163. The defects in the bastioned tracé and the modes proposed by different engineers to remedy them, particularly those of Choumara, have been sufficiently dwelt upon to show that, with the advantages inherent in this tracé of preserving the means of flanking the enceinte ditch to the last; of throwing the bastion salients into deep reënterings; and giving a better direction to the enceinte faces for sweeping the ground in advance of the demi-lune salients; it is susceptible of receiving all the means of casemated defences; of a great development of flank fire; of defensive arrangements of mines; of ample communications for an active defence; and an extension of the exterior side fortified commensurate with the improvements of late years in artillery and small-arms.

This last, together with a shorter perpendicular to the front, giving relatively shorter flanks, the breaking back of the parapet in the polygonal front for flanking the caponnières, the introduction of armored casemates and turrets for flanking the ditches, the extensive use of covered defences, the simplification of the outworks and reduction in their command in both systems, have materially diminished the marked points of difference, and have brought the two systems more nearly into equality for both the close and distant defence.

164. In the discussions which have taken place upon the merits of these two tracés, between engineers of the two rival schools, each has seemed disposed to exaggerate the defects, and to depreciate the advantages of the system analyzed, and has conducted his mode of attack accordingly. The true point, however, as to the inherent merits of the question, does not lie in a comparison of the means of resistance of a bastioned tracé with defective communications and without casemated defences and mines with that of the German system, but between the former with these additions, now regarded by engineers of every school as indispensable to a vigorous defence against the greatly improved means of attack of the present day, and the latter.

In these discussions many considerations arising from the

immediate vicinity of the protected city to the fronts of attack have been introduced.

The great range of modern guns has made it impossible to defend a city from its immediate suburbs, and has led to arranging for both close and distant defence the forts of the belt or belts encircling the place, leaving for the enceinte only the duty of protecting the city from the attack of an army (perhaps large) which may break through the outer line.

The enceinte to satisfy the conditions requisite for this defence must be proof against assault or escalade, but will not require elaborate outworks or interior retrenchments. The cheapest and simplest system, either polygonal or circular, or a combination of them, will be in general adopted.

The outworks will be restricted to those necessary to protect the gates; the interior retrenchments to those required to keep the disorderly element of the inhabitants in subjection.

For the detached works, subject to regular approaches, the relative values of the rival systems must be determined by the circumstances of the particular case to which they are to be applied.

CHAPTER VI.

DETACHED FORTS.

165. For reasons previously stated, the main line of defence of fortified places is now at the belt of detached forts instead of at the enceinte. These forts have acquired all the additional value due to this fact, and the latest developments in the art of fortification, for land fronts, are to be found in the newest detached works of the German, French, and Belgian engineers.

166. These forts are as a rule polygonal, the tracés generally adopted are a long straight front with two flanks and a gorge, which may be rectilinear, tenailled or bastioned; a lunette with a very obtuse salient; or a modification of the lunette which has three or sometimes four faces and two flanks. The character of the gorge is determined, in all cases, by the nature of the site or the individual views of the designing engineer.

The faces and flanks of these forts which give a direct fire to the front have together a length of from 300 to 700 yards. The depth of the forts from front to gorge is a minimum consistent with sufficient interior space for the accommodation of their garrisons which vary from 500 to 1000 men. The armament of the largest is about 30 guns. Plate 16, taken from a German authority, shows the details of one of these works.

Their parapets have a command of from 25 to 40 feet at the salients and fall off towards the flanks and gorge for defilade.

The faces and flanks receive a thickness of from 20 to 25 feet and the gorges about 15 to 18 feet. The ditches have a minimum depth of 20 and width of 30 feet.

The scarp walls are generally detached or semi-detached and loopholed for defence.

They have such height, usually not less than 16 feet, as to be well protected by the glacis.

The counterscarps are generally revetted with masonry walls with relieving arches, which lend themselves to the construction of counterscarp galleries for sweeping the ditches and for starting points for countermines. The faces are flanked by artillery, machine guns or infantry fire from caponnières, and the flanks by caponnières or scarp galleries, a sheltered emplacement for which is obtained by breaking back the scarp wall at the shoulder angles and forming a kind of orillon, in the rear face of which the casemates are placed.

167. The interiors of the forts are provided with abundant bomb-proof cover for the garrison and supplies, and with chambers in which the guns may be placed when temporarily silenced by the concentrated fire of the attack.

These bomb-proofs contain the wells, kitchens, bakeries, latrines, hospitals, telegraph stations, etc. The main magazines are placed in the capital traverse or under the flanks; service magazines near the guns, and niches for ammunition are sometimes made in the interior slope of the parapet.

The masonry arches are covered with earth of a thickness varying from 3 to 16 feet, depending upon the fire to which they are exposed.

For important points which must be held at all hazards and where a great command and wide field of fire is wanted, revolving turrets are proposed and are strongly advocated by many engineers, foremost among whom is General Brialmont.

When the gorges of the forts are exposed to the fire of the works in their rear, they are in general casemated masonry structures, which serve as barracks for the garrison, their outer walls being arranged for defence against assault; but when to hold a very important point to the last extremity the works are thrown so far to the front as to render it possible that they may be surrounded, the gorges are made similar to the faces, but may have less cover for their scarp walls against plunging fire.

Whenever practicable the bomb-proofs are arranged for defence by infantry and machine gun fire, and serve as a substitute for the older form of keeps, which have been generally abandoned.

168. The communication with the exterior is through the gorge only, by a postern provided with two or more barrier doors and a drawbridge, the ditch being crossed by a permanent bridge or causeway, which is protected by a casemated guard-house.

The main communication in the interior is usually a bomb-proof gallery from the gorge to the salient, under the capital traverse, which also covers a row of chambers on each side of this corridor. This central communication is sometimes replaced by an open passage similar to a *chemin de ronde* at the level of the parade and close to the parade wall or rampart slope, giving direct access to the chambers under the terre-pleins and traverses.

The necessary ramps, stairs, posterns, and lifts, are provided in either case.

169. When the work is small, and its importance justifies the expense, the whole area inside the interior crest, except the gun emplacements and the banquettes, may be covered by chambers and passages in arched masonry and earth.

170. These forts are surrounded by a glacis covering a sentinel's path extending around the fort. The outworks are restricted to flanking caponnières and redans or ravelins covering the caponnières and bridge at the gorge. When wet ditches are used the masonry scarp and counterscarp walls are replaced with earthen slopes.

171. If there is difficulty in providing places for the artillery within the fort, permanent or provisional batteries for 4 to 6 guns are constructed on one or both sides of the fort, resting their flank upon the gorge or shoulder angle, and having their interior crest at the height of the glacis. They are supplied with ammunition from the main work.

When they are intended to be worked independently, they are provided with the necessary masks, shelters, magazines, etc.

The forts are placed as before stated, from 4 to 8 miles from the enceinte and 2 to 3 miles apart.

172. The intermediate works are calculated for a small infantry garrison of from 60 to 100 men and 3 or 4 pieces of artillery, usually field guns.

They are generally half redoubts or lunettes with short flanks and straight or reëntering gorges. They have a command of 16 to 20 feet, their parapets are from 16 to 23 feet thick on the faces and about 13 on the gorge. Their scarp walls are high enough to resist assault (13 feet minimum).

The arrangement of their gorges and communications is similar to that of the larger forts. See Plate 16, Fig. 8.

CHAPTER VII.

I.

INFLUENCE OF IRREGULARITIES OF SITE ON THE FORMS AND COMBINATIONS OF THE ELEMENTS OF PERMANENT WORKS.

173. Although the same general principles are applicable, and the same conditions must be satisfied in planning a work, so that it shall have all the efficiency of which it is capable, whether the site is unbroken and sensibly horizontal, or presents a great variety of feature, within the range of cannon of the proposed work; still irregular sites, where the surface is of a diversified character, give greater scope than level ones for the science and skill of the engineer, and call for all the resources of his art in adapting his plans to the natural features of the site.

The principal conditions to be satisfied, and which are the same in all cases, are:

1. That every point exterior to the defences, over which the enemy must approach them, or from which he can annoy them by his fire, shall be brought under the fire of the defences.

2. That no point of the defences shall be left unguarded by their own fire, or present any position where the enemy, obtaining temporary shelter from fire, may gain time to renew an onset.

3. That the troops and *matériel* within the defences shall be sheltered from the enemy's fire in any position he may take exterior to them.

174. The problem presented for solution to the engineer in irregular sites is frequently one of no ordinary complexity; demanding a minute and laborious study of the natural features of the position in their relations to the defence; connected with a tentative process of which the object is so to modify the plan, relief and details ordinarily adopted, as to adapt them in the best manner to the given position.

No rules but of a very general character can be laid down for the guidance of the engineer in such cases; among which the following are the most essential, and, when, practicable, should be adhered to.

175. It has already been observed that, from the means used in the attack by regular approaches, the more plunging the fire of the work, the more efficacious will it prove in retarding the enemy's progress. The efficiency of this fire will depend upon two causes:

1. The command of the work over the point to be attained.

2. The direction of the ground with respect to the lines by which it is swept.

176. As to the command of the work over the exterior ground, it has already been shown that motives of economy restrict it, in most cases, within very narrow limits, where, to obtain it, artificial embankments have to be employed.

To augment, therefore, in the greatest degree this element of the defence, advantage should be taken of the natural features of the locality, by placing the principal lines, from which the exterior ground can be seen, on the most commanding points of the site.

If, with this position given to the principal lines, the ground swept falls or slopes towards them, the most favorable combination for an efficacious plunging fire will be obtained; for, with this direction of the ground, the enemy will meet with far greater difficulty, in putting himself under shelter by his works, than where the ground falls or slopes from the line by which it is swept; as the surface, in the latter case, descending in the rear of the cover thrown up by the enemy, will be screened to a greater extent than in the former, where it rises in the rear of the cover.

When this, however, cannot be effected, the next best thing to be done is, so to place the principal lines with respect to the surface to be swept that it shall be seen by a part of these lines, thus bringing to bear upon it a flank fire from these parts.

177. The general rule, therefore, which the engineer is to take as a guide, in order to satisfy the condition of bringing the exterior ground under an efficacious fire from the work, is:

1. *To place the principal lines of his work on the most commanding points of the site, and in such directions as to bring the exterior ground to be swept in a position sloping towards these lines in such a manner that they can*

bring their entire fire to bear upon it, or else bring a portion of it to sweep it in front.

This will generally be best effected by placing the salient points of the work on the most commanding and salient points of the site; as, in this position of the salients, the faces, which are usually the principal lines bearing on the exterior ground, will occupy the salient and commanding portions of the site, whilst the reënterings, being thrown on the reëntering and lower portions of the site, will be in the best position for sweeping the ground immediately in advance of the faces by a flank fire; and at the same time these reënterings will be masked by the faces from the enemy's view, and thus preserved from serious injury up to the moment when their action may be rendered most effective; that is when the enemy, despite the fire from the faces, has succeeded in planting himself upon points on which this fire cannot longer be brought to bear.

To carry these precepts, which are equally applicable to single works or to lines of detached works, into practice, a wide margin is left to the engineer's judgment, in which he will find it necessary in some cases to extend the lines of his works beyond what a strict regard to economy might prescribe, so as to include within his defences ground from which he can best sweep what is exterior to it, or which being occupied by the assailant, might make his own position less tenable, in this way forcing him to extend out his lines so as to embrace crests within them that overlook valleys beyond them; and in some cases to throw his own lines further back in order to avoid enfilading or plunging views from points which are too distant to be brought within his defences.

2. *The condition of leaving no point of the defences unguarded by the fire*, will depend in a great degree for its fulfilment on the same rule as the preceding. But where the irregularity of the site is such that all the exterior ground cannot be swept by the fire of the works, additional batteries, advanced works, or detached forts placed in defensive relations with the main works must be employed.

These works should satisfy the usual condition, that the more advanced must be taken before those in rear can be successfully attacked.

3. *The condition that the troops and matériel within the defences shall be sheltered from the enemy's fire from all commanding points without*, will depend upon the relative positions of the principal lines and the exterior commanding

points; and as far, therefore, as it can be done, without sacrificing either of the preceding and more important conditions, the plan of the work should be so arranged that the principal lines shall present themselves in the most favorable direction to the exterior ground to avoid plunging, enfilading or reverse views upon their terre-pleins from any point of it.

178. To effect these objects, when the work is in the vicinity of commanding heights within cannon range, and the crests of these heights, as seen from the work, present a nearly horizontal outline, the principal lines of the work, fronting the heights, should receive a direction as nearly parallel as practicable to that of the commanding crests.

When the outline of the crests presents a nearly continuous line, but one which declines or slopes towards the site of the work, the principal lines towards the height should receive a direction converging towards the point where the line of the crests, as seen, if prolonged, would join the site, if this point or points beyond it and within cannon range cannot be occupied by the enemy.

The reasons for the positions assigned to the principal lines in these cases respectively, may not, at a first glance, be obvious; but by examining the relative positions of the crests of the heights and of the principal lines, as here laid down, it will without difficulty be seen that they can be brought in the same plane, and the latter be so placed as to give a nearly uniform command to the parapets of the principal lines over the site; and that by keeping the terre-pleins of these lines in planes parallel to the one in which the crests of the heights and those of the parapets are held, and at suitable levels below it, the parapets will be made to cover the terre-pleins from the fire of the heights in the simplest manner.

179. Remarks. The foregoing general methods for determining the direction of the principal lines fronting commanding heights, so as to cover from direct fire, in the easiest manner, by their parapets, the space to the rear occupied by the troops and *matériel*, present, at the same time, the simplest cases of the adaptation of the plan of a work to the features of the locality, to subserve the object in view. In most cases, all that can be done is to avoid giving such directions to any of the principal lines as shall be favorable to enfilading or reverse views of the enemy; which may be effected by so placing them that their prolongations shall fall on points where the enemy cannot establish his

ELEMENTS OF PERMANENT FORTIFICATION.   101

works; or on those which, if occupied by him, will afford disadvantageous positions for his batteries either for enfilading or reverse fires.

As the attack derives its great advantage from its enveloping position, by which enfilading views and a concentrated fire can be brought to bear on the assailed point, so, in the general disposition of his defences, the engineer should endeavor to reduce these salient and assailable points to the fewest number. and to accumulate upon them such surplus strength that in spite of their natural weakness they will cost the assailant a great deal of time and a large sacrifice of means to get possession.

This consideration has led engineers to propose for the general outline of their defensive polygon a triangle in which the principal development of their work being a number of fronts on a right line, they can neither be enveloped nor their principal lines be enfiladed by the assailant's trenches, thus leaving only the three angular points as assailable, and which they propose to strengthen by an accumulation of works upon them.

Were the engineer untrammelled in all cases by other considerations, this method might do very well. But this is far from being the case. All that he can, therefore, do in planning his work is to keep this consideration in view, throwing as many fronts as he can on the same right line; making the angles of his general polygon as open as possible, so as to force the assailant to a great development of his works, to gain a concentrated and enfilading fire on them; placing these angles on points of difficult access to the assailant; and by taking advantage of such natural obstacles as water and rock, to give additional strength to these points. The skill and judgment of the engineer are here his main reliance in adapting his details to these general principles.

II.

DEFILEMENT OF PERMANENT WORKS.

180. Remarks. The greater importance of so adapting the plan and command of permanent works to the features of irregular sites as to satisfy the conditions of sweeping thoroughly by their fire all approaches exterior to the defences, and completely flanking the latter, seldom places it in the power of the engineer to fulfil the condition of withdrawing the interior of the defences from either enfilading or reverse views by a modification of either the plan or the command.

To mask, therefore, the terre-plein which would be exposed to these fires, as well as from such as would be attained by a plunging fire in front, resort must be had to the usual expedients of defilement; that is, giving to the terre-pleins such position with respect to their parapets that the troops and *matériel* upon them will be screened from a plunging fire in front by the parapets; and, when the terre-pleins are exposed to either enfilading or reverse views, by so placing earthen traverses or other masks as to intercept these views, and cover the troops, etc., from the enemy's projectiles.

The defilement of permanent works, like that of field works, proposes the same end, and employs nearly the same means. They differ mainly in their practical details; the latter being reduced to a simple practical operation on the field, while the former, from the usually greater complexity of the arrangements of permanent defences, requires the aid of mathematical methods, and demands the best attainable results.

Owing to the regularity of the trajectory of modern rifles and the resulting accuracy of fire even with an angle of fall up to $\frac{1}{4}$ or greater, it is generally impracticable to secure cover from cannon fire for any considerable area by the defilement of open defences. However, as the assailant must in general see the effect of his fire, both to correct his aim, and to learn whether his results justify the expenditure of ammunition, the necessity for defilement from the *view* of the attacking force, when it can be had at not too great cost, still exists.

The protection of the larger areas from plunging, reverse and enfilade fire must be secured by bomb-proofs; for limited areas it may be obtained by the free use of the traverse and parados.

181. For the solution of all problems of the defilement of permanent works, the engineer requires—

1. The limit exterior to the defences beyond which the effect of the enemy's fire may be regarded as so uncertain as to be neglected, and that beyond which he will be unable to see the point struck and the effect produced by his projectiles.

2. The presumed positions within this limit that the en-

emy may take up to bring his artillery to bear upon the works, or for observatories.

3. An accurate topographical map of all the ground within the above limits, as given by its horizontal curves referred to a plane of comparison.

4. The magistrals and interior crests of the works, as either definitely or proximately arranged, referred to the same plane.

182. The 15c. m. (6″) rifle, the largest considered available for siege purposes, is effective for accurate breaching fire for masonry up to 2000 yards, angle of fall about 3°; for flank fire against gun emplacements up to 3500 yards (angle of fall $6\frac{1}{2}°$). Its extreme range is about 10,500 yards, or 6 miles.

The distance at which the point of striking and effect of the shot can be determined by the use of field glasses and portable telescopes is from 1 to 2 miles.

183. These limits, and the importance of protecting any particular points within the work, will determine the character of defilade to be adopted.

The surface of the site embraced within the exterior limits and the line of defences may be divided into three zones, one lying between the limits and position of the first parallel of the attack; the second between the positions of the first and second parallels; the third between the positions of the second and third parallels.

184. At no stage of the attack will the assailant attempt to raise his batteries above the natural surface of the ground, in order to obtain command for his guns; the labor and additional exposure of his guns to the fire of the defence far more than counterbalancing the advantage gained by any attainable increase in command. This will restrict the vertical limit within which his fire may be delivered to about 5 feet above the surface of the ground.

185. Observatories or lookouts will be placed at the highest points which can be occupied with moderate security; but no great height can be given them above the general line of the works without an amount of work incommensurate with the small advantage gained in the first zone or exposing them to the destructive fire of the defence in the second and third.

These considerations will, in general, limit the height of the observatories to 10 feet above the ground in the first and second zones. In the third zone, the defilade will be against close fire and a nearly straight trajectory. In this zone the fire of infantry mounted on the parapets of the trenches may sometimes be used, and the work should be defiled against it. The maximum height of this plane of fire may also be taken at ten feet above the level of the site.

186. Taking, then, the extreme cannon range or the adopted limit of distinct sight, the dangerous ground exterior to line of the defences may be marked out on the topographical map of the site by drawing lines parallel to those connecting the most advanced salients and at this distance from them and then considering the references of the horizontal curves of the ground within the zones thus marked off to be increased 10 feet.

187. In the defilement of each part separately of the line of defences, those portions alone of these zones should be regarded as dangerous which are embraced within arcs, or other lines drawn at the foregoing distances from the salients, or the faces of the part to be defiled.

It may also happen that, within the limits of dangerous ground for one portion of the line of defences, there may be other portions which, from their positions, may mask the portion to be defiled from all the dangerous points beyond them; in which case the points thus shut off need not be regarded, in effecting the operations of defilement.

If, for example (Pl. 17, Fig 1), the limits of dangerous ground for the demi-lune A being marked off, it is found that the demi-lune B, masks the demi-lune A from all fire that might come from the ground beyond B; then this portion of the zones of danger need not be regarded in defiling A.

To ascertain this it will only be necessary to pass a plane through the interior crest of A tangent to the surface beyond B, raised 10 feet, and see whether it lies below B at all points. If so then will B serve as a mask for A.

188. All masonry should be covered by earthen masks from the plunging fire of the heaviest guns within the range at which this fire would prove destructive against it.

189. In the defilement of works of limited interior capacity, as, for example, the réduit of the reëntering place-of-arms, the double caponnière and the like, which are, moreover, not habitually occupied by troops, the extreme limits may be reduced.

190. Within the limits of the zones of danger, positions may be found for front, for reverse, and for enfilading fire.

If the two faces, for example, of a work be prolonged to intersect the extreme limit of dangerous ground, the sector which they embrace may be termed *the limit of direct* or *front fire;* since, from every position that can be taken up within this sector, a direct fire alone can be brought to bear upon the two faces.

The two sectors which lie adjacent to this may be termed *the limits of lateral,* or *reverse fire,* since they afford positions from which a reverse fire can be obtained against one of the faces, and a front fire upon the other. It is also only within these last limits that positions for enfilading the terre-pleins of the faces can be obtained.

191. Remarks. The problems of defilement which present themselves for solution may embrace one or more of these cases in any example; depending upon the relative positions of the interior crest of the work to be defiled, and of the dangerous ground embraced within the foregoing limits.

The terre-pleins may be screened from direct *view* by their parapets, from reverse or enfilade *view* on one face alone, in some cases by the parapet of the other, in others by traverses and parados.

A portion of the terre-pleins may be screened from plunging *fire* by the parapet, parados or traverses, but for protecting considerable areas, bomb-proof casemates or shelters are required, as previously stated.

III.

PROBLEMS OF DEFILEMENT.

192. It does not come within the scope of this summary to examine the many cases of defilement which may arise from irregularities in the site. Those alone will be discussed which are of most ordinary occurrence, and which require for their solution the usual geometrical constructions involved in planes and other surfaces tangent and secant to a surface defined by the projection of its horizontal curves. The cases which will here find their application may be arranged under two heads:

1. The plan and command of a work being definitely decided upon, to ascertain the exact portions of the zones of danger, from which any description of fire can be brought to bear upon its terre-pleins, and to defile them from it.

2. The plan of a work being definitely fixed, but its command only approximately within certain limits, to ascertain the easiest method of defiling the terre-pleins of the work.

by varying the command, or position of the interior crest, within the assigned limits.

193. (Prob. 1, Pl. 17, Fig. 2.) *The command or position of the interior crest of the faces of a work being fixed, to ascertain the dangerous points on the exterior, and to defile its terre-plein from these points.*

Let a b, a c, be the projections of the given crest; and the curves (26.0), (29.0), etc., those of the natural surface.

Prolong outwards to c and d, the faces; construct the scales of declivity of the two lines, a e, a d; and, from them, the scale of declivity, e f, of their plane.

From the salient, a, supposing an arc to be described with a radius of 3500 yards, the dangerous ground will be included between it and the two faces of the work.

Now, if the plane of the interior crests, of which e f is the scale of declivity, be indefinitely extended, and its intersection with the surface parallel to the natural surface and 10 feet above it be found, it is evident that the portion of this raised surface which lies below the plane may be disregarded, as the interior of the work is covered from it by the parapet. But from every point of the surface above the plane the interior is more or less exposed to view, depending upon the height of the point above the plane, its distance from the work, and the height of the interior crest above the terre-plein and parade.

Having drawn the horizontals of the plane, e f, and found their intersections with the corresponding horizontals of the raised surface (which last will be given by adding 10 feet to the references of the curves of the ground), of which x y z is the projection, that portion of the surface which lies above this curve will alone see the interior of the work, and will be the only portion for which defilement will be necessary.

Now, as this intersection falls entirely within the angle d a e, of the faces prolonged, or within the limits of front fire, it is evident that the terre-pleins will require to be defiled only from direct fire.

To effect this, let a plane be passed through the face, b a d, of the work, and tangent to the raised surface above x y z. This plane will pass above all the dangerous ground, except at its point of contact with it; and, being extended back from the face within the work, it is clear, if the terre-plein of this face be so taken with respect to this plane that no point of it shall be less than 8 feet below the plane, that then every point of the terre-plein will be screened from view by the parapet of the face a b. Now, if the same series of operations be gone through with for the face, c a e, then will its terre-plein be defiled in like manner; and thus the defilement of the whole work be completed for this case.

The tangent planes which satisfy the above conditions are termed *Planes of Direct Defilement;* and they may be defined as *the planes which, passed through the interior crest of a parapet, leave at least 10 feet below them, all the dangerous ground of front fire, and pass at least 8 feet above every point of the terre-plein behind the parapet.*

The terre-pleins are usually parallel to their respective planes of direct defilement and 8 feet below them. But when the declivity of the plane of defilement exceeds $\frac{1}{25}$, then the terre-plein, if it is to receive cannon mounted on travelling carriages, must be kept within this limit.

In Fig. 2, the references are given in feet. The tangent plane through b a d is determined in the usual manner, by finding the horizontal (in this case 45.0), among all those drawn to the curves of the raised surface, which makes the minimum angle with b d. The line h i, perpendicular to this horizontal, is the scale of declivity of this plane; and the point, p, that of contact. The line k l, is, in like manner, the scale of declivity of the other plane, and o its point of contact.

It might happen, from the steepness of the terre-pleins, that the reëntering or gutter formed at their intersection would be inconvenient, and it would therefore be desirable to have this position raised, when it can be done without exposure to a plunging fire.

This, in most cases, may be effected in this way: It will be seen, from an inspection of Fig. 2, that the points o and p are the only ones from which the enemy's fire passes exactly at 8 feet above all the points of the respective terre-pleins determined by the tangent planes; and that if, from these points, lines of fire, o a r and p a s, be drawn, every other line of fire through a, from the ground in the angle, p a o, will pass more than 8 feet above the portion of the terre-pleins embraced in the angle, s a r, since the ground within the exterior angle lies below the tangent planes.

If, then, a be taken as the vertex of a cone, the elements of which are tangent to the raised surface within the angle, p a o, and if these elements be prolonged within the work, their prolongation will form a cone of lines of fire, which will pass more than 8 feet above the terre-pleins. If these last, therefore, be connected by a surface parallel to this cone, and 8 feet below it, this surface may be taken as the portion of the terre-plein which, connecting the two plane portions, will remedy the inconvenience pointed out.

194. (Prob. 2, Fig. 3.) *The data being the same as in the preceding case, and the work being exposed to both direct and reverse views, to cover its interior from these views.*

Suppose the plane of the interior crest of the faces extended within the limits, and its intersection with the dangerous ground determined as in the preceding case; and let x y z, m n o, and p q r, be the curves of this intersection.

The face a b will be exposed to direct fire alone from the ground above the two curves x y z and m n o; and to reverse fire from that above the curve p q r. In like manner, the face a c will be exposed to direct fire from x y z and p q r, and to reverse fire from m n o.

The defilement of each face from the direct fire will be effected precisely in the same way as in the preceding Prob.

The lines h i and k l are the scales of declivity of the planes of direct defilement of the faces respectively.

For the reverse defilement, a plane is passed through a b, tangent to the surface above p q r; and one through a c, tangent to the surface above m n o, and their line of intersection a a′ found. The line u v is the scale of declivity of one of these planes, termed a *Plane of Reverse Defilement*, and s t that of the other.

Now, if a traverse is so placed that its crest shall occupy the position of the line a a′, it will cover all between it and the two faces, as high as the interior crests, from the reverse fire on each side. But as it is desirable to have the troops, when on the banquettes, screened from this fire, the crest of the traverse should be raised from 18 inches to 2 feet above the line a a′ to effect this.

The traverse should extend so far towards the gorge of the work that the entire line of each face shall be covered by it. To determine its length with this condition, lines are drawn from the extreme points b and c of the faces, tangent to the curves m n o and p q r, and their points of intersection with a a′ marked; the one that falls farthest from the salient will evidently give the required length.

If the line a a′ should fall so near either of the faces that the traverse, if placed along it, would incommode the service of that part of the work, it will be the best to place its crest in the vertical plane a a″ of the capital of the work.

When so placed, the intersection of this vertical plane with each of the planes of reverse defilement must be found, and the crest of the traverse be taken 18 inches above the one that lies highest.

195. The position of the crest of the traverse, as determined by either of the preceding methods, will be in a vertical plane passing through the salient, a, of the work.

From the thickness and slopes which traverses usually receive, they would ordinarily, if placed in this position, take up all the interior space within the salient, and leave no room there for dispositions either for artillery or musketry. To prevent this, a break is made in the direction of the crest, at some point on the vertical plane through the salient, from which it is directed on a point of either of the faces, so far from the salient that sufficient room will be left for the object in view. In (Fig. 4), which illustrates this arrangement, the traverse is withdrawn far enough from the salient to leave room for a barbette battery for several guns.

The face upon which the traverse is directed, will be determined by the condition of covering both faces in the most effective manner, by the position taken for the traverse.

196. The cross section of traverses for permanent works is similar to those used in field works. The top of the traverse receives a slight slope each way from the crest to the sides. The thickness at top is sufficient to render it shot-proof. The sides take the natural slope from the top, either to the lowest level at which they may be struck or to the terre-plein. If to gain interior space these slopes are terminated at the higher level, then the portions of the traverse below these planes are made more steep, and the earth supported by retaining walls. The top of the traverse, where it joins the parapet, being higher than the superior slope, is run out above this slope, upon which the side slopes fall; its extremity terminates in the plane of the exterior slope, extended above the exterior crest.

197. When, from any circumstance, a single traverse cannot be used for reverse defilement, resort must be had to several, which should be so combined that no line of fire can penetrate between their extremities to attain any point which they should cover.

Examples of this construction are found in several plates, and will suggest the manner of making others. The following case will serve as a further illustration:

Where a demi-lune is arranged with a réduit, a traverse

placed in its salient cannot be extended further back than the counterscarp of the réduit; and an open space, therefore, will be left at the ditch, through which a reverse fire would attain that portion of either face which is not covered either by the traverse in the salient, or by the parapet of the réduit.

To cover the part thus exposed, it will be necessary to place one or more traverses, which, in combination with the one in the salient, and the parapet of the redoubt, shall subserve this end.

To simplify the case, let the face a c, Pl. 17, Fig. 5, be the one exposed, and let the point x be one the fire of which is most dangerous. Having, in the first place arranged the traverse, t, as in the last example, and drawn the two lines of fire x b and x d from the point x, through the extremity of the traverse, and the top of the parapet of the redoubt at the salient, the length, b d, of the face intercepted between these l'nes will be the part to be covered. If a second traverse, t', be placed across the terre-plein of the other face of the demi-lune, and in a position such that one of its ends shall rest on x b, and the other on x d, it will evidently cover the portion b d.

198. In selecting the positions of several combined traverses, attention must be given to avoid those where, if one be placed, the assailant would find shelter behind it from the fire from the rear. In the example just taken, the slope of t, towards the salient, should be swept by the fire from the rear, through the réduit ditch; the like slope of t' should be swept by a portion of the réduit face near its salient; and neither so fall as to have the space behind it masked from fire by the one to its rear.

199. Remarks. Traverses usually present not only the easiest solution of all problems of reverse and enfilading defilement, but, affording the means of rendering the command independent of fire from without, they enable the engineer to regulate this element solely with a view to the effect which he desires to attain by his own fire.

From the space required for their erection, traverses may, as in the cases of narrow terre-pleins, like those of the covered-ways, and of the demi-lune with a redoubt, be inconvenient, both from embarrassing the communications, and from taking up ground that may be wanted for batteries.

200. (Prob. 3.) *The plan of a bastion being definitively fixed, and one point of its command approximately, to de-*

file the work in the most advantageous manner, by shifting the position of its interior crest within certain limits.

Let Fig. 6 be the plan of the work, and a the salient, the command of which can be varied within certain limits without impairing any of the other conditions; and let the dangerous ground be embraced within the arc m n, at 3500 yards from a, and the lines a u and a v supposed drawn from a, through covering masses on the right and left of the work.

The front limits of defilement in this case are embraced within the sector m a n; and the lateral limits within the other two m a u and n a v. Now, the most favorable case of defilement here will be that where a plane, containing a, taken within its extreme positions, shall pass above all the exterior ground, and give such a command to the interior crest throughout, when held in it, as shall satisfy the other conditions of defence. To ascertain the existence of such a plane, let a be taken as the vertex of a cone which envelops all the dangerous ground; any plane tangent to this cone will satisfy the condition of defilement, and it will, therefore, only be necessary to find whether any one of these planes of defilement will satisfy the other, of giving the points b c d, and e, a suitable command. If no such plane can be obtained, the next most favorable case will be to find one that shall satisfy all the requisite conditions of command, and intersect the ground only within the front limits. In this case it is clear, from the position of this plane, if the interior crests are held in it, that the interior of the work will be exposed only to the direct fire from that portion of the ground which lies above the plane.

Let x y z be the curve of intersection of the plane with the ground, found in the usual way. Through the faces a b and a d, let planes of direct defilement be passed; the terreplein of the faces being held parallel to them will be covered by their respective parapets from all plunging fire. But, in order that the planes of defilement of the faces shall also defile the flanks, it is necessary that each flank be placed in the plane of defilement of the adjacent face, and its terreplein in that of the terre-plein of the face. Now, in giving the interior crests of the flanks these new positions, they will lie below the plane that contains the curve, x y z, and in which the interior crests of the faces lie. This being the case, it may happen that the parapet of one of the flanks will not cover the opposite face from reverse fire, coming from the lateral limits opposite the flank. In this contingency, it will be necessary, in order to cover the face, to place the flank in the plane of the curve, x y z, as this plane defiles from the lateral limits; but, in doing this, the flank, d e, for example, will be exposed, in its turn, to the ground above x y z; and to cover it, the only remedy is to erect a traverse, at some suitable point, which shall intercept all this dangerous fire. The least inconvenient position for the traverse will usually be at the shoulder angle. From this point it must extend so far back as to intercept all fire from above x y z, both on the terre-pleins of the flank and curtain, where they unite, and be high enough to screen the troops on the banquette.

If the defilement cannot be effected by either of these processes, there remains no other means than, having first definitely fixed the command, to divide the bastion by a traverse, either along its capital, or some other convenient direction, and, having given it a suitable height, to cover each portion from direct fire by the usual method.

201. The foregoing problems embrace in their solution all of the more ordinary cases of defilement, and suggest the route to be followed in treating others.

In all cases of the defilement of combined works, like the enceinte and its outworks, etc., it must be borne in mind that the advanced works, which from their position, must first fall into the assailant's power, become thus a portion of the dangerous ground for the works more retired, and which must also be held after the fall of the others. The retired works, under such circumstances, must be defiled from the advanced; their planes of defilement being made to pass from 3 feet to 4.5 feet above the portion of the advanced work on which it is presumed the assailant may make a lodgment, and, which, from its position, may be re-regarded as the most dangerous to the retired work, it being assumed that in the close attack the artillery fire will be delivered at a height above the ground not greater than this.

202. Where a work has considerable command, and is open at the gorge like the cavalier retrenchments, for example, and the works in its rear do not mask its interior from reverse fire, it may be necessary to place a traverse, termed a *parados*, across its terre-plein at the gorge, giving it sufficient height to subserve the end in view.

A parados or traverse immediately in rear of a parapet exposed to front fire is open to objection, since shells passing over the parapet penetrate the traverse and by their explosion throw out splinters and portions of the traverse toward the parapet.

On the other hand, they intercept splinters coming from shells exploding in their rear, and when properly constructed, of soft earth, retain a very large portion of the splinters of shells exploding after striking them.

The following conclusions were drawn from the results of an exhaustive series of experiments recently carried on in Italy ("Fortifications of To-day," Washington, Government Printing Office, 1883):

"1. In temporary batteries, and also in permanent ones which can only be attacked by field or siege artillery, parados, even at short distances, are not only free from danger, but also in most cases advantageous.

"2. When in works subjected to fire of greater calibres, parados have to be used, well sifted earth should be chosen in preference to sand in their construction. Their distance from the battery, measured from the foot of the interior slope of the parados to the end of the gun platform should be not less than twenty metres (66 ft.) if the work is exposed to the fire of siege artillery of calibres not greater than 15 cm. (6"), nor less than thirty metres (99 ft.) if the work is exposed to more powerful artillery. These limits may be somewhat reduced for batteries high above the position of the attacking artillery.

"3. As the inconveniences resulting from parados placed at distances less than those indicated may in many cases be less than that proceeding from the fire of musketry or of artillery placed in commanding positions in rear of the battery, so in especial cases in which fortifications have to be constructed, the importance of the two dangers will have to be compared in order to judge whether it is better to place the parados at less distance or to expose the battery to reverse fire."

203. General Remarks. The methods of defilement here laid down are those now followed by engineers. They unite mathematical accuracy in results with great simplicity of detail; and render the defilement altogether secondary to the other conditions of defence, upon which the plan and command are made essentially to depend.

Before they were adopted, the results of the method then followed were, in most respects, like those obtained in the practical operations for defiling field works. A line was taken, the position of which was determined by a series of trials, having for their object to obtain the most satisfactory results both as to the economy of the requisite embankments and the best disposition of command of the various parts at, or in the rear of, the gorge of the work to be defiled; this position coinciding with the natural surface, or being above or beneath it as the case required. Through this line a plane was passed tangent to the dangerous ground. This plane, termed, as in field defilement, a *Rampant Plane*, was taken as the artificial site of the work, in reference to which the relative command of all the parts was arranged as upon a horizontal site. Or, in other words, the result was nearly the same as if the works had been arranged on a horizontal site, and then the whole combination turned around some fixed line of this site, until it was brought into the position of the required rampant plane. The defects of this method are evident at a glance. It preserves the relations of defence of the various works the same as in a horizontal site; but it, to a great extent, leaves out of consideration the bearing of the command on the exterior ground, and, in many cases, may lead to excessive excavations and embankments which the methods now followed enable the engineer, for the most part, to avoid.

In the preceding discussion fixed horizontal limits of defilade have been avoided, as they must be determined by considerations of relative cost and value to the defence.

The vertical limit is considered the maximum which is practicable or generally desirable. It is fixed with a view to preventing the commander of a battery seeing the effect of his own shot and correcting his aim by it. It is, of course, impracticable to prevent the effect being seen from other points; but when many guns are engaged this is of little value to the attack, since it is almost impossible to know to which gun any single shot belongs.

To recapitulate: against a plunging fire the protection given by the parapet depends only upon its height and the angle of fall of the projectile.

Defilade against this fire can be determined by passing a plane with the proper inclination through the interior crest without considering in any way the point from which the shot comes.

Against close direct fire or for concealment from view, the principles and problems given above illustrate the methods which may be employed.

To what extent these methods shall be used, if at all, will be determined by the circumstances surrounding each particular case.

CHAPTER VIII.

ACCESSORY MEANS OF DEFENCE.

I.

204. Water may be made a very important accessory means of defence in many localities—as in a flat, marshy country where the level of the natural surface lies but at a slight elevation above the water-level; or, as in the case of an undulating surface, where small streams, running through valleys, can be dammed back, so as to produce an inundation of some extent.

205. In the former case, the defensive works can be easily girdled by a zone of marshy ground, upon which it will give an assailant great trouble to construct his trenches and other siege-works, while the work itself can be secured from attempts at surprise, by keeping its ditches filled with water to the depth of six feet at least. In such a locality—moreover, if in a climate where the winters are mild—revetted scarps and counterscarps, the chief use of which is to prevent an attempt at open assault, may be replaced by earthen ones, a strong stockade being formed along a wide berm, answering as a corridor, to give greater security on the more exposed fronts of the work.

206. In the latter case, portions of the ground, in the immediate vicinity of the works, may be covered by a sheet of water, of sufficient depth to prevent their being used by the assailant in his approaches; and within the inundation thus artificially produced detached works may be erected, which, having flank and reverse views over other lines of approach of the assailant, may force him to make his approach upon other points which have been strongly fortified to meet this condition of things.

To form these artificial inundations the locality must lend itself to the construction of dams, in such a position that they cannot be reached by the assailant's missiles, and will be secure from any other means he may take to destroy them. This supposes, then, that the stream should either run through the works, so that the dam could be erected within them, or so near to them that, in combination with some advanced work, the dam may be made secure.

In a locality having these features, the inundation would, as a general rule, have to be formed on the up-stream side of the work, since, if made below it, the dam would have to be placed further from the work, and the inundation itself might spread up too far within. Besides these objections to this position, an assailant would evidently have greater facilities for tapping the inundation and running the water off than when it occupies the up-stream position.

The position and extent of the dams, and the other necessary constructions connected with them, as sluices, waste weirs, etc., will depend entirely upon the local features of the site, and will form a particular study in each case for the engineer.

207. Besides these uses of water as a passive obstruction, arrangements may be made, when the locality is favorable to it, for producing a powerful current to sweep away the assailant's works in the ditches by letting loose a large body of water, which has been dammed back for the purpose, with a rush into the ditches. This, in like manner, will require the same constructions as in the preceding case, and flash gates which can be suddenly turned about a horizontal or a vertical axis, so as to give an outlet to the water in considerable volume and with great velocity. These gates have to be placed in some very secure point of the ditches, inaccessible to the assailant and covered from his missiles, and, if effectively used, may prove a source of great annoyance to him by frequently frustrating his attempts to make a passage of the ditch.

II.

208. Solid hard rock, or even thin layers of soft rock alternating with layers of soil, as was the case at Sebastopol, are great obstructions to an assailant's siege works, as the rock has, in many cases, to be blasted out to gain partial cover, and a large amount of earth with trench materials, has to be brought forward at great risk of life to form the parapets.

In constructing a work, nothing should be omitted which, if placed on the line of the assailant's approaches, will delay his operations and force him to greater efforts and exposure. To this end, where fragments of rock can be readily had in sufficient quantities, it should be used in forming the embankments of the glacis, and also be thrown in upon other points, over which important lines of trenches must necessarily be run.

Besides these accessory means of delaying the progress of the besieger's works, a site of solid rock offers the further advantage of giving natural scarps and counterscarps, where the ditches are excavated out of the rock, of far greater resistance to the assailant's means of destruction than any masonry, however solidly and carefully constructed, can offer; besides forcing the assailant to construct galleries through the rock to attain the level of the bottom of the ditch where his passage of it is to be constructed.

209. With a similar purpose, the stumps of large trees may be left in like positions, and trees may be planted when the work is constructed with the object of cutting them down, using their timber, and leaving their stumps when the work is threatened with a siege.

210. Obstacles as described in field fortifications may also be used in the defence of a breach or as an aid to a weak scarp wall, for which they are even recommended by some engineers as a substitute.

III.

211. Mines, when properly arranged and well played, are so important a defensive means that they should constitute a part of the permanent dispositions of defence of every work where the character of the soil will admit of it, at least on those points which are otherwise weakest, and therefore most liable to be assailed.

As the general arrangement of a combination of galleries and mine chambers, as well as the details for their construction, is given in Military Mining, nothing further is called for here than to state that the principal galleries of the combination should be constructed with the work, and of durable materials, leaving the other parts to be done when the exigency calling for them may happen.

CHAPTER IX.

SEA-COAST DEFENCE.

I.

BATTERIES ON LAND.

212. The different character of the attacks to which sea-coast and interior fortifications are subject, leads to material differences in their construction.

The guns attacking sea-coast works being mounted on ships which by their constant movements prevent deliberate and accurate aim, it is impossible to break down the defensive works by placing shot after shot upon a limited area, as is done by breaching batteries on land.

On the other hand the ships, being able to carry the heaviest guns, can, by uniting in large fleets and concentrating their fire upon one or two works, generally have the advantage in number and weight of guns; while their tops, presenting poor targets to the defence, are particularly favorable for the use of machine guns against the shore batteries.

213. Stone casemates, which as previously stated, would, when built, stand single shots from the heaviest guns then in use, are now easily penetrated and the fragments of masonry add to the destruction produced by the projectile. Their use is given up by all nations.

Sea-coast guns are now protected either by earth, iron, or steel.

214. Earthen Batteries. The thickness of a sand parapet equal to once and a half the penetration of the heaviest shot is about 70 feet (see Table of Penetrations, Appendix I). This thickness is excessive, and would not be often used. An equal resistance with a thinner parapet may be obtained by using concrete or large blocks of granite set in cement, the resistance of the first being approximately twice and of the second three times that of sand.

215. As before remarked, the penetration of elongated projectiles in parapets is less than in experimental butts, and the result of the bombardment of Alexandria, in 1882, in which 80-ton guns were used, led to the conclusion that "No English gun afloat could send a projectile through or seriously damage a good earthen parapet 30 feet in thickness, at ordinary practicable ranges." *

216. The practice in Germany is to make earthen parapets of sea-coast works from 33 to 40 feet thick.

The tendency of American engineers is to use thicker parapets.

217. No matter what the thickness of parapet, a plunging shot striking near the interior crest generally passes through and cuts a furrow, throwing out the earth and diminishing the height of the parapet.

This, combined with the plunging fire of machine guns from the ship's tops, makes it necessary to give the greatest available height above the terre-plein to the interior crest in open batteries.

This height of interior crest is of little value if the gun, at all times, and its detachment, while loading, are exposed to the fire of the ship's cannon and machine guns, since even the smaller cannon can by a well directed shot dismount or disable the heaviest gun, or the machine guns sweep away its detachment.

218. Several forms of disappearing gun carriages have been devised which allow the gun to be lowered behind the parapet to load and to be raised above it to fire. Figs. 2, 3, and 4, Plate 7, illustrate three of these. The drawings show their general features.

219. The Moncrieff works well for the smaller guns but is not applicable to the larger calibres.

220. The Hydraulic or Hydro-pneumatic requires the use of steam power for its rapid working, but it may be applied to the heaviest guns if its parts are properly proportioned.

221. King's carriage has stood the test of exhaustive experiments with the 25-ton gun, may be worked by hand-power with a 50-ton, and if properly constructed would work with the 100-ton gun. Major King proposes with very heavy guns the use of hydraulic pressure instead of hand-power for manœuvring the carriage.

* NOTE.—Report of British Naval and Military Operations in Egypt, 1882, by Lieutenant-Commander C. F. Goodrich, U. S. Navy.

222. Open batteries exposed to slant and enfilade fire must be protected by high traverses with bonnets. One, or at most two, guns may be mounted between consecutive traverses.

The thickness and height of traverses are determined by the direction of the fire to which they may be exposed.

High traverses are open to the objection that they show the position of the guns to the enemy at great distances.

223. When the battery is only subject to front fire, the interior crest and the tops of the splinter-proof traverses should be held in the same plane.

The guns should be painted of the same color as the parapet or background and provided with shields to protect the gunners from small projectiles.

224. Powder magazines and shell rooms are made under the traverses communicating by a lift with the loading passage in the traverse at the level of the terre-plein and generally close to the interior slope, the gun being traversed so that it is presented at this passage for loading. Plate 7, Fig. 1.

A bomb-proof room for the relief detachment is also built in the traverse.

When hydraulic power is used, bomb-proof shelters for the steam boilers and pumps are built in a place secure from hostile fire.

225. When placed upon a commanding plateau, of ample area, the battery may consist of a series of gun-pits sunk in the earth and fitted up as previously described.

226. This construction is particularly well suited for mortar batteries, which may be set back from the crest of the height, the pits being made to contain from one to four mortars each; the traverses between the pits serving for magazines, shell-rooms, cover for the men, and firing points for the groups of mortars, which may be placed very close together and fired from the shelter provided.

Plate 2 is a battery for 12 mortars designed by Gen. H. L. Abbot, Corps of Engineers, described in No. XI. Printed Papers Essayons Club, March 3, 1869.

227. The increased accuracy of fire and weight of projectile of the rifled mortars has given them much greater value for use against ships, and will cause them to be extensively used in the defence of channels and anchorages. Their fire attacks a ship upon its flat deck, which, is its most vulnerable part above water. They can be silenced neither by the ship's cannons, machine guns, nor mortars on floating structures. Mortar batteries are not expensive either in construction or armament.

228. If the site of a battery be very high, 100 feet or more above the water, it is generally considered that guns mounted on simple barbette or embrasure carriages in open batteries will be able to hold their own against ships, owing to the difficulty which the latter experience in working their heavy guns at high elevations, and the loss of plunge in the fire of the machine guns. In this case, however, as in the low batteries, the guns should be provided with shields against small projectiles and the cannoniers should be covered with a sufficient height of parapet.

229. The Use of Armor. Where the sites are contracted, earthen batteries cannot be built, and when without considerable command open batteries are rendered untenable by the small arms and machine guns of the ships. For these sites covered defences of iron or steel are alone available.

These are either casemates or turrets; they are made of wrought-iron, compound-plates, steel or chilled cast-iron.

When a limited field of fire only is desired, casemates have the advantage of cheapness, but usually require a somewhat larger embrasure, which as well as the muzzle of the gun is constantly exposed to hostile fire.

Turrets give an all-round fire with the smallest possible embrasure and almost complete protection so long as the armor is not pierced, and allow the muzzles of the guns to be turned to the rear while loading.

They are more expensive than casemates in themselves, in their substructure and in the machinery for their working.

230. The great expense of iron and steel constructions will always limit their application to the protection of guns of the highest power, which cover important points. The smaller guns will generally be placed in open batteries. These smaller guns being much cheaper in themselves, their mounting and emplacements, as well as much more rapid in their fire, which is nearly as effective as that of the large guns against unarmored ships and the unprotected parts of iron-clads, they should be provided in as large numbers as practicable.

II.

231. Floating Batteries. In some harbors of large area or with marshy banks, emplacements for guns commanding the channels cannot be obtained on shore.

For these cases the defence will sometimes require floating armored batteries of small speed, light draught, and great thickness of armor, which may be placed in different points of the harbor passing over shoals to avoid being rammed, or to pass from one channel to another when desired. They will carry the heaviest guns with the best possible protection, and not being designed to go to sea, can be made stronger in guns and armor than the attacking ships. Their first cost and the constant expense of keeping them in serviceable condition prohibits their use except in harbors, which can be defended in no other way.

III.

232. Obstacles, Submarine Mines and Torpedoes. The defence of harbors is not possible without the use of a sufficient number of guns and mortars; but where the inducement is great enough to justify it, or the inner harbor is not well protected, vessels can, and, under favoring circumstances will, run by the outer batteries, however well constructed and armed, unless obstacles, passive or active, are placed in the channels which will hold them under the fire of the guns until they are disabled by this fire or by the action of the obstacles themselves.

A perfect defence requires, beside guns and mortars, passive obstacles and submarine mines or torpedoes.

233. Obstacles. The following general conditions should be fulfilled by a system of passive obstacles, viz.:

1st. They should be in readiness for use at short notice, and of such simple construction as to be readily placed in position by river and harbor tug-boats.

2d. They should be capable of withstanding the effects of currents and storms, and the action of marine insects and growths for a considerable time.

3d. They should either be so strong and rigid as to break through the bottoms of vessels striking them, or, if of a yielding character, their resistance should gradually increase until it stops a vessel coming against them.

4th. They should be so placed as to be thoroughly swept by the fire of both the large and small guns of the defence, and of a construction which will not be seriously injured by this or the hostile fire.

234. The passive obstacles generally used, and which satisfy the above conditions to a greater or less degree, depending upon their construction, the character of the bottom, the currents, the temperature of the water and their expense, are sunken vessels and cribs, piles driven and rigidly braced in a vertical or inclined position; piles driven nearly to the bottom with floating and pointed logs attached to them by chains, making artificial "sawyers;" booms and rafts stretched across the channel; floating nets of chains, wire or other rope supported by buoys and generally carrying ropes with loose ends to become entangled in the wheels of attacking vessels; and in shallow water *chevaux de frise* or any other extemporized devices.

Of these the fixed obstructions can be used only in channels intended to be closed somewhat permanently; the floating ones being used in those which it may be necessary to open for the passage of friendly vessels.

235. Submarine Mines and Torpedoes. Submarine mines and torpedoes were first tried in the war of the Revolution, but hardly passed the experimental stage. They were again used in the Crimean war to a very limited extent.

Their first successful application on a comparatively large scale was in the war of Secession, 1861–5.

236. A system of submarine mines to be efficient should satisfy the following conditions, viz.:

1st. The positions which they are to occupy should be selected, all parts of the permanent structures designed for their use prepared, and all the mines and their attachments provided, properly marked and stored during peace.

2d. The mines should be as strong, cheap, and simple, as is consistent with efficiency.

3d. They should, when used, be planted in multiple lines or groups so disposed as to close the channels; and their electrical connections should be so made that a limited number of cables being cut by enemy will not disable the mines in such a way as to open a channel through the lines.

4th. The lines and groups must be thoroughly swept by the fire of the large and small guns of the defence.

5th. Trained officers and men in sufficient number to place and work the mines must be always available.

237. Fixed torpedoes, known as submarine mines, serve to close the channel to hostile vessels while leaving it open to those of the defence.

Movable torpedoes, known as "*torpedoes*," may be used to harass the enemy either at anchor or in motion.

Torpedo boats of small size and great speed, using spar torpedoes or more frequently launching "*auto mobiles*," of the Whitehead type, may move out from the harbors and attack the fleet at distances entirely beyond cannon-range and even in the open sea.

238. These torpedo boats and floating batteries are connecting links between the defence by land and sea forces.

239. Submarine mines are either self-igniting or controlled from the shore. The self-acting, once placed, close the channels equally to friend and foe. Those controlled from the shore by electricity may at will be made active against hostile, or harmless toward friendly vessels.

The latter class only can be employed in harbors which are to be used for naval or commercial purposes.

240. Submarine mines of both kinds are either "buoyant" or "ground."

The latter rest on the bottom, and may be used in water not exceeding 40 feet in depth; the former in deeper water, being held in place by an anchor and a cable which hold them at the proper depth below the surface.

241. The buoyant self-acting mines are exploded by the contact of a vessel with the mine itself; the ground mines by contact with the buoy, the explosion being caused by the action of a very sensitive fuse.

242. In mines controlled from the shore, the buoyant mine itself and the buoy attached to the ground-mine carry a "circuit-closer" (or breaker) which, acting under the shock caused by the vessel striking them, either announces the contact to the operator in the electrical room, or fires the mine as may be desired. In some cases they are fired only by the action of the operator, the position of the vessel with reference to them being determined by observers on shore.

243. The details of the circuit-closers, annunciators and arrangements for firing the mines differ materially in different nations, and are taught in their special schools. An attempt is generally made to keep them concealed from other nations.

They necessarily are more or less complicated and delicate in their construction and adjustment, and require for their effective use operators skilled in electricity, familiar with delicate mechanisms, and of careful and non-excitable disposition, assisted by trained and reliable men.

244. That system is best which is designed to fulfil only the necessary requirements with the least possible complication of parts, and in which the parts are as simple, strong, easily accessible, and easily understood by simple inspection, as possible.

In addition to this, the electrical connections of the different parts should, so far as practicable, be permanently made by the manufacturer, leaving to the operator only the necessity of attaching the torpedo wires and batteries for testing and firing.

245. The requisites for the satisfactory working of the electrical system are that each mine and cable may be tested as to its condition, that contact with a mine must be signalled; and that any mine may be fired by the operator, whether it has or has not been struck by a passing vessel.

The electric connection between the mines and the operating-room is by insulated cables of the kind used for submarine telegraphs.

246. The cases of ground-mines may be of cast-iron of a hemispherical or similar shape, as are the anchors of the buoyant mines.

247. The cases of the buoyant mines in our service are made of mild steel of spherical shape. They have a volume which gives them sufficient buoyancy to sustain their own weight, that of the charge and mooring cable, and enough excess to prevent them from being too much depressed in depth by the action of the currents of the place where they are to be used.

248. They are charged with the most powerful explosive attainable which is safe to handle, and not liable to be injured by age or moisture. Gun cotton, dynamite and explosive gelatine, are the principal explosives now used.

249. Movable Torpedoes include, 1st. The "automobile" or self-propelling, of which the Whitehead and Howell are examples. They contain their own motive power, generally compressed air, and once launched, no further control can be exercised over them. 2d. The "fish torpedoes" of which the Lay and Simms are examples. They are driven by liquid carbonic acid and an electric motor respectively, and are directed by electricity through cables which they reel out as they run. Their effective range is about two miles. 3d. Drifting torpedoes, which float with the current and are intended to explode upon striking a vessel. 4th. Submarine boats designed to pass under a vessel, fix a mine to it, and retire before the explosion occurs. A description of these different torpedoes does not properly belong to the subject of fortifications.

250. The destructive range of submarine explosions being very limited, every effort is made to cause them to take place as near the vessel attacked as possible.

The law of diminution of pressure and kinetic energy, in the transmission of the shock from subaqueous explosions of the principal explosive compounds has been well determined by General Abbot and published in "Professional Papers, Corps of Engineers, U. S. A., No. 23, 1881."

The resistance of modern vessels to these shocks is not so well known, and can only be determined by many costly experiments, comparatively few of which have yet been made.

251. Organization of Fortifications, Mines, and Torpedoes for the Defence of Harbors. The torpedo boats working out beyond cannon-range form the first line of defence. When driven in, they retreat until covered by the forts, and come into action again if opportunity offers.

252. The fish torpedoes come into play about two miles from shore. They have not yet had the test of actual use in war.

253. The forts and submarine mines arranged in defensive relations form the main line of defence upon which the safety of the harbor will usually depend.

254. Submarine mines derive a moral effect from the destruction which is worked by a single one successfully exploded, which prohibits the passage of the hostile fleet until the mines are destroyed or rendered inert. To render them harmless the enemy must capture the fortifications covering the operating rooms, cut all the cables, destroy the mines by blowing them up with counter mines, or disable them by grappling and dragging.

That these operations could be carried on by ships or boats in narrow channels under the close, well-directed fire of powerful guns, and the action of movable torpedoes, and of the mines themselves, is, if not absolutely impossible, of evident improbability. It may be said that a harbor provided with an efficient torpedo defence, thoroughly supported by both large and small guns, is practically impregnable by naval attack.

If, however, the supporting guns are not covered by fortifications strong enough to enable them to hold their own against the heaviest ship's guns, they may be silenced and captured, and with their fall the torpedo defence falls also, as it is manifest that the torpedo defence can have no value whatever when the control of its firing arrangements falls into hostile hands.

255. The possibility that the enemy may break through

a single or even double line of mines by sacrificing one or two ships, by well-worked counter-mines, by cutting, one or two groups of cables by a fortunate shot, or by the occurrence of one of the many accidents which may disable somewhat delicate electrical apparatus, makes it necessary that the third condition above given, should be fulfilled.

256. Remarks. The more modern and better-developed systems of submarine mines as harbor defences have not as yet stood the test of actual attack. In all the wars which have occurred, since their development, their moral effect has deterred naval commanders from assailing harbors defended by forts and supposed to be supplied with a system of submarine mines.

CHAPTER X.

THE DEFENSIVE ORGANIZATION OF FRONTIERS WITH PERMANENT FORTIFICATIONS.

257. No State, in the present condition of civilization, can be regarded as secure from foreign military aggression, the accessible points of whose frontiers are not occupied by permanent fortifications of such strength as shall prevent an enemy from obtaining possession of them by a sudden assault, and thus procuring the means of penetrating into the interior. Guided by the experience of centuries of wars, and the daily increasing facilities which the improvement in the *matériel* of armies and their transportation afford for rapid and powerful offensive operations, the ruling states of Continental Europe have, within the last half-century, not only made every effort to place their frontiers in an unassailable condition, but also their great centres of population and wealth in the interior, beyond the chances of a sudden attack from an enemy who might force his way through the frontier defences and march rapidly upon them, thus making these positions the rallying points where a defeated army can find a safe resting-place until it can be reorganized and sufficiently strengthened to resume the offensive.

Such seems to be the result at which the generals and statesmen of Europe have arrived, after the most mature and careful consideration of the important problem of national defence; at a time when *the utility of permanent fortifications was seriously called in question*, by some who pointed, in support of their views, to the very inefficient part the great number of fortified places had played in the wars waged by Napoleon, when, by means of overwhelming numbers in the field, he was enabled to disregard such places, the garrisons of which were too feeble to make any efficient offensive movements, until the defeat of his adversary, in one or more great pitched battles, necessarily also threw them into his possession.

In view of the arguments based on these events, the opinions of Napoleon himself should carry great weight. In speaking of the bearing of permanent fortifications in a defensive war, he says: "If fortresses can neither secure a victory, nor arrest the progress of a conquering enemy, they can at least retard it, and thus give to the defence the means of gaining time—a most important advantage in all warfare." In like manner the Archduke Charles of Austria, who showed himself one of the ablest adversaries with whom Napoleon was called upon to cope, took the ground "that a defensive warfare cannot be systematically and successfully carried on in a country which is not provided with fortresses that have been planned and distributed according to strategical requirements." Like views were held by the Duke of Wellington; and it is probable that no great general, from the earliest period of military operations down to the present moment, has ever entertained the contrary.

Without going further back than the Franco-Prussian war of 1870–71, we find that while the entrance of the German army upon French territory was easily accomplished, owing to its superiority in numbers, organization, and rapid mobilization at the first stage of the war, it was necessary to detach from the advancing army the large forces investing Metz, Strasburg, Belfort, and other fortified places.

These forces, with their artillery, were occupied from 30 to 100 days in reducing these strong places, which were upon their lines of communication and could not be neglected.

The fortifications of Paris, although their scarp walls were exposed and their casemates not strong enough to resist the German artillery, held the German army in check from the middle of September until the end of January, affording four and one half months for the organization of an army of relief in the other parts of France.

The fact that this opportunity was not made use of has no bearing upon the value of the fortifications, which more than fulfilled their original design.

That this value was appreciated by both sides, is shown in the immense sums spent by them since that time in building new forts and remodelling the old. The only question, then, on this subject that remains for solution by a State is, in what way such a means of security from aggression can be best adapted to its own geographical, political, and military status.

258. In a country like our own, with so vast an extent

of sea-coast and inland frontier, and with political and social institutions which are so antagonistic to every approach to a large standing army as a measure of national safety, this question is one of peculiar importance, both from the open character of this extensive frontier, and from the almost incredible facility with which considerable armies, with all their *matériel*, can be concentrated on distant points by the aid of steam. The weakness of our immediate neighbors on the one side, and the daily increasing mutual commercial interests between us and the greatest naval power in the world, by which we might be seriously threatened both along our seaboard and our extensive line of inland frontier, it is true, would seem to favor the hope that the day is still remote, and from present appearances, may never arrive, in which our country will have to apprehend anything in the shape of invasion except along the sea-coast; and we may, therefore, dismiss from our consideration any other provision against this eventuality (which, should it happen, looking to our resources in men and means, will hardly extend inland beyond a few marches), except what we have already attempted, viz., the securing of our principal harbors, naval stations, and commercial marts from a naval attack, or from one combined with the operations of a land force, which, from the causes above alluded to, could be but of short duration.

259. In the organization of the inland frontier fortifications of a state, the points to be principally regarded are the principal avenues of access to it, and their topographical features as they lend themselves more or less to strengthen the artificial defences. In conducting an invasion across an inland frontier, the march of the enemy must necessarily be along the roads that intersect it, as these afford the only means for transporting the *matériel*, etc., of the army. The points, therefore, or places in their neighborhood where the principal roads or other avenues of communication cross the frontier, particularly those which lead to the great centres of population and wealth, are the ones which would necessarily call for permanent defences. No absolute rule can be laid down for the distribution and strength of such works along a frontier. Everything must depend upon the greater or less of facility presented to an enemy for penetrating at one point rather than another, and upon the ulterior advantages the one may present to him over another.

260. Rivers and mountain ranges are the natural fortifications of states; and where they form the frontiers they greatly facilitate the application of artificial defensive means, as they present but few, and those in general important, points of access.

When these points on a river are fortified, an invading force, however powerful, cannot, without great risk, cross the river without first gaining possession of them; for, even should a sufficient detachment be left to observe and blockade the fortresses, the main army, in case of retreat or any disaster, might be placed in an extremely critical position, in its movements to recross the river, with the garrisons of the fortresses threatening its flanks and rear.

261. In offensive operations, fortresses upon a river frontier form one of the strongest bases of operations. If a river intersects the frontier, the point where it crosses it, or some one in its vicinity, should be occupied by a permanent work; among such points those are more peculiarly necessary to be held where a river forming the frontier is intersected by another navigable one which lies wholly within the frontier.

The importance of thoroughly occupying such points is obvious, as they afford an army on the defensive the means of passing readily and safely from one side to the other of the river, either to evade a force too powerful for it to cope with in the open field, or, when an opportunity offers, from any imprudent movement of an invading force on one side, to throw itself suddenly from the other on its flank or rear, and thus force it to a retrograde movement.

262. With respect to mountain passes, the main roads alone will require permanent works. If the passes are independent of each other, a work will be necessary for each one separately; but where several unite at the same point, upon or within the frontier, a single work placed upon this point will suffice. Local circumstances will determine the point in each pass which, occupied, will offer the greatest advantage for obstructing the march of an invading force and retarding the bringing forward its *matériel*. The only rule that can be given is that, while the position selected shall satisfy these conditions, there shall be every facility of communication between the fortress and the interior for receiving supplies and reinforcements. This rule would lead generally to the selection of some point of the outlet within the frontier as the proper one.

263. The number of fine natural harbors and roadsteads on our seaboard, where the largest fleets can find a secure anchorage at all seasons; the proximity to the ocean of many of our most important cities, towns, and populous villages, by which they are not only exposed to the usual dangers of naval attacks, but to incursions from an enemy's land forces; together with the large rivers which, having their outlets on this seaboard frontier, are navigable for long distances within it by vessels of the greatest burden—have given to the subject of sea-coast defences a particular prominence among ourselves.

The means of defence disposable for the security of such points consists in permanent works arranged to meet an attack both by sea and land, and of such strength as the presumed nature of the attack will demand; of such temporary fortifications as the exigency of the moment may point out; of movable land forces; and of floating defences to act in aid of the others.

264. The character of the permanent defences will depend upon the object in view. Where this is simply to exclude an enemy's fleet from the use of a harbor or roadstead, which offers to him no other inducement for its occupation but that afforded by a secure anchorage, one or more small works of sufficient strength to prevent the success of an open assault upon them, armed with heavy mortars and guns with long ranges, that can reach by their fire every point where an enemy's ship could safely anchor, will be sufficient.

The points to be occupied by these works, as well as their plan, will depend upon the natural features of the harbor or roadstead itself.

They will usually consist either of open works with guns in barbette and mortars sweeping all points of approach to and within the harbor; or of a combination of covered and barbette batteries; with ditches or other obstacles, and bomb-proof barracks of sufficient capacity to hold the garrison necessary to beat off an open assault on the battery by land, and to be secure from a *coup-de-main*.

Like defences will also be sufficient for the security of the smaller classes of towns and villages, which would probably offer a temptation only to a small naval force.

265. In the case of important commercial cities and large naval depôts lying within harbors more or less accessible both to sea and land attacks, the character of the defences called for must necessarily be commensurate with the magnitude of the interests to be guarded, and the consequent temptation to an enemy to put forth great efforts for their occupation and destruction.

The avenues of approach to these objects by sea, which can be brought within range of cannon and mortars in fortifications on the shore, or in armored forts erected on natural or artificial islands, should be occupied to a distance that will prevent a fleet from approaching near enough to open a bombardment, and if practicable also force the enemy, if he ventures a land attack, to disembark his forces either at so great a distance from the object to be reached that he will not be able, by a sudden movement of this nature, to effect a surprise; or to limit his landing to such points on the coast as, from their exposed position, may render the coöperation of the naval and land forces very uncertain, and, in case of a storm, place the latter in a very perilous condition if attacked.

These works will form the exterior chain of the defences. Within these, batteries, either open or casemated, as the locality may seem to demand, should occupy all the most suitable positions for sweeping the path that a fleet must follow by powerful cross, direct, and enfilading fires, and for reaching every point of anchorage within the harbor.

The batteries commanding the inner harbor within easy range of the city have especial value in attacking and destroying, by their cross-fire, any ships which might run past the outer forts. The presence of such batteries will probably deter the ships from attempting this kind of attack.

On the land approaches, points should be occupied by forts of a permanent character, which will prevent a sufficiently near approach to bombard the city or depôt, and, in combination with temporary works, will afford an intrenched field of battle for the troops on the defensive. These will form the exterior line of the land defences, the interior line being either a continuous enceinte strong enough to resist assault, or else a suitable combination of either continuous or detached field works of such strength and armament that the enemy, in any attempt to carry them by an open assault, will be made to suffer heavily, even if he is not repulsed.

The security of objects of this character will be greatly increased when they lie at some distance within the sea-coast frontier, and can only be approached by water through such comparatively narrow defiles as even our largest rivers present, and by land after one or more marches. These defiles will, for the most part, not only present admirable positions on their banks from which an assailant's fleet can be enfiladed within the range of the heaviest guns, but frequently others, at points where the river narrows, or changes its course, where works occupying the opposite banks will give the means of rendering the river impassable by torpedoes, booms, rafts, or other floating and sunken obstructions, which cannot be removed except by getting possession by a land attack of the defences which guard them.

266. Wherever harbors or bays are of such extent that their entrance cannot be interdicted to an enemy's fleet, nor secure anchorage within them be prevented, of which we have examples on our own coast, the case falls beyond the province of fortification, and must be left to floating defences for a solution. Here even some fortified harbors on the shores of such extensive estuaries may give secure places of refuge for ships-of-war, from which they may at any moment sally when they can take the enemy at a disadvantage, or into which they can retreat if attacked by a superior force.

267. In the great military states of Continental Europe, the question as to what extent the great centres of population and wealth in the *interior* should be covered by fortifications, has been submitted to the investigation of the ablest engineers and statesmen, from the time of Vauban down to the present day; but more particularly since the fall of Napoleon, a catastrophe which might not have taken place had Paris been secured by fortifications which would have prevented a *coup-de-main*, when the armies of the Allies gained possession of it as the result of a pitched battle. Whatever differences of opinion have been called forth as to the mode of accomplishing this object, as shown in the published views on the proposition to fortify Paris, there seems to have been none among those best qualified to decide upon it as to the great importance of so fortifying this capital and other large places in the interior, as Lyons, etc., which from their position must be of the highest strategical value in the case of a successful invasion by a large army, as not only to prevent their wealth and resources from falling into the possession of the invading force, but to make them safe rallying-points for beaten and dispersed forces, and depôts for organizing new armies.

The plan that has been adopted for this end, both in France and in most of the other cities of Europe which have been either newly fortified or had their old work strengthened within this period, is to surround the city by a continuous enceinte of greater or less strength, but one secure from a *coup-de-main*, and to occupy with forts of a permanent character the most suitable points in advance of the enceinte, to prevent an enemy from bombarding the city, or penetrating between them without first gaining possession of them. By this plan, it is proposed to gain all the advantages offered by the passive resistance of fortifications and the activity of a disposable movable force occupying the zone between the enceinte and the forts as an intrenched camp, upon which the forts and temporary works thrown up between them would render an open assault too perilous to be attempted.

268. The fortifications of Paris, of 1840, consist of a continuous bastioned enceinte, without outworks, with a revetted scarp of the usual height, to secure it from escalade, and a ditch with a counterscarp of earth. The advanced forts are either quadrangular or pentagonal bastioned works, inclosing all the means of security for their garrisons, as bomb-proofs, etc., their plan being skilfully adapted to the site, and their mutual bearing on the defence.

After the siege of 1870–71, these fortifications were increased by the addition of an exterior line of forts occupying the outer crest of the basin of Paris approximately upon the circumference of a circle of 24 miles diameter, that of the inner belt being about 12 miles and the enceinte about 6 miles.

The new detached forts are polygonal without outworks.

The fortifications of Lyons present more diversity, both in the plan and details of the enceinte and forts; although the general system is the same as that of Paris. There is here seen a more extensive application of casemated and gallery defences, both for exterior flanking and for the defence of the interior forts, growing out of the more broken features of the site generally, and frequently the more confined space occupied by them.

In Germany the same general system of a continuous enceinte, with strong advanced isolated works, has been followed; the whole being so planned and combined as to meet the distinctive features of what is known as the German system of fortification. The principal changes in those have already been described.

269. In our own country, where the important centres of population and wealth lie almost immediately upon the seaboard, it would seem impracticable, in view of the rapid spread of population around them, and the consequent changes in local features, to resort to any defences of a permanent character to secure them from a land attack, even were the nation willing to assume the burden of the great outlay for such an object; as, in a few years, the works of to-day might be rendered useless by the changes referred to. Even in Europe, the strongest despotic governments have been obliged to cede what seemed military exigencies to the demands of the social condition; and either to raze the fortifications of cities, to give room to a crowded population, or else to suffer such encroachments on the ground necessary for their action as to render them nearly useless. The only defensive resource that seems left to ourselves, in like cases, is in the use of field-works—one which our military experience shows may be relied upon with confidence, so long as the military aptitude of our population remains unchanged from what it has thus far proved itself to be.

CHAPTER XI.

SUMMARY OF THE PROGRESS AND CHANGES OF FORTIFICATION.

I.

270. The records of history and the vestiges of remote civilization show that the art of fortification, in some guise or another, has been in practice throughout all nations, even in the lowest stages of social progress; and that, wherever it has been cultivated, its character has been more or less influenced, not only by the natural features of the country, but by the political and social conditions of its inhabitants.

In its earliest applications, we find men resorting to one or more simple enclosures of earthen walls; or of these surmounted by stakes placed in juxtaposition; or of stakes alone firmly planted in the ground, with a strong wattling between them; or of timber in its natural state, having its branches and the undergrowth strongly interlaced to form an impervious obstruction, with tortuous paths through it only known to the defenders.

A resort to such feeble means shows not only a very low state of this branch of the military art, but also of that of the attack; as defence of this kind would present but a slight obstacle, except against an enemy whose habitual mode of fighting was as cavalry, or against one not yet conversant with the ordinary plans for scaling. This class of fortifications for the defence of entire frontiers has been mostly met with in the east of Europe, and was doubtless, at the time, found to be a sufficient protection against those nomadic tribes that for ages have roamed over its vast plains, and who are only formidable as a mounted force.

271. To secure greater permanence and strength, the next step was to form walls either of rough blocks of stone alone, or of these intermixed with the trunks of heavy trees. Obstructions of this kind could only be used to a limited extent, and were confined to the defences of places forming the early centres of population. As human invention was developed, these, in their turn, were found to present no serious obstacle to an assault by escalade; giving to the assailed only the temporary advantage of a more commanding position; and they gave place to walls of dressed stone, or brick, whose height and perpendicular face alike bade defiance to individual attempts to climb them, or the combined effort of an escalade. From the tops of these inaccessible heights, sheltered in front by a parapet of stone, and, in some cases, by a covered corridor behind them, the assailed could readily keep at bay any enemy, so long as he was exposed to their missiles; but having reached the foot of the wall, he here found shelter from these, and, by procuring any cover that would protect him from objects thrown from above, could securely work at effecting a breach by mining. It was probably to remedy this defect of simple walls that towers, which at first were nothing more than square or semicircular projections built, from distance to distance, in the wall itself, were first devised; and which subsequently were not only enclosed throughout, but divided into stories, each of which was provided with loop-holes, to flank the adjacent towers and the straight portions of the wall between them. Each tower could be isolated from the straight portion of the walls adjacent to it, by an interruption at the top of the wall, over which a communication between the tower and wall could be established by a temporary bridge.

272. These formidable defences were, in their turn, found to be insufficient against the ingenuity and skill of the assailant, who, by means of covered galleries of timber, sometimes above ground and sometimes beneath, gradually won his way to the foot of the wall, where, by breaking his way through it, or by undermining and supporting it on timber props to be subsequently destroyed by fire, he removed the sole obstruction to a bodily collision with the assailed.

These methods of assault were in some cases supported by means of high mounds of earth which were raised in an inclined plane towards the walls, and sometimes carried forward to them, from the top of which the assailant, by the erection of wooden towers, covered with raw hides to secure them from being burnt, could command the interior, and, driving the assailed from the walls, gain a foothold on them by lowering a drawbridge from the wooden tower.

273. These changes in the attack led to new modifications in the defence, which consisted in surrounding the place by wide and deep ditches, of which the walls formed the scarp, the counterscarp being either of earth or revetted. This placed a formidable obstacle to the mode of attack by mining, and also to the use of earthen mounds, as these last had to be constructed across the ditch before they could gain sufficient proximity to the wall either to form a communication with its top, or to breach it by means of the battering-ram; the ditches also were filled with water whenever this obstruction could be procured, and when dry they formed a defile through which the assailed often sallied upon the assailant with success when found at a disadvantage in it.

274. The gigantic profile often given to the fortifications of antiquity seems almost incredible, as well as their extent. In many cases a double wall of stone or brick was filled in between with earth, forming a wide rampart upon which several vehicles could go abreast. Not only was the space enclosed by some of these fortifications that requisite for the habitations, but ground enough was taken in to add considerably to the food of the inhabitants and cattle, for the long periods to which blockades were in many cases extended, when all other means of reducing the place had failed.

The wall built by the Romans, between Carlisle and Newcastle, to restrain the incursions of the Picts into the southern portions of the island, was seventy-three miles in extent, about twelve feet in height, and nine feet in thickness. The extent and dimensions of this work sink almost into insignificance when compared with those of the celebrated wall of China, built to restrain the incursions of the Tartars. This structure is about 1500 English miles in length; has a height of 27 feet; its thickness at top is 14 feet. The lower portion of it is built of dressed stone, the upper of well-burned brick. It is flanked at distances of about 80 yards apart by towers in which iron cannon are found.

In the great extent it embraces, it necessarily crosses hills and valleys, and in many places important defiles. An examination of its parts has shown that in its plan there was an evident design to adapt it to those features of its site, as it is well thrown back to the rear of difficult passes; and at points where there is most danger to be apprehended from attempts of invasion, there are several walls in succession.

275. The mode of attack of fortified places resorted to by the ancients was reduced to settled rules, and brought to the highest state of perfection by the Greeks, about the epoch of Alexander the Great and the immediate successors to his vast conquests. An essential feature in it, whether in the sieges of inland fortresses or those on the seaboard, was to cut off all communication between the place and the exterior, by hemming it in by sea and land, with stationary forces, covered themselves by lines of intrenchments strengthened by towers, and, in the case of sea-coast places, also by fleets, from all assaults both from without and from the place invested.

Having selected the portions of the place on which the attack was to be directed, a second line was formed parallel to the first, which was covered, and constructed of timber and wicker-work, and secured with raw hides to prevent its being set on fire. From this sheltered position, which served also the purposes of a lodging for the besiegers, the besieged were annoyed with missiles thrown from all the artillery known in that day, consisting of the ordinary bow, the cross-bow, and the various machines for projecting heavy stones and other projectiles.

Under the diversion thus made, the besiegers pushed forward from this line several covered approaches of a like construction directly upon the place, for the purpose of gaining the counterscarp of the place, and from that position filling up the ditch with stones, earth, heavy logs, etc., to prepare the way for placing the battering-ram in position to breach the wall. The tower in which this machine was placed usually consisted of several stories, and was occupied by troops who cleared the top of the wall assailed of the besieged. This operation was frequently aided by other high towers, which were advanced either along the natural level of the ground, or upon artificial mounds forming inclined planes, towards the place, by means of which the towers could be given any desirable command over the interior.

276. The defence was mostly of a passive character; the besieged trusting mainly to the strength of their defences, under cover of which they resorted to all the means used by the besiegers for assailing the latter when they came within reach of their missiles; using cranes and other devices to seize upon the implements planted at the foot of the wall, and carrying out galleries of countermines to overwhelm the artificial mounds and their towers.

277. The Romans evinced their decided military aptitude, not only in the employment of the ordinary systematic methods of the attack and defence of fortified places, but in their application of the cardinal principle of mutual defensive relations between the parts of a fortified position, obtained by advanced and retired portions of the enceinte; and also in the adaptation of intrenchments to the natural features of the site, as shown in the fortifications of some of the permanent frontier camps of their military colonies. These principles have also been noticed in some of the fortified positions of India, which consist of a mural enceinte with the earthen ramparts flanked by round towers, and of round towers in advance of the enceinte connected with it by caponnières.

With the decadence of the Roman Empire, the art of fortification, like the other branches of the military art, was brought to so low a stage that strongholds which, skilfully defended with energy, would have baffled the efforts of a well-trained assailant in the art of attack, fell, almost without resistance, into the possession of the fierce northern hordes, by which the whole of civilized Europe was overrun.

278. The remains of the structures raised for defensive purposes, during the prosperous days of the Empire, were probably the sole means of protection afforded to the inhabitants of the towns that still maintained a nucleus of population, until the rise of the Western Empire, under Charlemagne; and it was the necessity felt by this conqueror, not only of securing his conquests, but of checking the irruptions of the barbarous tribes along his extended frontier, which led him to erect *têtes-de-pont* on the frontier rivers, and a line of strong towers, for garrisons of a few men, upon the most inaccessible and prominent points of this frontier; the latter being a means which was subsequently resorted to for a like purpose in the Spanish peninsula.

Henry I., of Germany, introduced a more important and more systematic addition to these permanent frontier defences, by surrounding the frontier towns and villages, occupied by military colonists, with walls and ditches, to secure them from such attacks as they might be exposed to, and subsequently adding a second line of strongholds within the frontier, by which an irruption through the frontier line might still be checked.

279. During the general disorganization of States under the feudal system, the free cities which depended for their defence on the burghers composing the different crafts, every individual who could maintain a few retainers in his pay, and the clergy, even, resorted—each according to their separate views—to such means of defence as would best secure them from the attacks of others in a like condition, and would enable them to carry out that system of pillage which had become general amongst the nobles and other military chieftains.

280. From this state of society sprang up those castles, placed in the most inaccessible positions on the lines of communication which the little inland commerce that was still carried on was obliged to traverse. These were provided with every possible device for an obstinate passive defence, being surrounded by a wide and deep ditch, or moat, over which a drawbridge was the only communication to the main entrance, which was flanked by towers on the exterior, and closed with massive doors; the tortuous passage which led from them to the interior of the castle being further secured by a grated portcullis, which could be let drop at a moment's notice, to arrest a sudden assault.

To these means were often joined, besides the ordinary measures of loop-holes and machicoulis in the walls and towers for annoying the assailant, a high interior tower, termed a keep, or donjon, which, commanding the exterior defences, was also a watch-tower over the adjacent country.

The keep, which was the last defensible point, was, in some cases, provided with a secret subterranean passage, having its outlet in some distant concealed spot, through which succor could be introduced into the beleaguered castle; and, in the last extremity, the garrison find safety in a stealthy flight.

281. The fortifications of towns partook of the same characteristics as those of castles. From the custom of assigning to the different burgher crafts, each of which had an independent military organization, the exclusive guardianship of portions of the enceinte, as well as their erection and repairs, great diversity, and frequently a whimsicality, in the defensive arrangements was the natural result; the evidence of which still exists in the remains of the walls of some of the old Continental cities. The art, for the most part, was practised by ambulatory engineers, who, like the secret orders by whom the bridges and churches of the same period were built, offered their services wherever they were wanted. Many ideas were also introduced from the East by the Crusaders, as exhibited in the fortifications of castles and cities belonging to the Templars and other religious military orders.

282. With the invention of gunpowder, and its application to military purposes, a gradual revolution took place in the general forms and details of fortification. It was soon seen that naked walls alone did not offer either suitable conveniences for the new military machines, or sufficient protection against the projectiles thrown from them. This led to the introduction of earthen ramparts and parapets, which were placed against the walls and suitably arranged to meet the exigencies of the moment. The art received something like a scientific basis about this time in Italy, from which the names and forms of most of the elements of fortification now in use are derived. The Italian engineers, like their predecessors, went from state to state to offer their services wherever they were needed, and in this way disseminated the principles of their school throughout Europe.

283. It was at this epoch that the bastioned form of fortification first appeared, but the precise date and the author of the invention are both unknown. With its introduction the importance of separating the parts of a line of fortification into advanced and retired parts, the latter flanking and defending the former, seems to have been recognized as an essential principle of the art. With these changes in the form of the enceinte, the art was gradually improved by the addition of outworks to increase the amount of cross and flank fire; the introduction of bomb-proof shelters for the troops and other purposes; the substitution of earthen for stone parapets; and the attempt to conceal the scarp walls from the enemy's batteries by decreasing the command and deepening the ditches of the enceinte.

By these gradual changes stone walls, which in the old fortifications were the essential defensive features, came at length to be regarded in their true character, simply as passive obstacles to an open assault by escalade. The property of earthen parapets, of resisting without material loss of strength the long-continued fire of the assailant's heaviest guns, showed that the same defensive means were applicable both to works of a permanent and of a temporary character; and were equally available for the purposes of the assailant and the assailed. The measures for the attack and the defence of positions were thus reduced to the same general principles, differing only in the forms and dimensions of the elementary parts, as circumstances seemed to demand.

284. Italian School. As above stated, the first employment of bastions as they now exist was made by the Italian engineers; and, as far as has been ascertained, towards the close of the fifteenth or the commencement of the sixteenth century. To whom the credit of their invention is due is not known. In the earlier fronts of the Italian school the bastions are very small, and they are connected by curtains varying from 250 to 500 yards in length. The bastion flanks, which were perpendicular to the curtains, were divided into two portions; that next to the curtain, which was one-third of the entire flank, was thrown back and covered by the portion in advance, which thus formed what received the name of the orillon. The lower part of the retired portion was casemated for cannon; and behind this, and separated from it by a dry ditch, rose a second flank, having the same command as the other parts of the enceinte parapet. In some cases a small and very obtuse bastion was erected at the middle of long curtains.

The ditches of the enceinte were usually about 100 feet wide and 24 feet deep; the counterscarps being parallel to the bastion-faces.

A scarp gallery, for the purpose of mining, ran throughout the enceinte scarp, and communicated with galleries leading to other points.

The parapets, at first of masonry, were afterwards of earth, and from 18 to 24 feet thick. The earth of the rampart was sustained on the interior by a wall. Ramps established a communication between the interior and the rampart.

The defects of these early fronts were soon felt, and a more complicated but improved method adopted, in which the bastions were enlarged and the curtains diminished. The retired flanks were still retained, but the orillon instead of being angular was rounded. To these improvements, cavaliers were sometimes added to the bastions, which in those cases were made without retired flanks; or placed on the curtains, when, from the configuration of the site, some portion of the ground within cannon-range could not be swept from the enceinte parapet. The covered-way was introduced and became an integral part of the front; and a small demi-lune or ravelin was placed in advance of the enceinte ditch, forming a *tête-de-pont* to cover the communication, at the middle of the curtain across the main ditch, between the enceinte and the exterior. The covered-way, which at first was of uniform width and bordered the main and demi-lune ditches, was subsequently provided with salient and reëntering places-of-arms. These various essential parts of a fortified front were gradually ameliorated by the Italian engineers, but not before the Italian school had left its impress upon the fortification of all the other states of Europe; as the Italian engineers, from their superior acquirements, were in demand throughout these states.

285. Spanish School. From the existing fortifications of Spain, the influence of the Italian school may be traced, but modified by national characteristics; the works seem organized more for a purely passive defence; the covered-way, that essential outwork to an active defence, being in many cases omitted; the means of annoying the besiegers by fires being greatly multiplied; and the outworks generally being arranged with a view to a purely passive defence. Besides this, the dimensions of the profile and height of scarp were increased as a greater security against escalade; interior retrenchments were multiplied, sometimes enclosing a bomb-proof keep to render the defence more obstinate.

The Spaniards, although resorting but little to sorties, show great skill and pertinacity in the defence of breaches, and in availing themselves of all obstructions for prolonging resistance.

From the broken character of many of the sites of their fortresses, the Spaniards resorted very much also to detached works to occupy commanding points from which the main work could be annoyed.

These they also generally organized for a strictly passive defence, leaving them more to their own resources than to any coöperation with the main work.

286. Dutch School. This school took its rise in the political necessities of the times, in which the national spirit was aroused to throw off an onerous foreign yoke. The aquatic character of the country, and the want of time and pecuniary means, led to those expedients of defence which are never wanting under like circumstances. The deficiency of earth led to the formation of low parapets for the main enceinte and wide ditches filled with water. The main enceinte was usually preceded by a second one with a very low parapet to sweep the surface of the wet ditch; and this second enceinte was separated from the first by a dry ditch, which favored sorties, and which was provided with all the means, as palisades, tambours, and block-houses, for offensive returns and surprises. The second enceinte was generally covered from an exterior command by a glacis in advance of the main ditch. The covered-way between the glacis and the ditches was, to a great extent, deprived of its essential offensive feature by an exterior wet ditch made at the foot of the glacis and enclosing it, over which communication with the exterior was kept open by temporary bridges.

The works were usually very much multiplied and their combination complicated; features the less objectionable where their defence chiefly rested upon the inhabitants who had become familiar with all their turnings, and as offering obscurity of design to an assailant who might force his way into them. The whole of the defensive measures of this school seem to have had solely for their object a strictly passive resistance. With this view long lines of intrenchments, supported from distance to distance by forts, connected their frontier towns and villages, affording a sufficient obstacle to marauding expeditions, and requiring the efforts of a strong force to break through them. At a later period, taught by the experience of their earlier efforts against the most military state of that epoch, covers that would afford security against incendiary modes of attack were provided; and revetments of masonry substituted for the earthen slopes of the ramparts, particularly where the ditches were dry. These successive changes, partly influenced by the Italian and Spanish schools, with which the Dutch engineers were brought into contact through their connection with Spain, were the natural precursors of the system of Coehoorn, the most distinguished engineer of the Dutch school, whose works are characterized by many of its essential features.

287. German School. The Germans reckon a number of original writers on fortification, among the most noted of whom are the celebrated painter, Albert Durer, Daniel Speckles, and Rimpler. In the propositions of these writers are to be found the influence which the Italian school naturally exercised throughout civilized Europe, and the germs of many of the views held by the German school of the present day; which last seem, however, to have been taken more immediately from the propositions of Montalembert and Carnot.

288. Swedish School. The part played by Sweden upon the theatre of Europe, under her two celebrated monarchs, Gustavus Adolphus and Charles XII., served to develop in this nation every branch of the military art, and produced a number of distinguished generals and engineers, who combined with the practice of their profession a study of its theory. Among the engineers of this school, Virgin holds the first place.

The climate and the nautical habits of the country seem to have led to land defences analogous to those of ships, as shown in the uses of casemated batteries in several tiers, both for sea-coast and inland fortifications. In this school the bastioned system seems to have been generally adopted for the enceinte, great attention being paid to covering the faces of the works from enfilading fire; in providing casemates having reverse views on the besiegers' works; and particularly in so arranging the interior dispositions that each part should not only contribute to the defence of the others, but be capable of an independent resistance. These dispositions necessarily led to great complication and multiplicity of works, as shown in the writings of Virgin.

289. French School. What may be termed the characteristics of this school are to be seen rather in the method of Cormontaigne, and the teachings of the two celebrated schools of Mézières and Metz for the education of engineers, than in the practice of Vauban, although his authority has exercised a preponderating influence throughout Europe, and is still appealed to, in all great problems of the art, by each side in polemical disputes.

The French have evinced in this, as in all the other arts, that spirit of systematic combination which forms one of their most striking national traits. Without excluding an active defence, the most noted authors of this school have based their methods upon a combination of elements by which the besieger's progress can be checked step by step by the fire of the works rather than by sorties. Within the last twenty years all schools have been rapidly tending towards a common system, which is the logical outcome of the weapons now available, and the means of resisting their action.

The freedom of intercourse between nations, no less than the general and free discussion of all projects by all engineers, leads to the development and adoption of the simplest, cheapest, and most effective methods of defence. That a universal system is yet adopted can hardly be said, but the disposition to depend mainly upon a defence by detached works, as previously described, is too manifest to leave room for a reasonable doubt that for many years it will be the only one employed.

II.

PROGRESS OF THE ATTACK SINCE THE INVENTION OF FIRE-ARMS.

290. The introduction of cannon, although it led to important changes in the measures both of the attack and defence, still did not, for a considerable period, bring about any very decisive results in the length of sieges. The means which it afforded the defence of reaching the besiegers at a distance, and of destroying all the methods of approaching and annoying the place which had been hitherto used, led to the substitution of the ordinary trenches of the present day for the wooden galleries and other similar expedients for approaching under cover, and to the erection of batteries at distant points to open breaches in the walls.

Lines of circumvallation and countervallation, which formed so prominent a feature previously to this epoch, was the only one which still kept its place, as it has done to a greater or less extent to the present day. For the purpose of effecting an entrance into the place, breaching batteries were erected opposite the points deemed most favorable. They were placed either on natural elevations of the ground, or upon artificial mounds, with the object of striking the wall to be opened near its foot, and forming a breach of easy ascent. These batteries were enclosed in works of sufficient size and strength to hold garrisons to secure them from sorties. The approaches were made as at present, by zigzags along the capitals of the salients to the counterscarp, where a covered descent was made into the ditch opposite the breach preparatory to its assault. When the wall was not exposed to a distant fire, the besiegers were obliged to carry the covered-way by assault, and establish their breaching batteries on the crest of the glacis.

In carrying forward these works the besiegers were subjected to great losses and delays, owing to the magnitude and multiplicity of the works they were obliged to complete, to the imperfect character of their artillery and the faulty position of their batteries, by which they were unable to keep under the fire of the place; the want of connection between the separate approaches, and the consequent exposure of the workmen in the trenches to sorties, the troops for their support being too distant in the enclosed works in the rear to give them timely succor; besides which, as these enclosed works naturally became the chief objects for the fire of the besieged, this agglomeration of troops in them added materially to the losses of the besiegers.

Owing to these imperfections in the measures of attack, the besieged were able to make a vigorous and prolonged defence; and sieges became the most important military operations of this period, in which captains of the greatest celebrity sought for opportunities of distinction.

291. But little deviation was made in the methods just described until Vauban appeared upon the scene. Previous to him, Montluc, a distinguished French general and engineer, had introduced short branches of trenches, which were run out from the angles of the zigzags, to post a few troops for the immediate protection of the workmen; but these were found to be very insufficient in repelling sorties of any strength.

The event which seems to have had the greatest influence on the subsequent progress of both the attack and defence was the memorable siege of Candia, in which volunteers from all parts of Europe engaged, who, after its close, disseminated throughout their respective countries the results of the experience they had there acquired.

Whether the idea of the parallels, now in use in the attack, originated there, or with Vauban, this eminent man was the first to establish them in a systematic manner, and to demonstrate by experience their controlling importance in repressing sorties. The introduction of this important element in the attack; the concentration of the fire of batteries, by giving them enfilading positions; the invention of the ricochet, as the most powerful destructive means against the defences; the avoidance of open assaults, which, even when successful, are made at a great sacrifice of life, preferring to them the less brilliant but slower method of skill and industry, by which the blood of the soldier is spared, and the end more surely attained,—such are the important services which the attack owes to Vauban, which gave it its marked superiority over the means of defence.

From the preceding brief summary, it will be seen that the art of fortification, in its progress, has kept pace with the measures of the attack; its successive changes having been brought about by changes either in the arms used by the assailant, or by the introduction of some new mode of assault. The same causes must continue to produce the same effects. At no past period has mechanical invention, in its bearing on the military art, been more active than at the present day. The improvement that has been made in the range and accuracy of aim of both small-arms and cannon, the adoption of wrought iron and steel for floating batteries and sea-coast defences, form the commencement of another epoch in the engineer's art. The great improvements in cannon give to the assailant a still wider range in the selection of positions for his batteries, and thus increase the difficulties of the engineer in adapting his works to the site, and in giving adequate shelter to the garrison and armament. Whilst the defence is to this extent weakened, the approaches of the besieger are rendered more perilous and more difficult from the greater range and accuracy of small-arms.

The great destruction of life in open assaults by columns, exposed within so long a range, gives an additional value to intrenched fields of battle; and we will again see fieldworks play the part they did in the defence of Sebastopol and Plevna, and positions so chosen and fortified that not only will the assailant be forced to intrench himself to assail them, but will find the varying phases of his attack met by corresponding changes in the defensive dispositions.

292. In our own country, from the circumstances of our position, permanent fortification has met with its most frequent applications in works planned for sea-coast defence, in which our engineers, without servilely copying any of the systems in vogue in Europe, have followed the bastioned system, wherever the works were of such an extent as to admit of its application.

In the larger works erected by them for sea-coast defence, the water-fronts consist of one or more tiers of casemated batteries, surmounted by one in barbette, whilst the land fronts consist of the usual rampart and parapet arranged for open defences.

In the smaller works, which, from the limited extent of their fronts, did not admit of the adoption of the bastioned system, flanking dispositions have been made, either by casemated caponnières or counterscarp galleries.

Wherever the site was very limited, and a large amount of fire in a given direction was desirable, as in the cases of islands (either natural or artificial) to be occupied on the line of a channel to a roadstead or harbor, the castellated form, consisting of several tiers of casemates, surmounted by a barbette battery, has been adopted. These works are generally so surrounded by water as to be secure from an open assault, and therefore not requiring flanking dispositions.

Where, however, it has been thought necessary to place these, small bastioned towers have been added at the salient angles of the work.

Whilst thus adhering to well-settled principles, and following the practice of the best European authorities, our engineers have contributed their share to the improvement of the details of the art. The works erected by them are remarkable for the excellence of the materials employed, the great skill shown in their construction, and the care with which every detail was worked out to subserve the object in view. In these respects, in the inventive genius often displayed, and in the adaptation of the plan to the site, it is not claiming too much to say that the works erected by them are not surpassed, and in some points not equalled, by any similar works in Europe.

Our engineers have for many years reported that these works are now entirely inadequate for the defence of our harbors, and have urgently advocated that they be replaced at once by those which can resist modern guns as well as afford emplacements for them.

A popular interest in this subject seems at last to have been awakened, and it is to be hoped that measures will soon be taken to provide our harbors and exposed cities with a suitable defence, by supplying them with fortifications and guns.

293. The further changes that will be required in fortifications both for attack and defence, so far as indicated by the progressive improvements in arms, the increased use of mortars and the proposed employment of dynamite and other high explosives in shells, will consist principally in giving greater strength to parapets and armor, extending still further the use of armored constructions and bomb-proof covers, giving them greater thickness, and in so constructing splinter proofs that they will give protection from splinters whose velocity, arising from a high explosive, will not only give them greater penetration, but, by exceeding that of the shell from which they come, will take the parapets and shelters in reverse.

None of these involve changes in principle nor great changes in detail, and it is probable that fortifications built in accordance with methods now adopted and approved will for many years fulfil all the requirements of an efficient defence.

CHAPTER XII.

MODERN CONSTRUCTIONS IN IRON AND STEEL.

294. Iron armor, although advocated by Gen. Paixhan, and Robert Stevens, of Hoboken, N. J., so early as 1841-42, received its first test in actual conflict in the attack of the French and English iron-clad batteries on the Kinburn forts in the Crimean war in 1855.

The results of this attack led to its further application, in both France and England, for naval purposes; but a new and marked impulse was given by the startling results obtained by its use in the civil war of 1861-65.

295. In the development of armor, wrought-iron naturally took the lead, although experimental constructions in steel were made so early as 1857, and in compound plates in 1859.

In its earlier application, both singly and in combination with iron, steel was found brittle and easily broken up by the projectiles.

It was not, however, abandoned, but continued experiments were made by English and French manufacturers, who produced the first successful compound plate in 1867, and steel plate in 1876.

Meanwhile the manufacturers had improved the quality and increased the thickness of iron plates, producing them of guaranteed quality 12 inches thick, and of good quality up to 22 inches thick which were tested in competition with steel plates of 22 inches in the last-named year.

Competitive trials of compound plates and those made of steel, each 18.9 inches thick, were also carried on in 1882, the results of both trials being rather in favor of the steel plates.

Although some of these proved quite brittle, constant improvement was made in the manufacture of both compound and steel plates; the introduction of a small per cent of nickel in the latter by Schneider et Cie of Creusôt marking a very material advance.

In the United States, the recent development of nickel-steel armor with the face hardened by the Harvey process has resulted (1892) in the production of plates which combine toughness and hardness to an extent hitherto unknown, and which have a resisting power far greater than any others made.

Chilled cast-iron was first introduced by Grüson, in Germany, in 1868, and has been gaining ground for land defence since that time, its great weight precluding its use on vessels.

296. Under the impact of projectiles, wrought-iron, by means of its ductility and relative lack of tenacity, is penetrated by the projectile in a manner similar to that of a plate of lead by a punch. The injury is, with the best plates, almost entirely local, and if the plate be not pierced it has nearly as much resisting power as before, in points a little removed from that struck.

In the immediate vicinity of a previous blow the resistance is diminished, because the metal flows laterally into the hole produced by the preceding shot.

When the blows are of great energy, and the plate is not large, or is of poor quality, it is generally destroyed by cracking and breaking.

The best steel projectiles are not materially deformed even by the thickest iron plates, their energy being expended upon the plate and not upon themselves. Their penetration can be quite closely calculated.

297. Compound armor behaves quite differently. Its hard steel face is either very slightly penetrated, and shows but little injury from the shot, or radial and concentric cracks of greater or less depth are produced about the point of impact, and the projectile gets through the armor more by a process of breaking up and displacing, than by penetrating it.

The best steel projectiles are frequently broken up by the plates.

298. Steel plates with a less per cent of carbon than the face of the compound plates, behave in a manner intermediate between wrought-iron and compound plates. They are penetrated more deeply than the compound but less than the iron plates, while they crack more readily than the iron, and perhaps less so than the compound. The cracks are almost exclusively radial.

The projectiles may pierce, but more frequently destroy

the plate by breaking it up. Steel projectiles are usually broken up, but occasionally rebound after striking, or pass through unbroken.

299. Chilled iron has an extremely hard surface. No projectile has yet been made which produces a deep penetration or which has not been broken into pieces when fired against it. It can hardly be called penetrable. Under repeated blows it is split into blocks, along the planes of weakness arising from crystallization, which, by their wedge shape, frequently resist a number of blows without displacement.

Its protective value is destroyed by the displacement of the broken parts or by the bodily movement of the shield under the blows of the projectiles.

Being a cast metal, the shields are easily made of any thickness required, with surfaces of double curvature of any desired convexity.

300. In designing armor for land defences, engineers are not hampered by many considerations which attach to ironclad ships. On land the weight of armor, as previously stated, is sometimes an advantage. This allows the use of chilled iron or wrought iron of any desired thickness. The necessity for covering a definite height with armor is obviated by the use of impenetrable substructures of masonry and earth.

This permits the application of spheroidal and dome-shaped structures which only admit of oblique impacts and present the smallest and most indistinct targets to the enemy.

The domes recently introduced by the Germans (Schumann's design, Grüson's make,) will probably be largely used. They are made in the shape of spherical segments of such slight convexity that they admit of the use of wrought iron, steel, or compound metal.

301. In the armored forts constructed by England since 1860, as previotisly stated, iron shields are in some cases used to cover the gun chambers in granite structures, of several tiers of fire. These shields are of wrought iron, usually consisting of three plates each about 5 inches thick separated by concrete, the embrasures being fitted for the old type of carriages.

In the large forts on Horse Shoal and No Man's Land at Portsmouth, circular in form and to mount 49 guns in two tiers, the exterior superstructure is entirely of iron, the front being of a construction about the same as the shields above described.

302. The English engineers have also used wrought iron turrets in their sea-coast works; the cylindrical type being selected, probably because, at the time they were built, their armor-makers had such large experience and skill in building turrets of this shape, and from the simplicity of their construction. They are still preferred by some engineers.

303. Plate 18, Fig. 7, is a vertical section of the turret at the outer end of the pier at Dover. Its interior diameter is 32 feet, height of armor, 9 feet; thickness of armor, 25 inches, in three plates of 7 inches and two of 2 inches. The roof, 2 inches thick, is only splinter proof, is partly grating, and the parts directly over the guns are removable to allow the guns to be taken out or replaced. The weight of the turret, without guns, is 460 tons. The total weight of turret, mounting, guns, and carriages, is about 895 tons.

304. The turret itself is carried on a framed support of steel turning on a central pivot and carried by 32 rollers running on a track placed on a masonry substructure.

The central pivot is built up of wrought iron, and is very strong. It is enclosed in a cylinder of Bessemer steel, and outside this is a heavy casting firmly fastened to the masonry. The turret is turned by a pinion and toothed wheel driven by steam-power.

The engines and magazines are about 30 feet below the level of the guns, and the shell-rooms in the intermediate story.

The turret is armed with two 80-ton muzzle-loading guns, which are capable of 7° elevation and 2° depression. They are drawn back into the turret, and depressed so as to be loaded from under the glacis. The glacis is of stone masonry covered with concrete, finished on the inside with a ring of plates 5 inches and 3 inches thick, resting on a circle of 2-inch plates.

305. Plate 18, Fig. 2, is a section and interior elevation of an experimental turret for land defences of French construction (Mougin, designer; St. Chamond manufacture.) Its exterior diameter is 15¾ feet; height of armor, 4 feet; thickness, 17.7 inches single plate; three plates make up the cylinder.

The top is of flat plates, in two parts, 7 inches thick, rabbeted and screwed into the vertical plates. The turret itself rests upon a structure of plates supported in the centre by a pivot, which serves as the plunger of a hydraulic press, by which the turret and its armament may be raised for turning, and lowered before firing. Around the exterior are 10 rollers whose axes are horizontal, running on a circular track, and 6 with vertical axes which press against a vertical ring.

These rollers do not carry the weight of the turret, but serve only to balance and direct it, and to relieve the pivot from shocks. The pivot is $16\frac{1}{2}$ inches thick.

The hydraulic pressure is obtained by a pump worked by hand. It enables the turret to be raised through considerable distance to free it if jammed by splinters, and allows it to be turned with very little friction. The turning is done by a winch, worked by four men, which turns a pinion engaging with a toothed wheel attached to the turret platform.

The substructure is of two stories, the lower being used as a magazine, and for the rotating and hydraulic machinery; the second, for working the guns and serving the ammunition. The guns, with their attachments, occupy the turret itself.

The turret is armed with two 15.5 c.m. (6") De Bange guns, with minimum embrasure carriages, admitting of an elevation of 20° and a depression of 5°. They allow a very small recoil. The gun and carriage are balanced by a counterweight.

306. In pointing, the guns are given the proper elevation by an arc attached to the slides in the usual manner. For horizontal direction, a graduated arc is placed under the turret, provided with a movable index for each gun; these are clamped on the arc at points corresponding to the azimuth of the object aimed at, the sighting being done through the bore of the gun.

Electric contact points are attached to the turret so as to touch these indices when the guns have the correct direction, and firing takes place automatically when the turret is turned in the right direction up to these contacts.

The glacis armor is made up of four pieces of chilled cast-iron, and is covered with concrete and sand in front.

The weight of the armor is about 73 tons, and that of the glacis about 68 tons; total, 141 tons.

The weight of each gun is about 6400 pounds and each carriage about 7500 pounds. Twenty-nine officers and men are considered necessary to work the turret and guns.

307. Plate 18, Fig. 1, shows a vertical section and interior elevation of an experimental turret of German manufacture (Schumann's design, Grüson's make).

The top is a spherical segment of $19\frac{1}{2}$ feet greatest diameter, 17 feet radius, and 3 feet rise.

The armor, 8 inches thick, consists of six arched sectors

and a six-sided central plate. The plates are dowelled together and screwed to a skin of two plates each, about ¾ inch thick, riveted together.

The embrasure plate, the two next it, and the top plate are of wrought iron; the other three of compound armor.

The turret is supported on a construction of plate iron, carried by a central pivot, and is provided with four rollers with elastic bearings, under the periphery at 90° apart.

These rollers run on a circular track attached to the glacis.

The pivot is about 7 inches in diameter, and rests at the bottom on a screw which is supported by a wooden block for elasticity. By the screw the turret may be raised or lowered to relieve the rollers from a part of the weight.

The substructure and the cupola are arranged in a single story. Recesses in the side walls serve for storing ammunition.

The glacis armor consists of eight chilled-iron plates. Their thickness at top is 14 inches, at bottom 8½ inches.

They are covered on the outside with concrete.

The turret is turned with a winch worked by 4 to 6 men.

It is armed with two 25 cal. 15 c.m. (6″) Krupp guns mounted on non-recoil carriages. The chase of the gun in the embrasure is supported by a trunnion ring, the trunnions resting in beds in the armor plates about which the gun turns for elevation and depression, which are 25° and 5° respectively. Horizontal direction is given in the usual way by revolving the turret.

308. The pointing is done by thrusting the head through a hole in the roof, the sights being fitted to the top; or by sighting through a hole in the back of the turret, and then revolving it 180°; a graduated circle and pointer providing for this, as well as for pointing in a fixed direction without sighting after the direction is once established.

The elevation is given in the usual way by an arc and pointer.

The embrasures are made horizontal. The guns and carriages are counterpoised by a heavy weight. The recoil is taken up by arcs attached to the turret.

The weight of the armor plates is about 46 tons, that of the glacis about 65 tons; total, 111 tons.

It is stated that the guns and turret may be worked by 14 officers and men. Grüson's price for a turret of this type is about $45,000.

309. This and the French turret previously described,

were subjected to competitive trial at Bucharest, in December, 1885, and January, 1886. Figs. 3, 4, 5 and 6, taken from photographs, show their appearance after the trial, *during which neither turret was penetrated or disabled.*

Fig. 4 shows the back of the French turret after 95 shots and 66 hits with the 15 c.m. gun at 1100 yards range. Striking energy 1146 foot tons. Fig. 6 shows its embrasure after 4 shots at 55 yards range with same striking energy.

Fig. 3 shows the back of the German turret after 135 shots and 71 hits; and Fig. 5, the front, after 7 hits with the same ranges and guns.

They illustrate the behavior of wrought iron under direct and oblique impact and that of compound plates under oblique only.

310. Plate 19, Fig. 1, is a plan vertical section and interior elevation of a revolving turret caponnière for machine guns for use at salient and shoulder angles.

It consists of a vaulted roof of wrought iron and a front ring of chilled iron, pierced for two revolving machine guns, with a chilled-iron glacis covered with masonry. The thickness of the armor is determined by the character of fire to which it may be exposed: the roof being made bomb-proof, and both roof and front proof against the oblique blows to which only they are subject. The dimensions will vary with the position and armament. A thickness of roof of 4 inches steel or $5\frac{1}{2}$ inches wrought-iron is considered sufficient for very small turrets. This turret is 7 feet interior diameter without central pivot. It is supported on a system of rollers and is turned either by a pinion and toothed wheel or by a lever. Entrance to it is obtained through a postern under the parapet, as shown. The size here represented, weighs about 18 tons, and costs at the manufactory about $6500.

The details and dimensions may be determined from the figure.

311. Fig. 2 is a half plan, half horizontal, and a vertical section with interior elevation of a fixed turret caponnière for use at salient angles. It is somewhat larger than the revolving turret. It is pierced for two machine guns on each side, with intermediate loopholes for musketry.

The chilled-iron armor in the vicinity of the machine guns which look down the ditches is made thicker than on the side toward the salient, being exposed to more direct fire. Entrance to the caponnière is by a postern, as in the other case. The machine guns have sufficient horizontal traverse to sweep the whole width of the ditch, and an elevation and depression of about 15° and 5° respectively.

312. Figs. 3 and 4, are sections and interior elevations of a disappearing turret for a 37 mm. (1".45) machine gun.

In this construction the roof is made bomb-proof, varying as previously stated (art. 310) from 4 inches in steel to $5\frac{1}{2}$ inches in iron. The vertical wall through which the gun fires is of steel and varies in thickness from $\frac{1}{2}$ inch to 3 inches in different constructions, depending upon the fire to which it is exposed.

The turret gun and carriage are supported on a framed structure carried by a central pivot which terminates in a rounded end.

The end of the pivot rests upon and turns in a bearing which is carried by a stirrup sliding vertically in a slot in a hollow cylinder, outside of which is a counterweight. The counterweight and stirrup are connected by chains passing over pulleys.

Attached to the bottom of the stirrup and passing down through the axis of the hollow cylinder is a chain which is led to a windlass in the postern.

The windlass is supplied with a crank and brake. When the brake is loosened, the counterweight falls and raises the turret to its firing position 16 inches above its lowest position. It is lowered by the windlass and chain which draw down the stirrup and raise the counterweight. When down, the bomb-proof top rests on the glacis plates.

Three conical rollers attached to the vertical cylinder serve to centre the turret in its firing position by bearing against the inner edge of the glacis plates.

The gun and carriage are supported on two levers joined to the floor of the chamber and the gun-carriage by pin bearings, so as to allow the gun to be drawn back within the turret as shown in the dotted lines, or to be thrust out for firing, in which position it is held by a catch attached to the armor. Three men are sufficient to work the gun and turret.

Accurate aim is taken by the motion of the carriage, an approximate pointing by turning the turret.

313. This turret costs at the factory about $4500, and the gun about $1250. A similar one for a 53 mm. (2") gun costs about $7000, and the gun about $3500.

314. These small disappearing turrets are applicable to ditch defence, but were also designed for use in the parapet of the forts for sweeping the ground in front; the small calibres for repelling assaults and general fire against troops; and the larger for retarding the besieger's approaches in in addition.

Figs. 1, 2, 3, and 4, are from designs of Major Schumann, Prussian Engineers, and are made by Grüson.

The construction of disappearing turrets for 6-inch guns is now seriously considered in France.

315. The frontispiece, taken from a photograph, of Battery St. Marie, at Antwerp, shows the use of chilled-iron armor in casemates. The mortised channel in the edge of the plates is filled with zinc solder to fasten the plate to its neighbor. The chill does not extend quite to this channel. The details of construction are shown by the figure.

APPENDIX I.

PENETRATION OF PROJECTILES AND THICKNESS OF PARAPETS.

FORMULAS.

All formulas have been reduced to the form $E = f(t)$, in which E represents the energy, in foot-tons per inch of shot's circumference, required to perforate an un-backed wrought-iron plate whose thickness in inches is t, and $f(t)$ the particular function of t.

AUTHOR.	ORIGINAL.	REDUCED.	REMARKS.
Maj. W. H. Noble, Royal Artillery.	$t = \sqrt{\dfrac{3WV^2}{\pi rgk}}$.	$E = 1.384 t^2$. ($r = 6$ inches.)	V = velocity on impact in ft. per sec. W = wt. of shot, lbs. g = accelerating force of gravity. r = radius of shot, in. k = constant, depends on kind of iron and nature and form of head of shot.
Maj. W. R. King, U. S. Engineers.	$E = a.t \times \log(b.t+1)$. $a = 39.$ $b = 0.1.$	$E = 39.t \times \log(0.1t + 1)$.	
M. Hélie.	$E = 4.40 t^{\frac{3}{2}}$.	$E = 4.40 t^{\frac{3}{2}}$.	
Maj W. H. Noble, Royal Artillery.	$t = \sqrt[1.6]{\dfrac{E}{2.53}}$.	$E = 2.53 t^{1 \cdot 6}$.	
Andrew Noble.	$t = \sqrt[1.5]{\dfrac{E}{3.18}}$.	$E = 3.18 t^{1 \cdot 5}$.	
Col. Maitland.	$t = \dfrac{e}{4.733 \pi r^2}$.	$E = 14.199 t$. ($r = 6$ inches.)	e = total energy on impact in ft.-tons.
English, For thick plates.	$t = \sqrt[2.035]{\dfrac{E}{0.86}}$.	$E = 0.86 t^{2 \cdot 035}$.	
Italian.	$t = \sqrt[1.4]{\dfrac{E}{4.154}}$.	$E = 4.154 t^{1 \cdot 4}$,	
Gen. Froloff.	$t = \dfrac{X}{360} - 1''.5$.	$X = \dfrac{W}{d^2} V.$ $E = \dfrac{WV^2}{4\pi r g 2240}$.	d = diam. shot, in.
Capt. Orde Browne, Royal Artillery.	$t = \sqrt{\dfrac{E}{c}}$.	$E = ct^2$.	*c depends for its value on the ratio of the thickness of the plate to diam. of shot.
Col. M. de Brettes.	$Zf = .10 S^2 + 110 S$.	$E = \dfrac{r}{2}(.0136 t^2 + 5.87 t)$.	Zf = energy in metre kilogrammes per square cm. of shot's cross-section. S = thickness of plates in centimetres. D = diam. of shot in centimetres.
Adts.	$Zf = 1.43156 S^2 + 85.1364 S$.	$E = \dfrac{r}{2}\left(\dfrac{.1939 t^2}{+ 4.5412 t}\right)$.	
Krupp.	$Zf = .10 S \sqrt[3]{\dfrac{S}{D}}$.	$E = \dfrac{r}{2}\sqrt[3]{\dfrac{t^4}{.0135 r}}$.	

* $\dfrac{t}{d}=$ 0.5 .6 .7 .8 .9 1.0 1.1 1.2 1.3 1.4 1.5 1.6 1.7 1.8 1.9 2.0
$c =$ 1.300 1.250 1.178 1.125 1.083 1.050 1.022 1.000 0.981 0.964 0.950 0.938 0.926 0.917 0.908 0.900

Capt. Orde Browne gives the following approximate rule for penetration: "The penetration of projectiles into wrought-iron is one calibre for every thousand feet of velocity." Very accurate results are obtained by its use.

162　　APPENDIX.

Krupp's B. L. Cannon.	Weight. (Tons)	Powder, Weight of Charge. (Lbs.)	Projectile, Weight of. (Lbs.)	Initial Velocity. (Feet)	At Muzzle.			At 1000 Yards.			At 2000 Yards.			At 3500 Yards.		
					Heavy Clay. (Feet)	Sand mixed with Gravel. (Feet)	Granite. (Feet)	Heavy Clay. (Feet)	Sand mixed with Gravel. (Feet)	Granite. (Feet)	Heavy Clay. (Feet)	Sand mixed with Gravel. (Feet)	Granite. (Feet)	Heavy Clay. (Feet)	Sand mixed with Gravel. (Feet)	Granite. (Feet)
40cm gun, 35 calibres length	108 / 119	750 / 615	2,240 / 1,632	1,885 / 2,017	85.5 / 69.1	51.1 / 40.9	10.2 / 8.2	82.5 / 64.8	48.9 / 38.4	9.7 / 7.6	78.6 / 60.9	46.5 / 36.1	9.3 / 7.2	73.2 / 55.3	43.3 / 32.8	8.7 / 6.6
40cm " 25 "	71	462	1,762	1,695	62.2	37.2	7.5	59.1	34.9	7.0	55.5	32.8	6.6	48.1	28.3	5.7
35.5cm " 35 "	75.3	520 / 462	1,560 / 1,155	1,835 / 1,965	76.2 / 71.0	45.1 / 36.1	9.0 / 7.2	72.3 / 57.0	42.9 / 38.7	8.5 / 6.7	68.5 / 53.1	40.6 / 31.5	8.1 / 6.3	63.3 / 47.5	37.5 / 28.2	7.5 / 5.5
35.5cm " 25 "	51.1	297	1,155	1,617	49.8	29.4	5.8	46.2	27.4	5.4	42.9	25.5	5.1	38.4	22.8	4.5
30.5cm " 35 "	48	357	1,008	1,857	67.2	39.9	7.9	63.3	37.5	7.5	59.5	35.2	7.0	54.1	32.1	6.3
28cm " 35 "	37	253	760	1,837	59.8	35.4	7.0	55.8	33.1	6.6	52.2	30.9	6.1	46.9	28.5	5.5
26cm " 35 "	27.2	183	614	1,768	53.8	31.9	6.4	50.1	29.7	6.0	46.5	27.6	5.5	41.5	24.6	4.9
24cm " 35 "	20.5	150	476	1,791	49.6	29.4	5.8	45.9	27.1	5.0	42.3	25.0	5.0	37.3	22.0	4.3
24cm " 30 "	18.9	150	476	1,726	47.8	28.3	5.7	44.1	26.1	5.2	40.6	24.1	4.8	36.0	21.3	4.2
21cm " 35 "	13.3	99	310	1,808	43.0	25.5	5.1	39.1	23.2	4.6	35.5	21.1	4.2	30.9	18.3	3.6
17cm " 30 "	7.0	57	172	1,772	35.4	21.0	4.2	31.6	18.7	3.7	28.2	16.6	3.3	23.8	14.2	2.7
15cm " 35 "	4.7	37.4 / 39.6	113 / 111	1,773 / 1,827	30.1 / 30.6	17.8 / 18.1	3.6 / 3.6	26.5 / 26.5	15.7 / 15.8	3.1 / 3.1	23.2 / 23.4	13.7 / 13.8	2.7 / 2.7	19.3 / 19.3	11.4 / 11.4	2.2 / 2.2

* The above computations were made by Lieut. F. E. Hobbs, Ordnance Department, U. S. A., from General Froloff's formula.

APPENDIX. 163

ACTUAL PENETRATION OF RIFLED CANNON INTO EARTH, GRANITE, CONCRETE, ETC.*

Place and Date.	Material.	Distance.	Gun.	Calibre.	Weight of Proj.	Velocity at Impact.	Penetration.	Remarks.
		Yds.		in.	lbs.	Feet.		
Dungeness, 1881	Concrete, 6 parts; shingle; 1 part sand; 1 part concrete	145	Woolwich.	10	408	1,424	13' 10" to 17"	
" 1881	" "	145	M. L. R.	6	80	1,893	10' 9" to 12' 7"	
" 1881	" "	145	M. L. R.	6.6	100	1,497	8' 2" to 8' 5"	
" 1881	Earth (clay, chalk, stones, and brick)	195	M. L. R.	10	408	1,416	34' 6"	
" 1881	Same	195	B. L. R.	6	80	1,875	12' 3".5	
" 1881	Earth	195	M. L. R.	6.6	100	1,452	14' to 14' 6"	
" 1881	Sand	195	M. L. R.	6.6	100	1,452	11' 6"	
Shoeburyness, Aug., 1883	Concrete, granite and concrete, broken granite	200	M. L. R.	80 tons.	1,700	1,586	34'	
Spezia, May, 1880	Sand	......	{ Arms.	17.7	2,200	1,512	39' to 46'	Mean of 48 shots.
" March, 1881	Soft rock and sand	437	{ B. L. R	17.7	..	......	20'	
Shoeburyness, 1865	Stiff marsh clay	......	......	9.22	......	......	32' to 40'	
Calais	Clay half, sand half	1100	......	9.62	397	1,329	26' 2"	
Shoeburyness and New Haven	Earth	......	......	12	......	......	50'	
" "	"	......	......	10	......	......	45'	
" "	"	......	......	9	......	......	40'	
" "	Concrete or brick	......	......	12	......	......	15'	
" "	" "	......	......	10	......	......	14'	
" "	" "	......	......	9	......	......	12'	
" "	Stone masonry	......	......	12	......	......	10'	
" "	" "	......	......	10	......	......	9'	
" "	" "	......	......	9	......	......	8'	

* This table is taken from "Report of the Board on Fortifications or Other Defences," 1886.

The following thicknesses of parapets were prescribed for German fortifications in 1884:

Kinds of Guns.	Thickness.			Snow well packed.
	Earth.	Masonry.	Wr'ght-iron and Bessemer steel.	
	Feet.	Feet.	Inches.	Feet.
Small-arms and shrapnell..	2 to 3	3	0.25 to 0.50	6
Field guns.................	10 to 12	4.5 to 5	4.5 to 5.0	26
Siege and fortress guns....	17 to 23	....	....	....
Ship's guns....	33 to 40	....	....	....

From experiments made by the Germans it was found that chilled projectiles penetrate rolled iron from $\frac{5}{4}$ to $\frac{6}{4}$ diameters; that small-arms will penetrate 9″ of oak and 10″ of fir.

APPENDIX II.

FRONTIER AND INTERIOR FORTIFICATIONS OF FRANCE, GERMANY, ITALY, AUSTRIA-HUNGARY, AND RUSSIA IN EUROPE.

FRANCE.

SINCE the war of 1870-71, the defensive frontier of France has been remodelled. Many of the old works have been abandoned, others ameliorated, and new works constructed in positions of modern strategical importance.

THE BELGIAN FRONTIER.—This frontier presenting no natural obstacle, a line of strong works has been constructed along it by the amelioration of the old fortifications. Detached forts have been placed around the most important centres, converting them into intrenched camps. The first line of defence consists of four groups of works: *Dunkerque, Lille, Valenciennes,* and *Maubeuge.* The first group comprises *Dunkerque, Bergues,* and *Gravelines,* and is being strengthened by the construction of detached forts. The second, *Lille,* which is to have a cordon of forts, *Aire* and *Douai.* The third, *Valenciennes,* which is to have a cordon of forts (some already constructed), *Condé, Bouchain,* and *Quesnoy.* The fourth, *Maubeuge,* which has a cordon of forts, *Landrecies, Hirson,* and *Rocroy.* In the second line, on the river Somme, are the citadel at *Amiens,* and the fortresses of *Péronne* and *Ham;* farther south, the strategic triangle of *La Fère, Laon, Soissons.* This triangle, when the fortifications about these places are completed, will form an immense intrenched camp; the base of armies operating in the north of France. *Rheims, further south, is also an intrenched camp with detached forts.*

THE GERMAN FRONTIER.—The defensive works along this frontier are constructed along the river Meuse from *Givet* to *Toul,* and thence along the Moselle to *Belfort. Givet* is a small fortress of minor importance. *Mezières* is a fortress which bars the valley of the Meuse, and occupies an important railroad junction. *Verdun* is an intrenched camp on the railroad from Metz to Paris. *Toul* is an intrenched camp on the railroad from Strasburg to Paris. *Verdun* and *Toul* are connected by a line of forts. *Epinal* is an intrenched camp on the upper Moselle. *Belfort* is a large intrenched camp near the frontier of Switzerland. *Epinal* and *Belfort* are connected by a line of forts. *Montmédy* and *Longwy* are small fortresses along the railroad from Luxemburg and Thionville to Mezières. In the rear of this frontier line are the intrenched camps of *Langres*, *Dijon*, and *Besançon*. The intrenched position, *Belfort, Epinal, Langres, Dijon* and *Besançon*, will form the base of an army operating from the south along this frontier.

THE ITALIAN AND SWISS FRONTIERS.—The line of the Alps is defended by numerous small forts in the passes, supported in the rear by the intrenched camps of *Besançon, Lyons,* and *Grenoble.*

SPANISH FRONTIER.—The line of the Pyrenees is defended by numerous old works which have been only slightly changed since the time of Vauban. The principal ones are those at *Perpignan*, on the Mediterranean side, and *Bayonne* on the Atlantic.

SEA-COAST FORTIFICATIONS.—The principal sea-coast works are, on the English Channel: *Cherbourg, St. Malo,* and *Havre;* on the Atlantic: *Rochefort, Lorient, Brest, La Rochelle, Oléron,* and *Belle Isle;* on the Mediterranean: *Toulon* and *Antibes.*

The capital, *Paris*, the centre of the defensive system, has been converted into an immense intrenched camp, having a cordon of forts at a distance of about nine miles from the city.

GERMANY.

Nearly all of the existing fortifications of Germany have either been built or ameliorated since 1870. The intrenched camps have usually an enceinte surrounded by a line of detached forts at a distance of four to five miles from the enceinte, and from two to two and a half miles from each other; between these forts are constructed intermediate works and batteries.

THE WESTERN FRONTIER.—The main line of defence against an army coming from the west is along the river Rhine; but beyond this are the intrenched camp of *Metz*, and the *fortress of Thionville on the Moselle*, the *tetê-de-*

APPENDIX. 167

pont at *Saar Louis*, and the old fortress of *Bitche*. On the Rhine are the fortress and *tête-de-pont* of *Neu Brisach;* the intrenched camp of *Strasburg*, the *tête-de-pont* of *Germersheim*, the intrenched camp of *Mainz*, with *Castel* on the opposite side of the river; forts *Alexander*, *François*, and *Ehrenbreitstein*, at *Coblenz ;* the intrenched camp at *Cologne*, with *Deutz* on the opposite bank, a *tête-de-pont* at *Dusseldorf*, and two forts protecting the river-crossing at *Wesel*. These works control all the principal bridges across the Rhine from Bâle to Wesel. On the east bank of the Rhine is the intrenched camp of *Rastadt*.

SOUTHERN FRONTIER.—On the Danube are the intrenched camps of *Ulm* and *Ingolstadt ;* on the Elbe, the fort of *Königstein ;* and in Prussia, the old fortified places of *Glatz* and *Neisse*.

EASTERN FRONTIER.—This frontier is now protected by three intrenched camps of the first order. *Königsberg* in eastern Prussia, *Thorn* on the Vistula, and *Posen* on the Warthe. In addition to these are *têtes-de-pont* at *Marienburg*, on the Nogat; *Derschau* and *Graudenz* on the Vistula, and the fortress of *Glogau* on the Oder.

The capital, *Berlin*, is not fortified, but its approaches are defended by the intrenched camp at *Magdeburg;* the old fortress at *Torgau*, on the Elbe, and the intrenched camp of *Cüstrin*, on the Oder. An intrenched camp is also being constructed at *Spandau*, in the immediate vicinity of Berlin.

SEA-COAST FORTIFICATIONS.—The principal naval port on the North Sea is that of *Wilhelmshaven*, and on the Baltic that of *Kiel*, protected by the works of *Friedrichsort*. In addition to these, on the North Sea, are the works *Cuxhaven* at the mouth of the Elbe, and *Geestemunde* at the mouth of the Weser; on the Baltic, *Sonderburg-Duppel*, *Stralsund; Travemunde*, at the entrance of the port of *Lubeck; Swinemunde*, at the mouth of the Oder *; Kolberg*, *Danzig*, *Pillau*, and *Memel*.

ITALY.

Italy possesses a large number of old fortresses and fortified towns; the only ones, however, of modern strategical importance are *Alexandria*, *Casale*, *Bologna*, *Capua*, *Legnano*, *Mantua*, *Peschiera*, *Placencia*, *Pizzeghettone*, *Verona*, and *Rome*. *Rome* has been converted into an intrenched camp by the construction of a cordon of forts, and the fortifications of *Capua* are being ameliorated, but none of the other places can be considered as strong places according to the modern idea.

In the last few years much attention has been paid to the construction of works in the passes of the Alps, to bar the advance of armies coming from France and Austria. The principal works of this class are those of *Fort Bard, Exille, Fenestrelle, Venadio, Monte Argentera, Ventimiglia,* on the *French frontier,* and *Rivoli* on the *Austrian.*

SEA-COAST FORTIFICATIONS.—Particular attention has been paid to the reconstruction of the sea-coast fortifications. *Spezia* on the Mediterranean, is the principal naval port, and is being thoroughly fortified; work is also going on at *Genoa, Gaëta, Porto-Ferraio* on the island of Elba; the *Island of Maddalena,* and *Messina,* on the Atlantic; *Ancona Venice,* and *Tarento,* on the Adriatic. *Civita Vecchia* is also a fortified port.

AUSTRIA-HUNGARY.

Austria-Hungary has numerous old fortifications, some of which have been ameliorated. The great extent of assailable frontier making a thorough defence impossible, the Austrian engineers have limited themselves generally to the construction of small works, simply intended to impede invasion by obstructing the principal lines of communication leading into the country.

BAVARIAN FRONTIER.—There is a fortress at *Küfstein* on the Inn; a fort at *Pass Lüeg,* south of Salzburg, and an old intrenched camp at *Linz*

SAXON AND PRUSSIAN FRONTIER.—On the Elbe is the intrenched camp at *Theresienstadt,* the old fortifications of *Josephstadt* and *Königgratz* on the Elbe, and on the March an intrenched camp at *Olmutz.*

RUSSIAN FRONTIER.—The fortifications consist of intrenched camps at *Cracow,* on the Vistula, and at *Przemysl,* on the San, a tributary of the same. In the second line is the fortress *Eperies,* on the Tarcza, a tributary of the Theiss. The intrenched camp at *Przemysl,* for which 5,500,000 florins have been appropriated, will, when completed, be the strongest fortification of Austria.

ROUMANIAN FRONTIER.—There are numerous old fortified places in Transylvania, the principal ones of which are *Kronstadt* and *Orsova;* in Hungary, on the Danube, is the intrenched camp at *Komorn,* and fortifications at *Peterwardein;* on the Maros, *Karlsburg* and *Arad;* on the

APPENDIX. 169

Drave, *Eszek;* in Croatia and Dalmatia, on the Save, *Brod, Gradiska,* and *Karlstadt.*

THE ITALIAN FRONTIER is protected by numerous forts constructed at the passes through the Alps.

SEA-COAST FORTIFICATIONS.—The principal naval port is *Pola,* on the Adriatic; fortifications also exist at *Trieste, Fiume, Zara, Sebenico, Spalatro, Ragusa,* lately abandoned, and the island of *Lissa.*

The capital, *Vienna,* is not fortified.

RUSSIA IN EUROPE.

PRUSSIAN AND AUSTRIAN FRONTIER.—The Polish possessions of Russia are protected by three strongly fortified places: *Novo-Georgievsk* (Modlin), at the junction of the Bug and Vistula; *Warsaw,* the capital of Poland, and an important railroad centre on the Vistula; and *Ivangorod,* on the same river. In rear of this line on the Bug is the strongly fortified place of *Brest-Litovsk.* In the rear of these frontier fortresses are *Bjelostok,* a small fortress at the junction of the railways from Warsaw to St. Petersburg, and Königsberg to Brest-Litovsk; the intrenched camp of *Kovno,* on the Niemen, the citadel of *Wilna;* the intrenched camp of *Dünaberg,* on the *Düna;* the old fortifications of *Smolensk,* on the Dnieper; the old fortress of *Luzk,* and the fortifications in process of construction at *Doubno,* on the railways leading from Poland and Galicia towards Kiev; and the intrenched camp of *Kiev* on the Dnieper.

ROUMANIAN FRONTIER.—In the vicinity of this frontier are the old fortresses of *Kamenez-Podolsk, Chotin, Bendery,* and *Tiraspol.*

SEA-COAST FORTIFICATIONS.—The principal naval ports on the Baltic are *Helsingfors,* protected by the fortifications on the Sveaborg Islands, and the harbor of Kronstadt; in addition to these are the forts *Hangö, Ruotsinsalmi, Fredrikshamn, Viborg,* and *Baltischport,* on the Gulf of Finland; and *Riga,* on the Gulf of Riga, is protected by the fortifications of *Dünamünde.*

The principal naval port on the Black Sea is *Nikolaifsk,* protected by the works of *Otschakow* and *Kinburn;* in addition there are the works of *Akkerman, Sebastopol,* and the fortifications on the *Kertch Strait.*

THE CAUCASUS.—There are numerous old fortifications between the Black and Caspian Seas. The most important of these are *Kars* and *Alexandropol.*

APPENDIX III.

BOOKS OF REFERENCE.

THE following list comprises a few of the many valuable works upon permanent fortifications, and its allied branches of Military Engineering.

In the books mentioned will be found references to many others treating fully upon the different branches of the subject.

It is not considered necessary to repeat the names of all the works referred to in the text; nor to enumerate the writings of Vauban, Cormontaigne, Coehoorn, Montalembert, Chasseloup, La Chiche, Virgin, Choumara, Dufour, Noizet, and other standard authors.

Adams, Capt. H. M.: Report on Trial of Chilled-iron Armor at Spezia. Washington, 1886.
Barnard, Gen. J. G.: Dangers and Defences of New York. New York, 1859.
―― Notes on Sea-coast Defence. New York, 1861.
―― Wright & Michie: Fabrication of Iron for Defensive Purposes, with Supplement. Washington, 1871.
Barnes: Submarine Warfare. New York, 1869.
Bixby, Capt. W. H.: Report on Fortification and Ordnance, published in "Engineering News." 1885.
Brialmont: Études sur la Défence des Etats et de la Fortification. Paris, 1863.
―― Traité de Fortification Polygonal. Paris, 1869.
―― La Fortification à Fossés secs. Paris, 1872.
―― Études sur la Fortification des Capitales et l'investissement des Camps Retranchés. Paris, 1873.
―― La Fortification du Temp Présent. Brussels, 1885.
Craighill: Guns Afloat and Guns Ashore. Essayons Club Paper, No. 6. 1868.
Delafield: Report on Art of War in Europe in 1854-56. Washington, 1860.
Douglas: Observations on Modern System of Fortification. London, 1859.
Fortifications of To-day: Translated from Italian. Washington, 1883.

APPENDIX.   171

Fraser: The Attack of Fortresses of the Future. London, 1877.
Girard: Traité d'application Tactiques de la Fortification. Paris, 1874.
Gillmore: Siege of Fort Pulaski. Washington, 1864.
Goodrich: Report of British Military and Naval Operations in Egypt. Washington, 1885.
Giese: Constructions of Iron as applied to Fortification. Washington, 1867.
Griffin: Our Sea-coast Defences. New York, 1885.
Humfrey, J. H.: Essay on Modern Systems, etc. London, 1838.
King, Major W. R.: Armor Plating for Land Defences. Washington, 1870.
—— Torpedoes. Washington, 1866.
—— Economy in Sea-coast Defences; Essayons Club Paper, No. 19. 1871.
King, J. W.: European Ships of War. Washington, 1877.
Kunka: Die Panzerthurme. Vienna. 1876.
Lendy: A Treatise on Fortification. London, 1862.
Mangin: Mémoire sur la Fortification Polygonal; construite in Allemagne depuis 1815. Paris, 1851.
—— Die Polygonal Befestigung. Leipzig. 1855.
Maguire: Attack and Defence of Coast Fortifications. New York, 1884.
Prevost, F.: Études Historiques sur la Fortification. Paris, 1869.
Prevost de Vernois: De la Fortification depuis Vauban. Paris, 1861.
Ratheau: Traité de Fortification. Paris, 1866.
—— Attaque et Defence des Places Fortes. Paris, 1877.
Report of Board on Fortification or other Defences. Washington, 1886.
—— Of Select Committee on Ordnance and War Ships. Washington, 1886.
—— With Reference to Progress in Construction of Fortifications for Dockyards, etc. London, 1867.
—— Of Committee on Gibraltar Shield. London, 1868.
—— Upon Practice in Europe with Heavy Guns. Prof. Paper, Corps of Engineers, No. 25. Washington, 1883.
Record of Experimental Firing at Fort Monroe. Washington, 1870.
Schueler Leitfaden für den Unterricht in der Befestigung, etc. Berlin, 1884.
Schütz, J. von: Expériences de Bucharest. Brussels, 1886.
Sellon, Maurice de: Various Writings. Paris, 1845 et seq.
Sleeman: Torpedoes and Torpedo Warfare. Portsmouth, England, 1880.
Stotherd: Notes on Torpedoes Offensive and Defensive (Reprint). Washington, 1872.
Totten: Casemate Embrasures. Washington, 1857.
Tripier: La Fortification de son Histoire. Paris, 1886.
Ténot: Paris et ses Fortifications. Paris, 1880,
Very: The Navies of the World. Washington, 1880.
—— The Development of Armor for Naval Use. Annapolis, 1883.
Viollet-le-duc: Annals of a Fortress. Boston, 1876.
Von Schelliha: Treatise on Coast Defence, etc. London, 1868.
Woolwich: Text Book on Fortification. London, 1877.
Zastrow: Histoire de la Fortification Permanente. Paris, 1866.

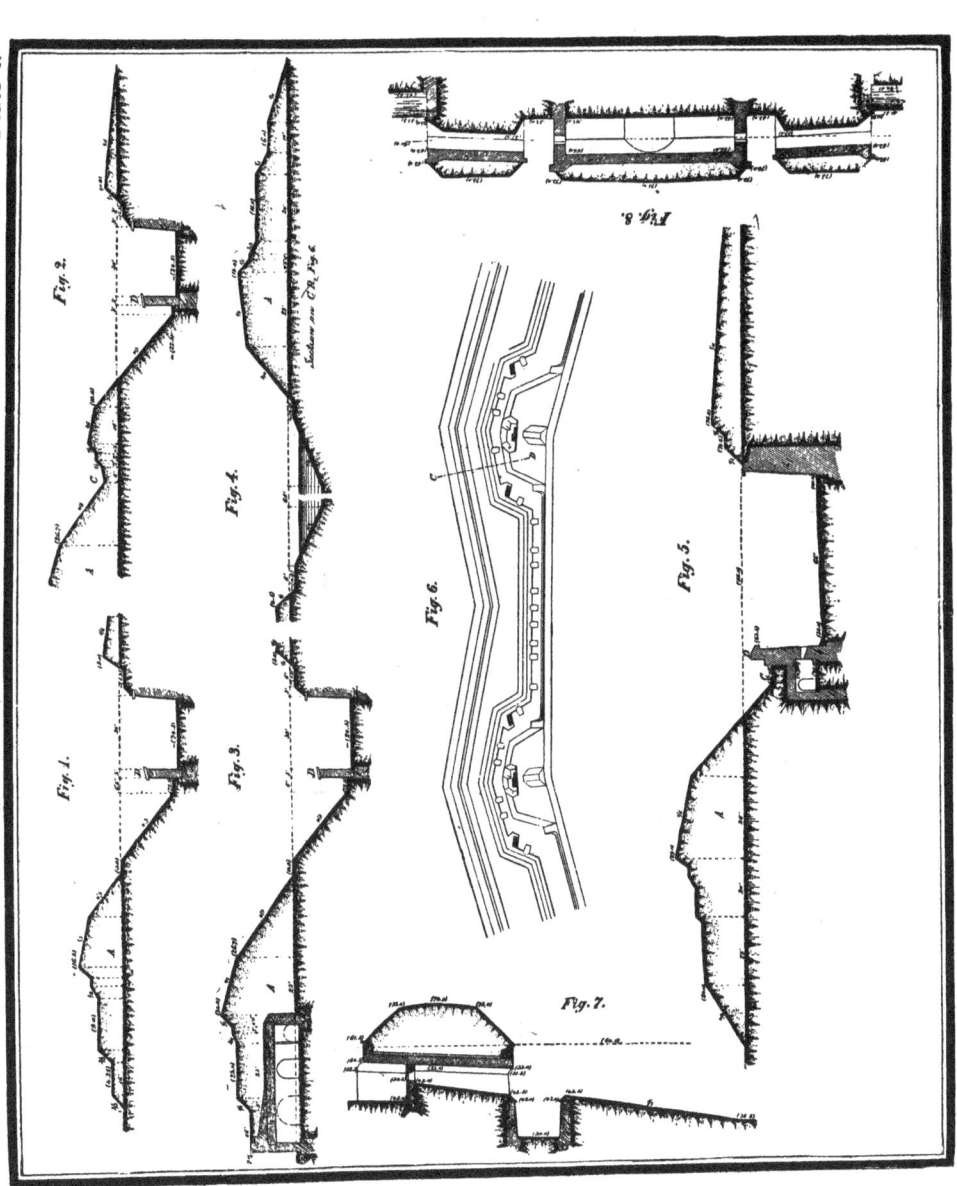

Plate 2.

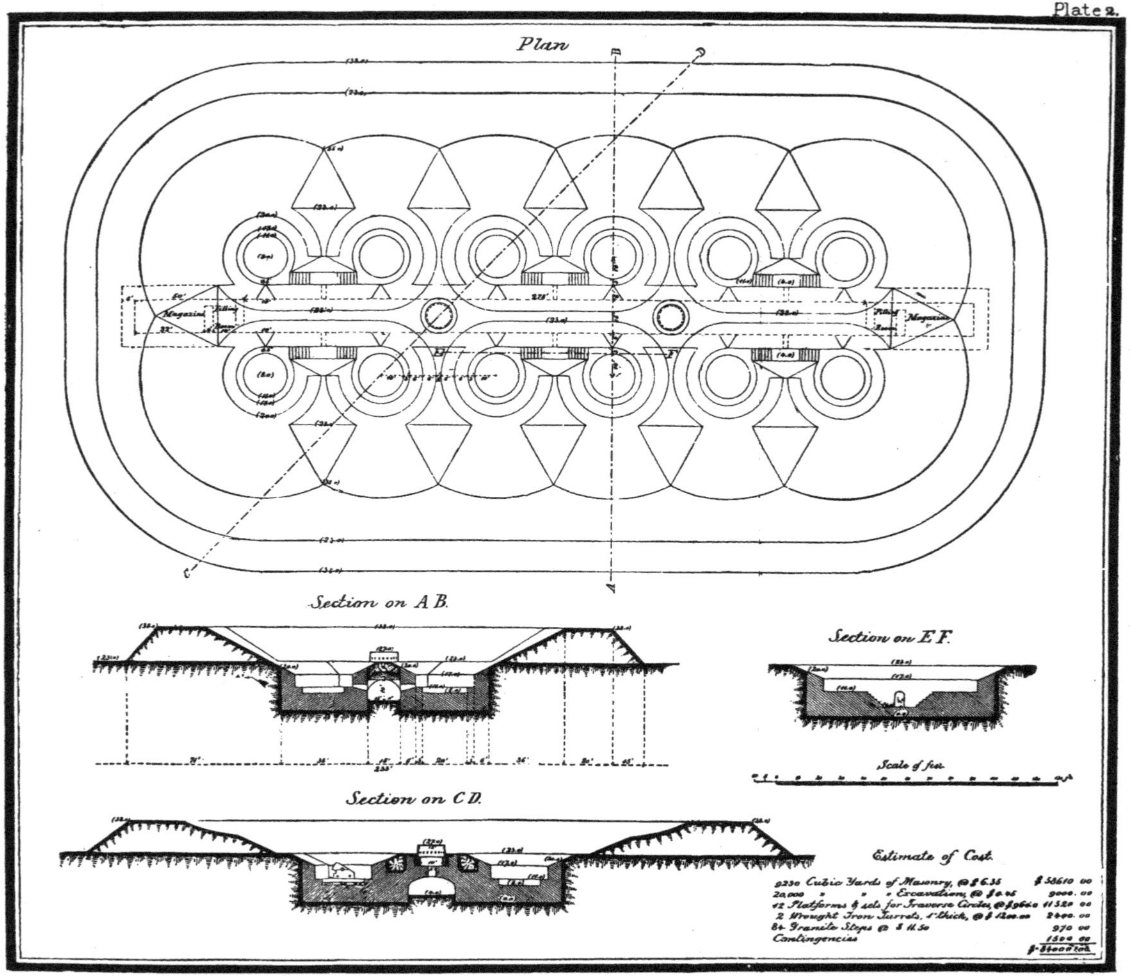
Plan
Magazine
Filling Room
Section on A B.
Section on E F.
Scale of feet.
Section on C D.
Estimate of Cost.
9230 Cubic Yards of Masonry, @ $ 6.35 $ 58610 00
20,000 " " " Excavation, @ $ 0.45 9000. 00
12 Platforms & sets for Traverse Circles, @ $ 960.00 11520 00
2 Wrought Iron Turrets, 1" thick, @ $ 1200.00 2400. 00
84 Granite Steps @ $ 11.50 970 00
Contingencies 1500 00
$ 84000.00

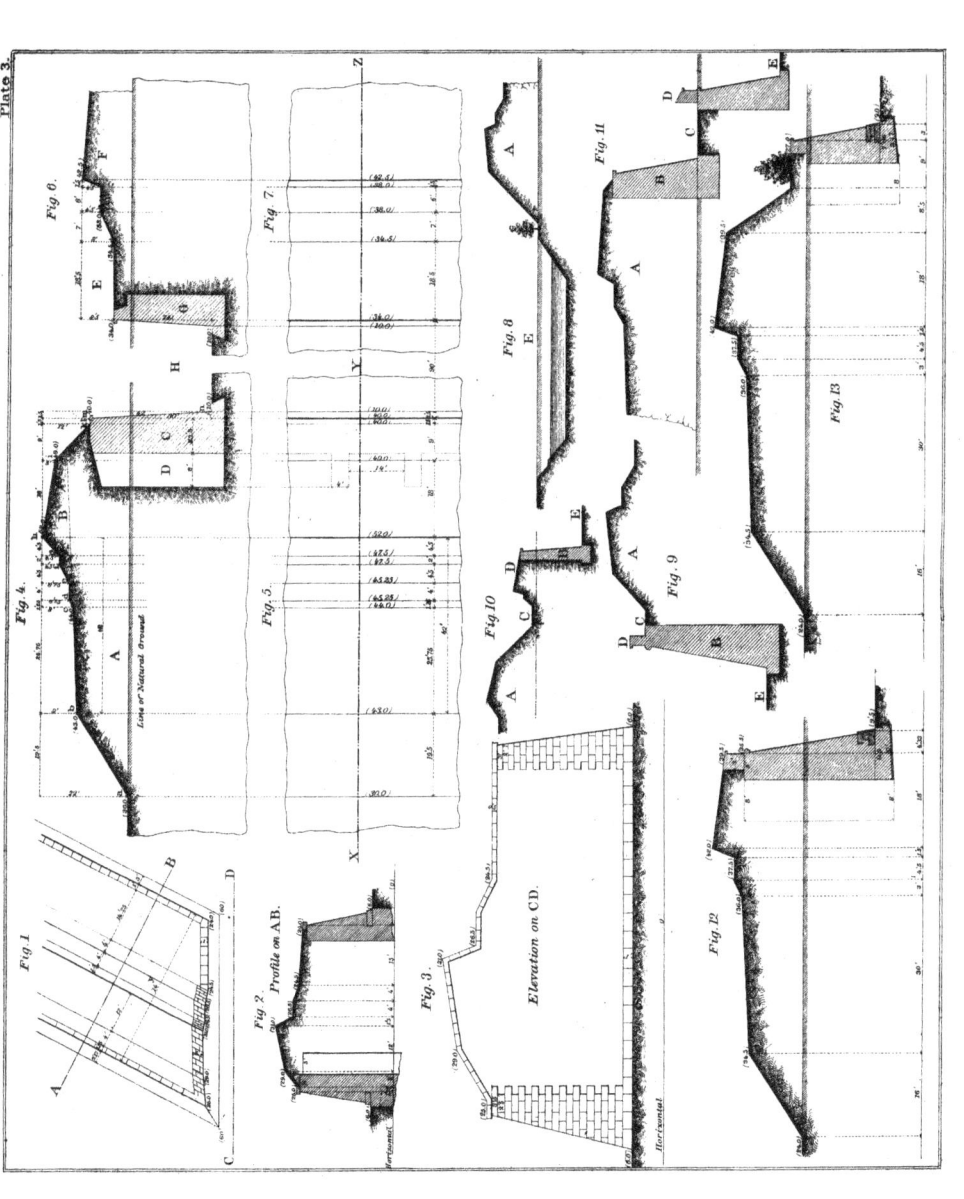

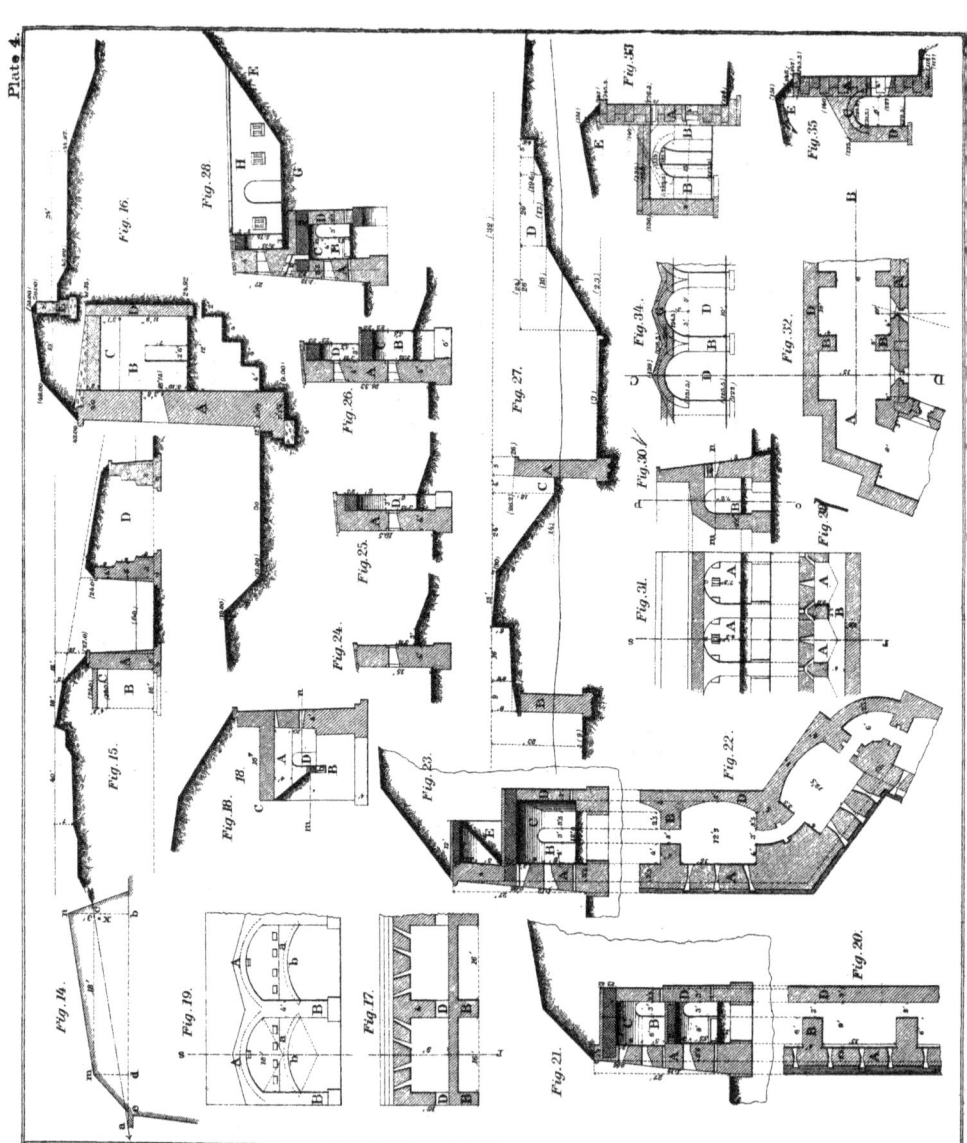

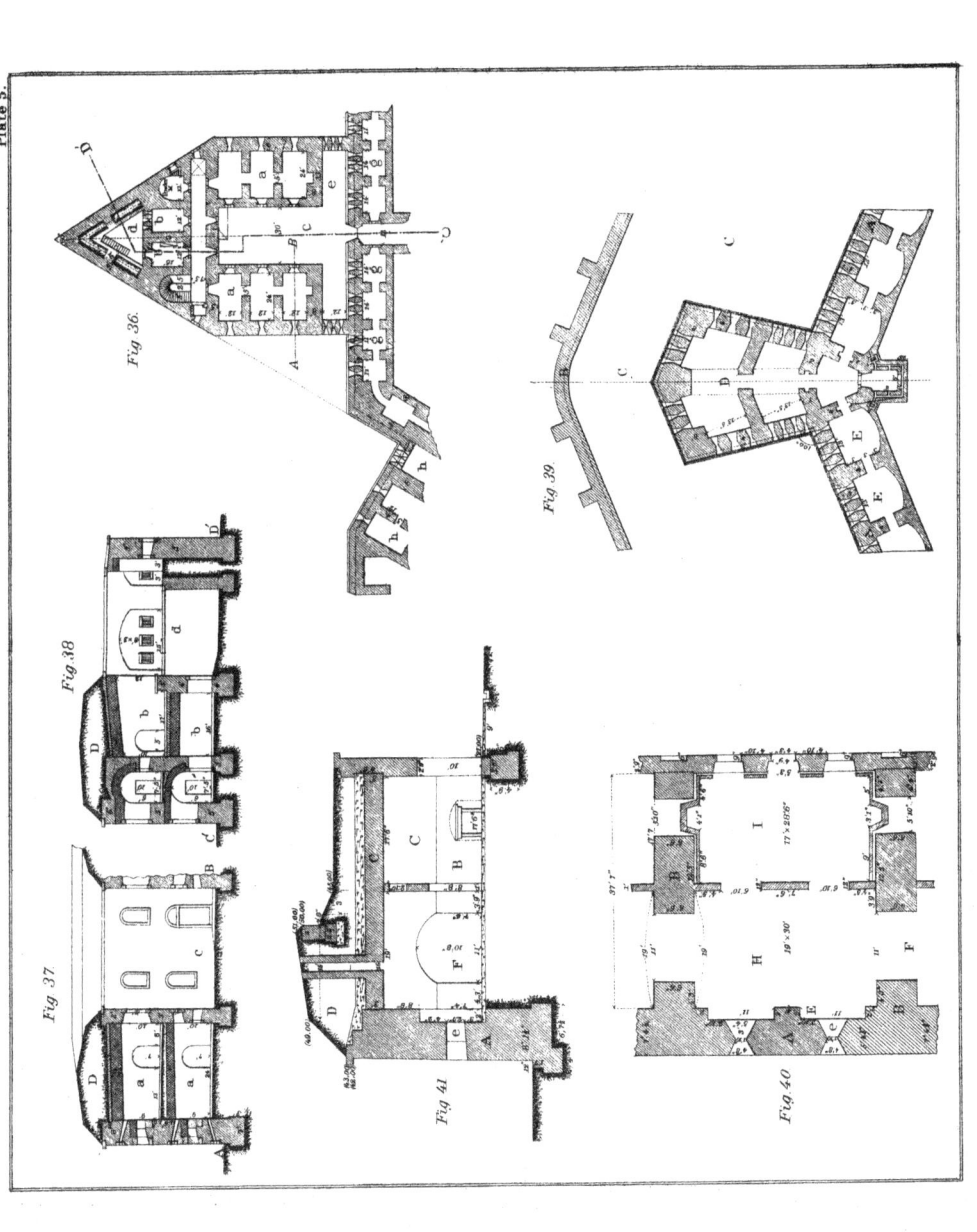

Plate 6.

Fig. 45
Fig. 46
Fig. 47
Fig. 50
Fig. 44
Fig. 48
Fig. 42
Fig. 49
Fig. 43

Plate 7.

Fig. 3
KING'S COUNTERPOISE GUN-CARRIAGE
FOR 35 TON GUN

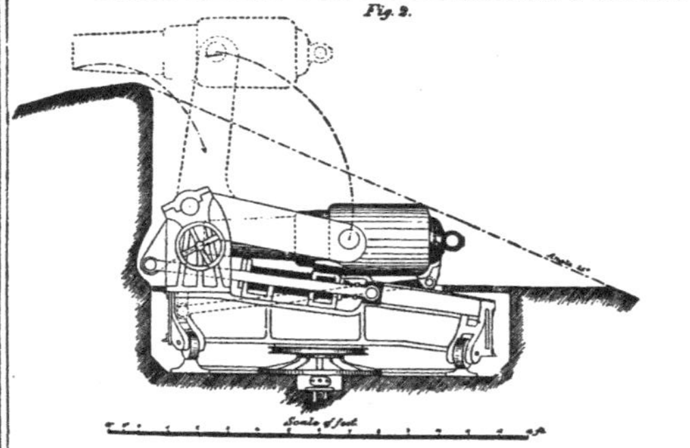

MONCRIEFF CARRIAGE FOR 12½ TON GUN.
Fig. 4.

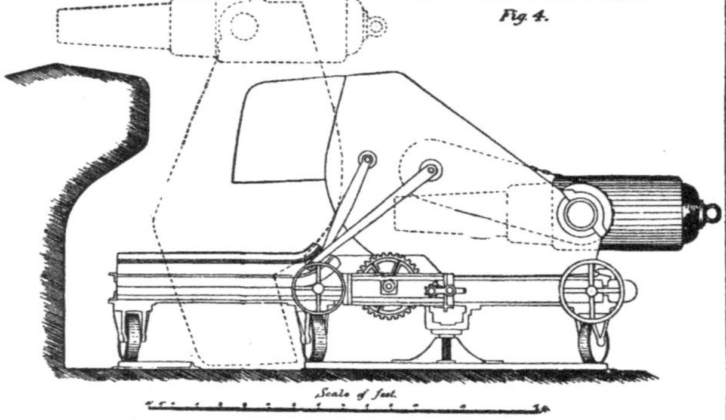

BARBETTE BATTERY DEPRESSING GUN CARRIAGE
Fig. 1

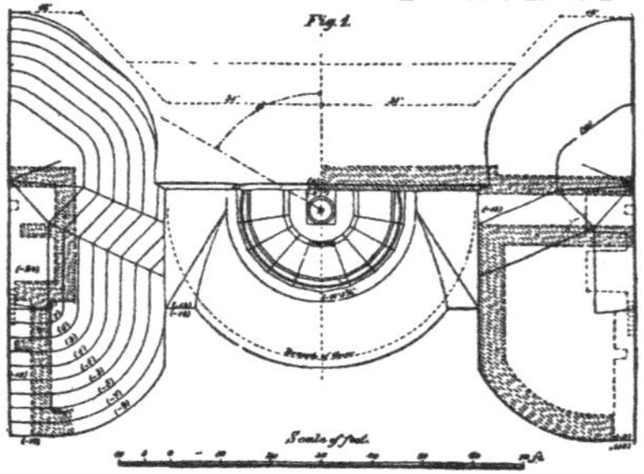

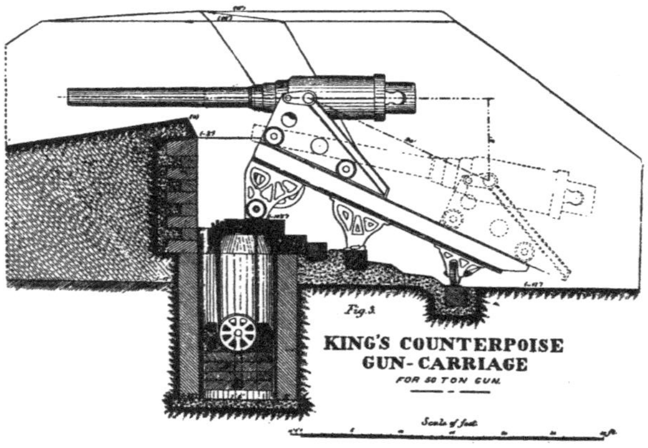

DISAPPEARING GUN ON HYDRAULIC SYSTEM.
Fig. 2.

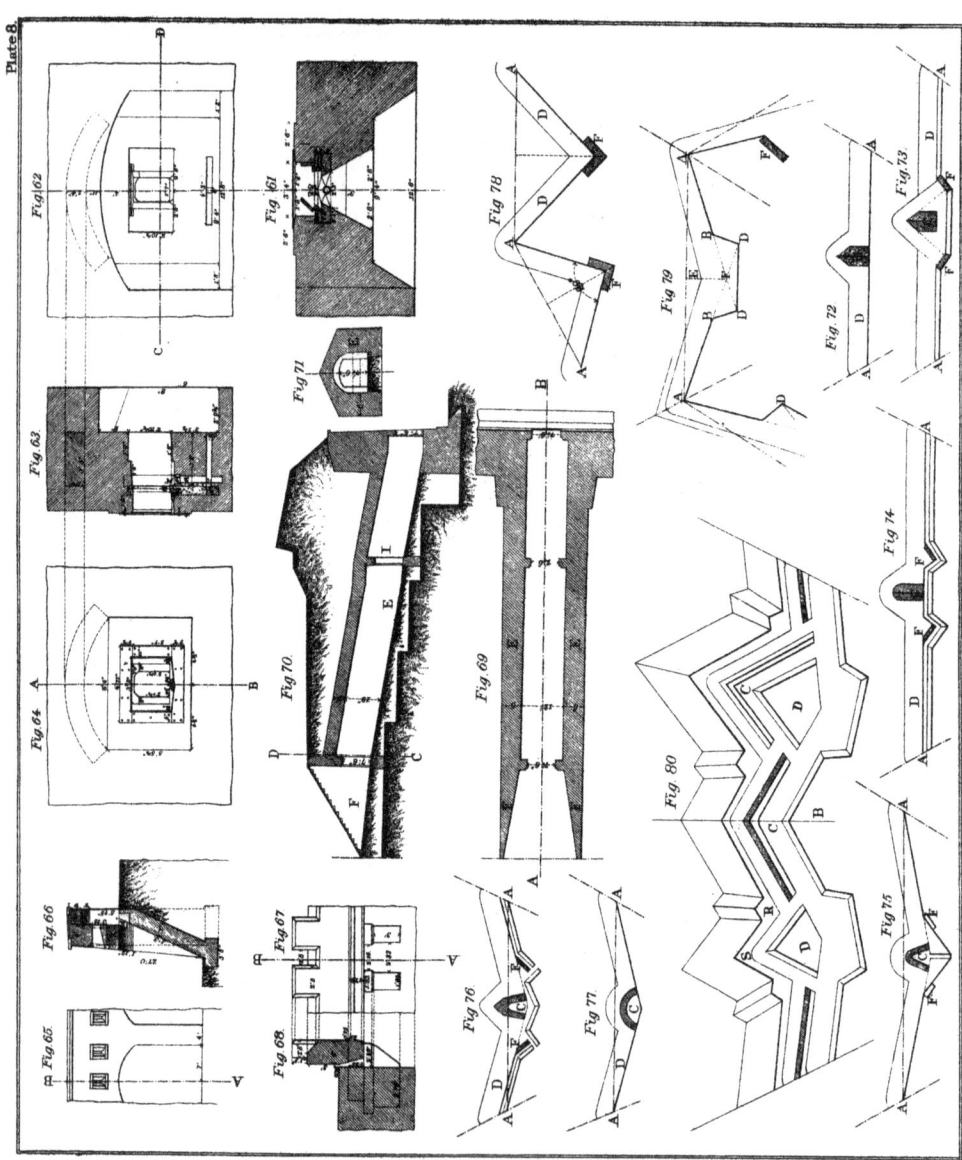

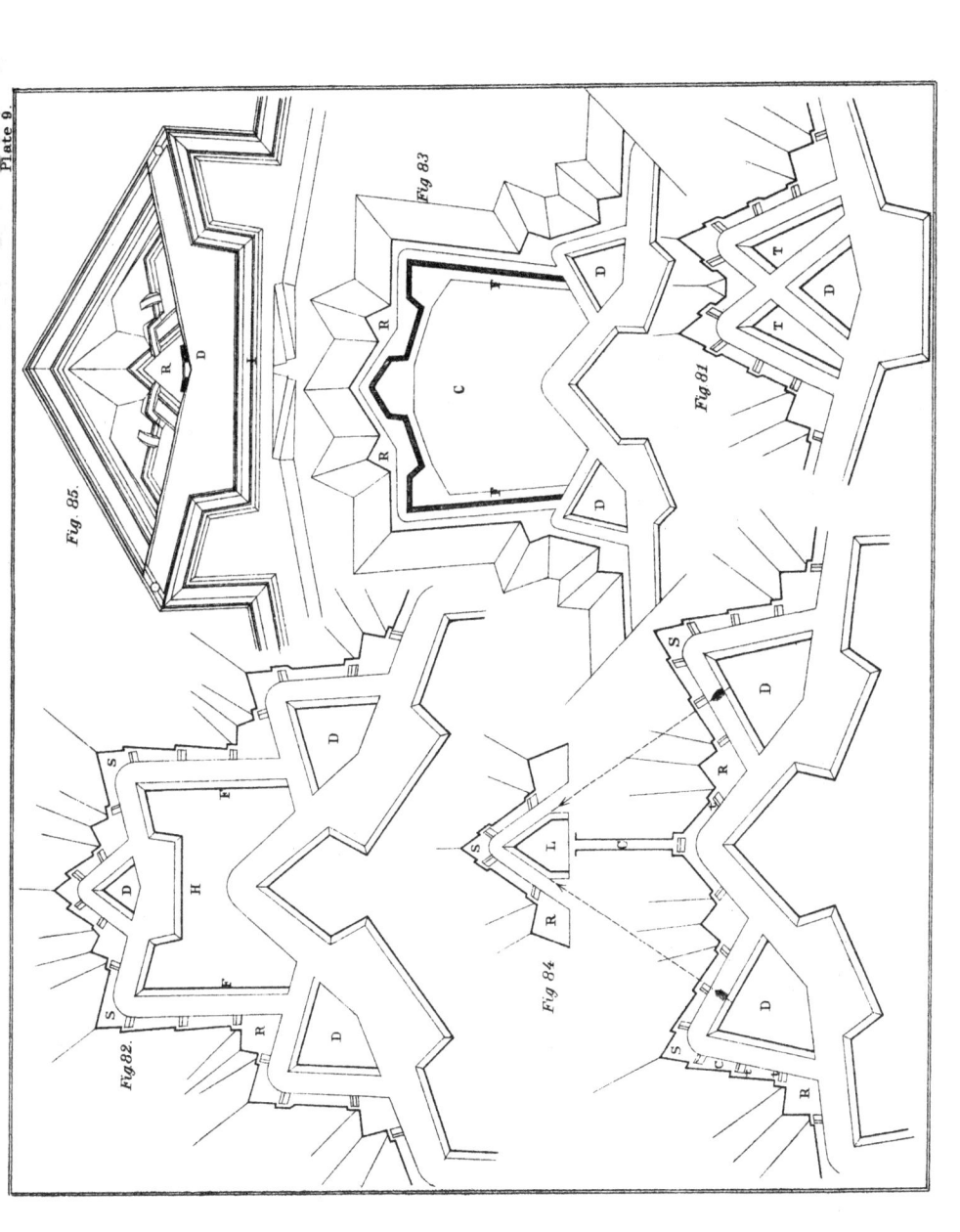

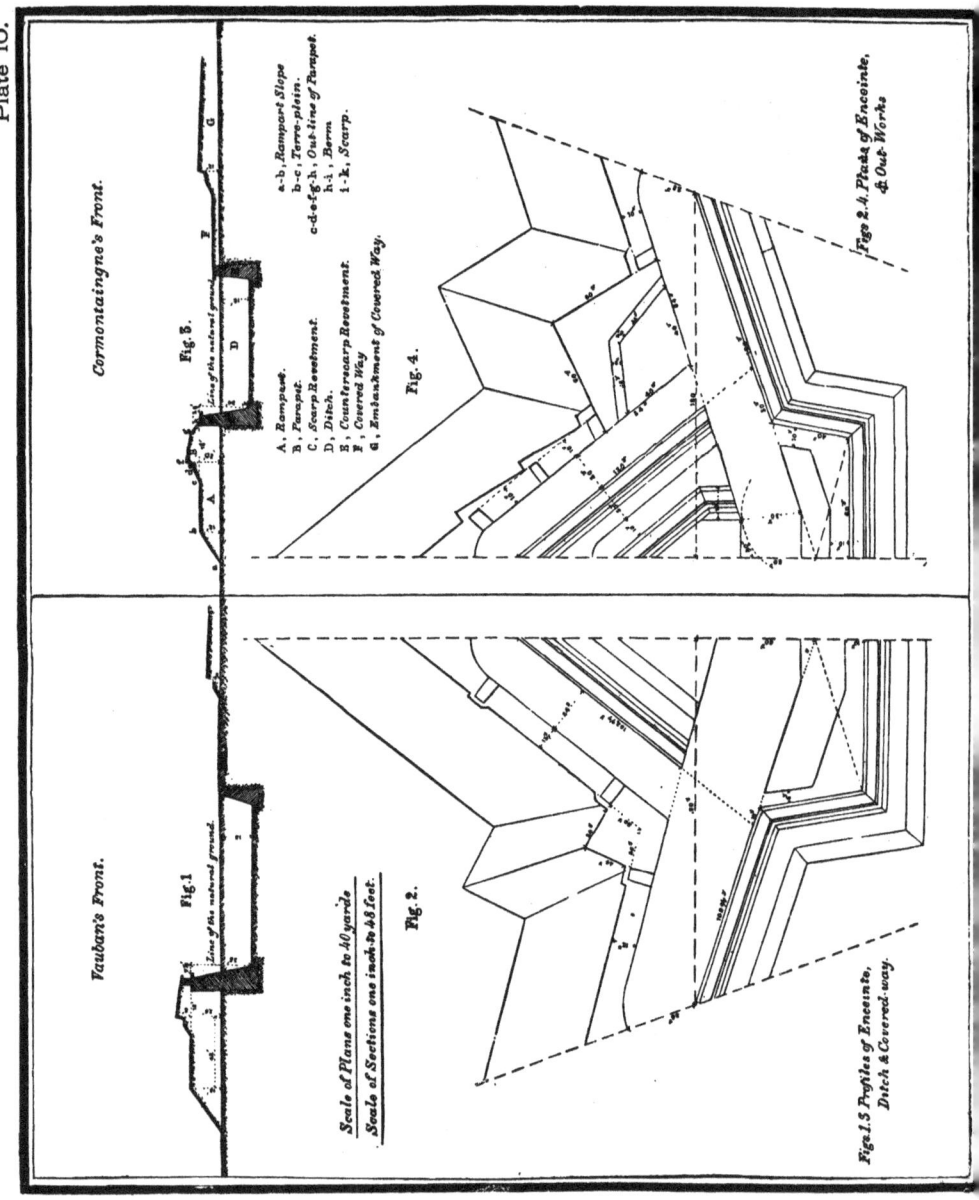

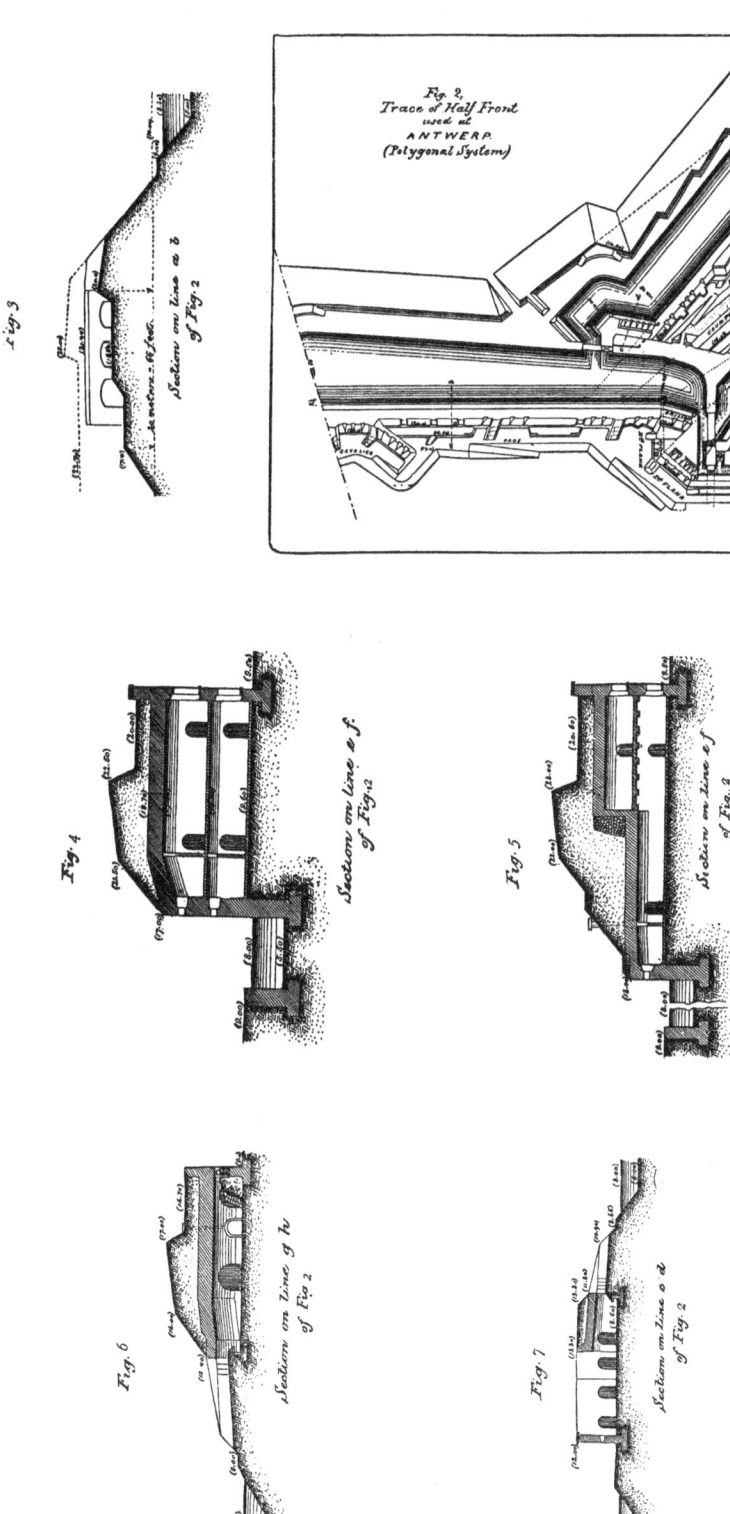

Plate 11a

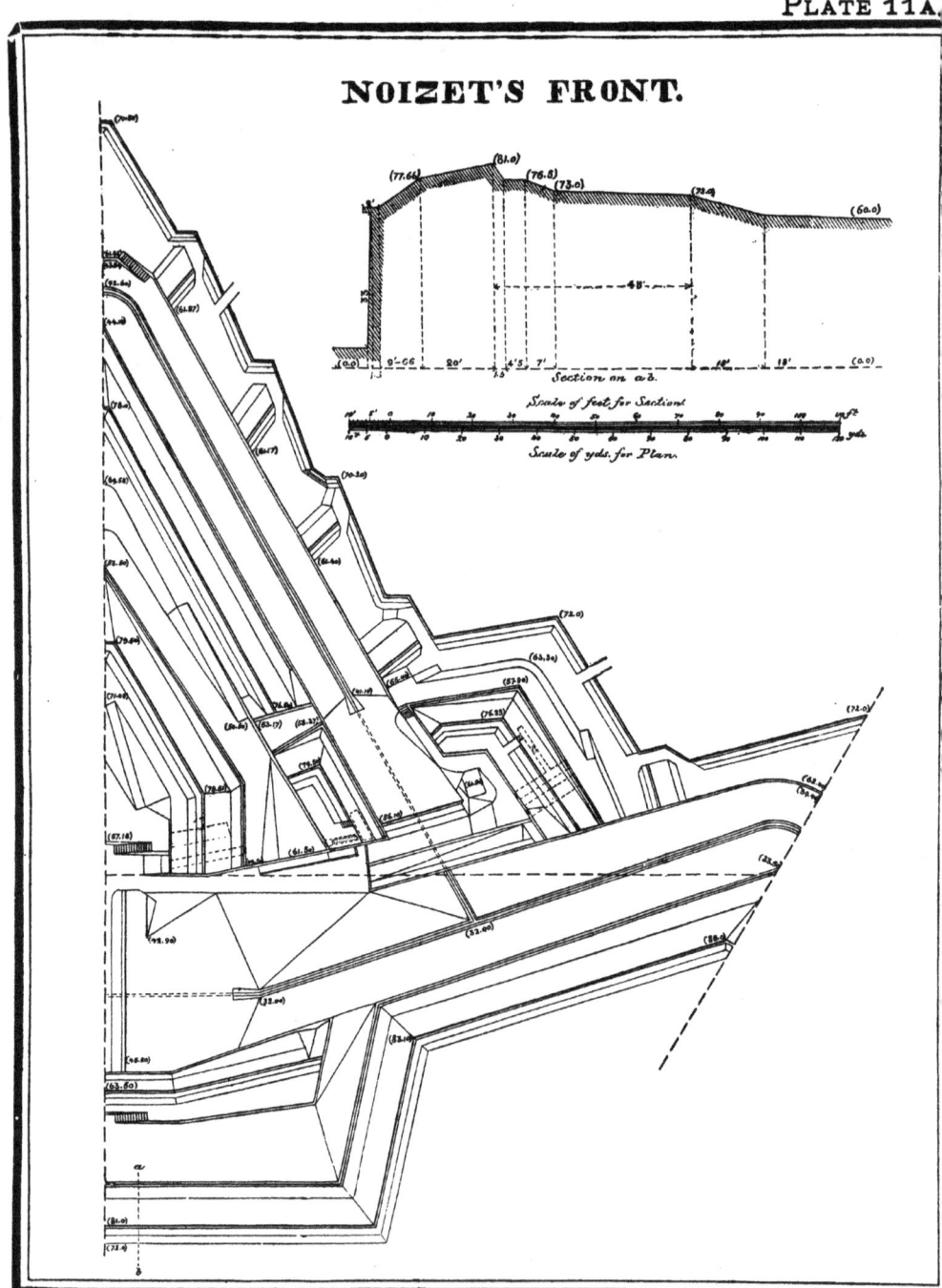

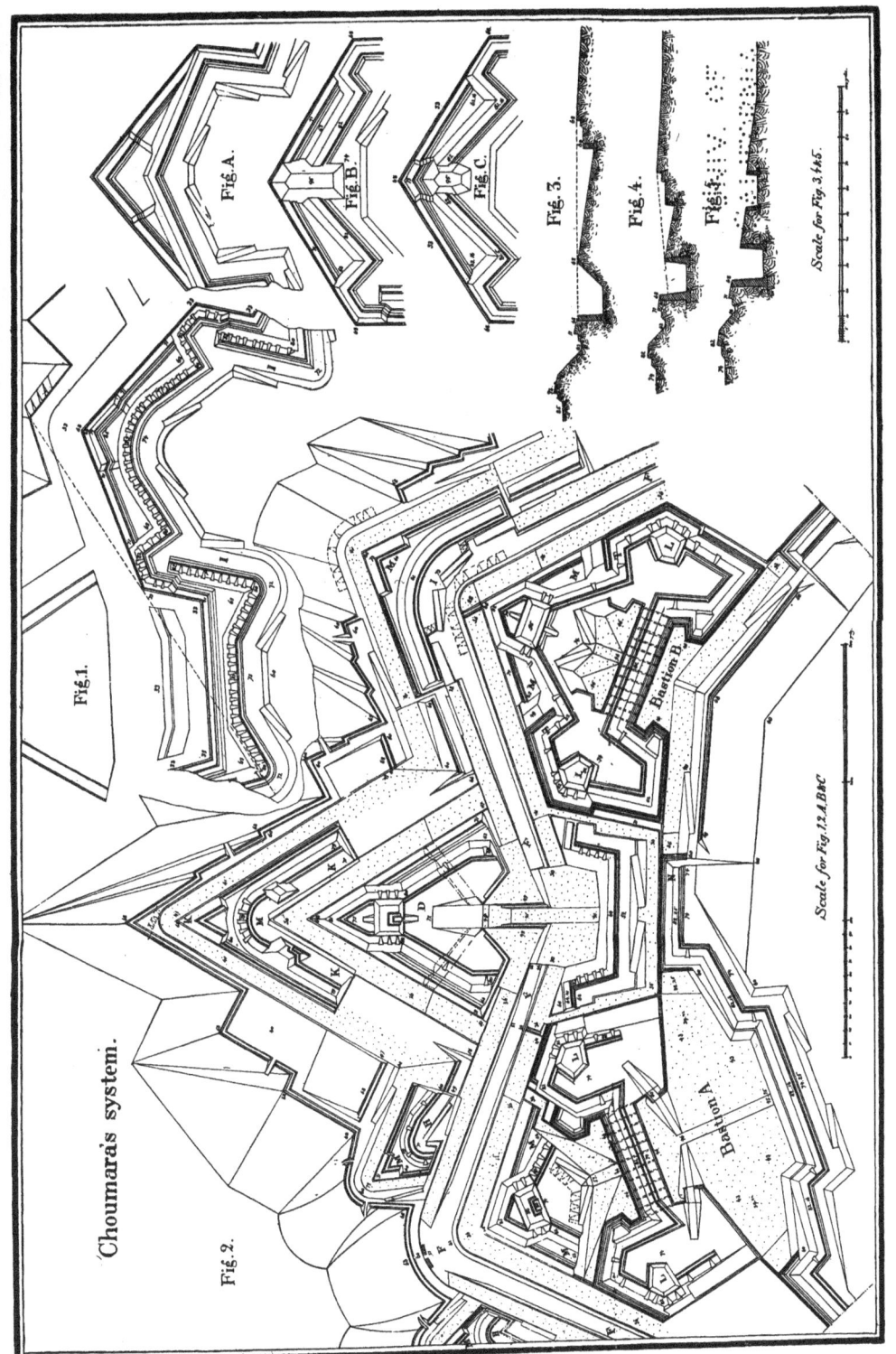

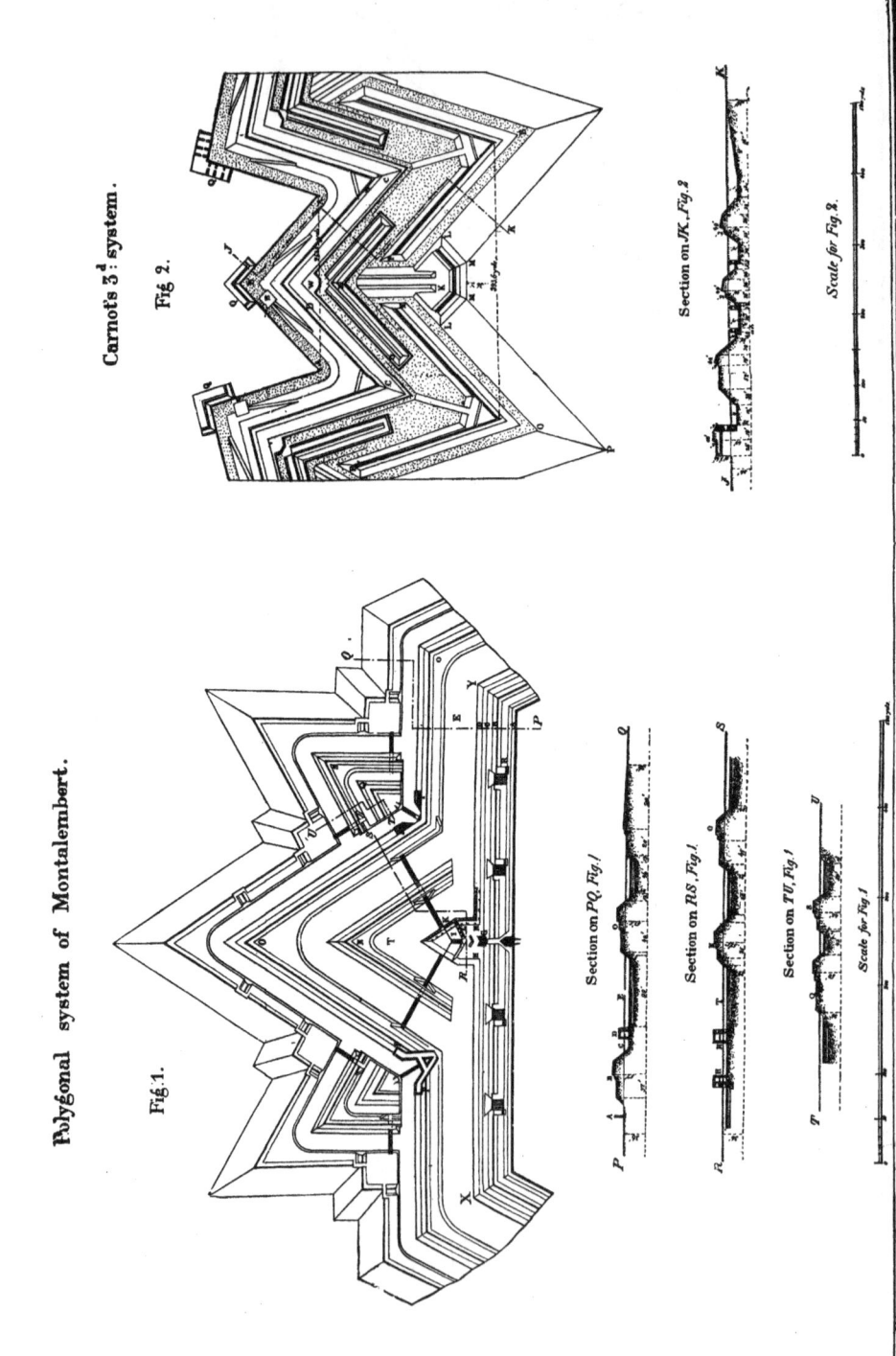

PLATE 13.

Polygonal system of Montalembert.
Fig. 1.

Carnot's 3d system.
Fig. 2.

Section on PQ, Fig. 1.
Section on RS, Fig. 1.
Section on TU, Fig. 1.
Scale for Fig. 1.

Section on JK, Fig. 2.
Scale for Fig. 2.

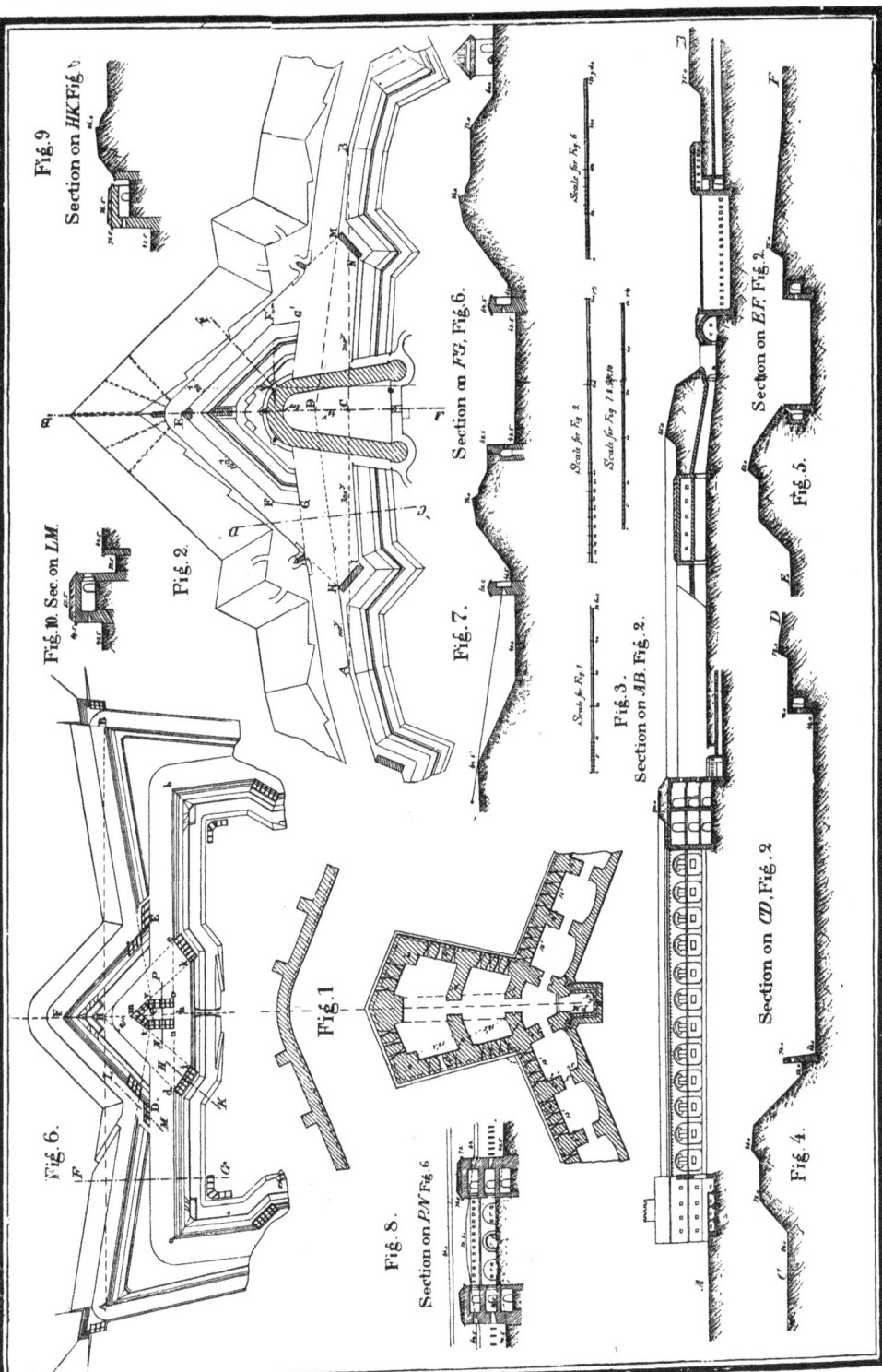

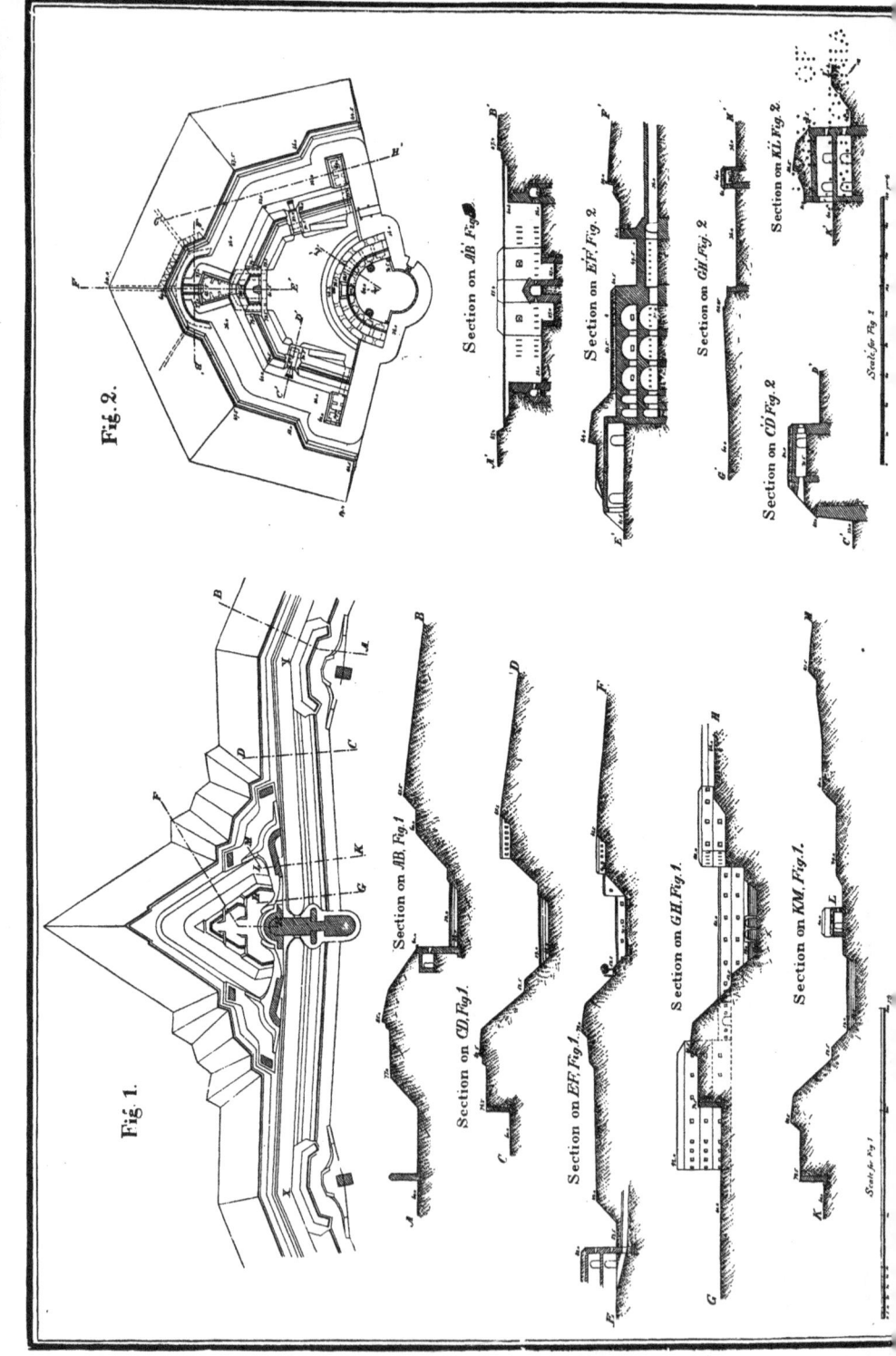

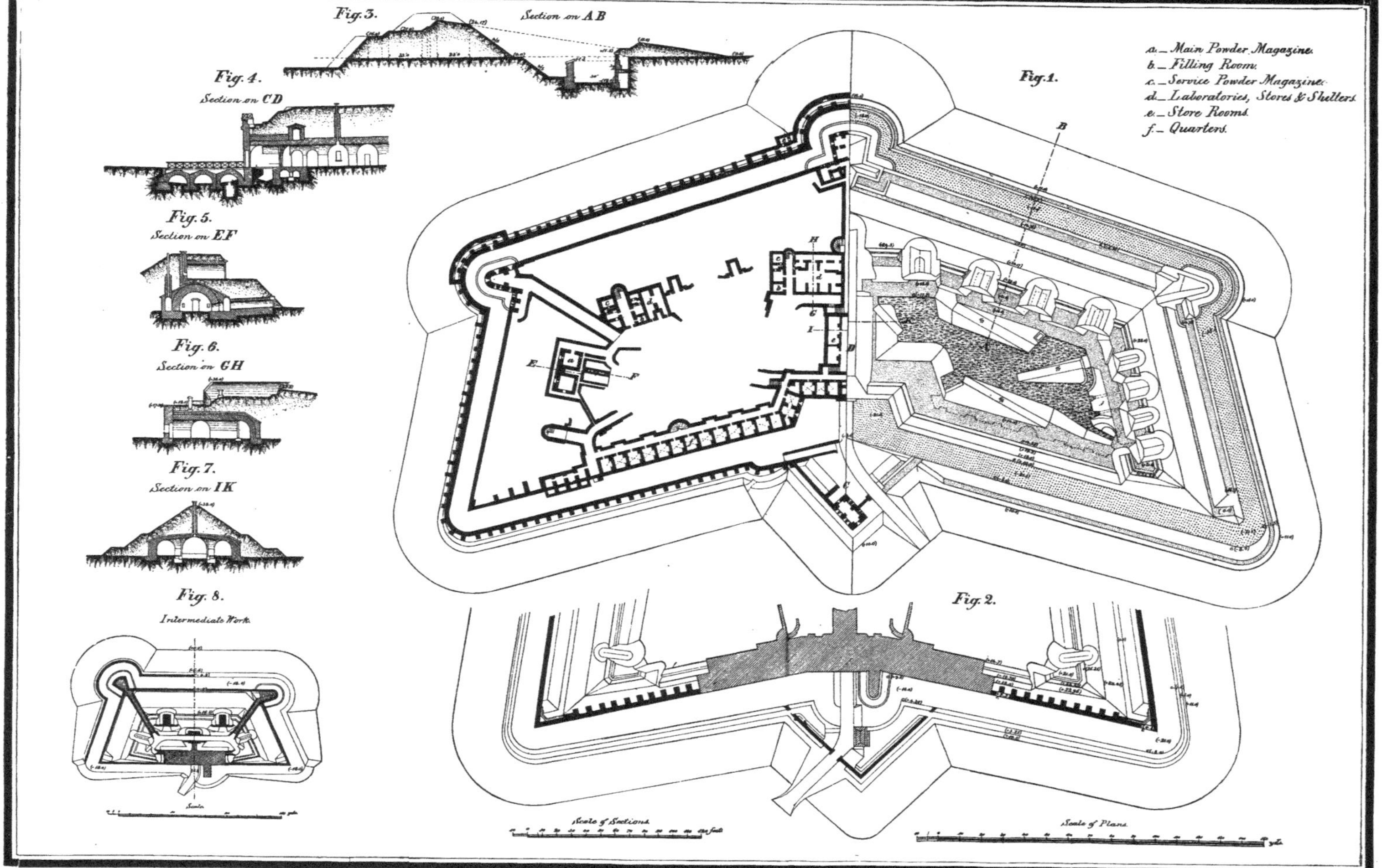

Plate 16.

a — Main Powder Magazine.
b — Filling Room.
c — Service Powder Magazine.
d — Laboratories, Stores & Shelters
e — Store Rooms.
f — Quarters.

Fig. 1.

Fig. 2.

Fig. 3. Section on AB

Fig. 4. Section on CD

Fig. 5. Section on EF

Fig. 6. Section on GH

Fig. 7. Section on IK

Fig. 8. Intermediate Work.

Scale of Plans.

Scale of Sections.

Plate 47.

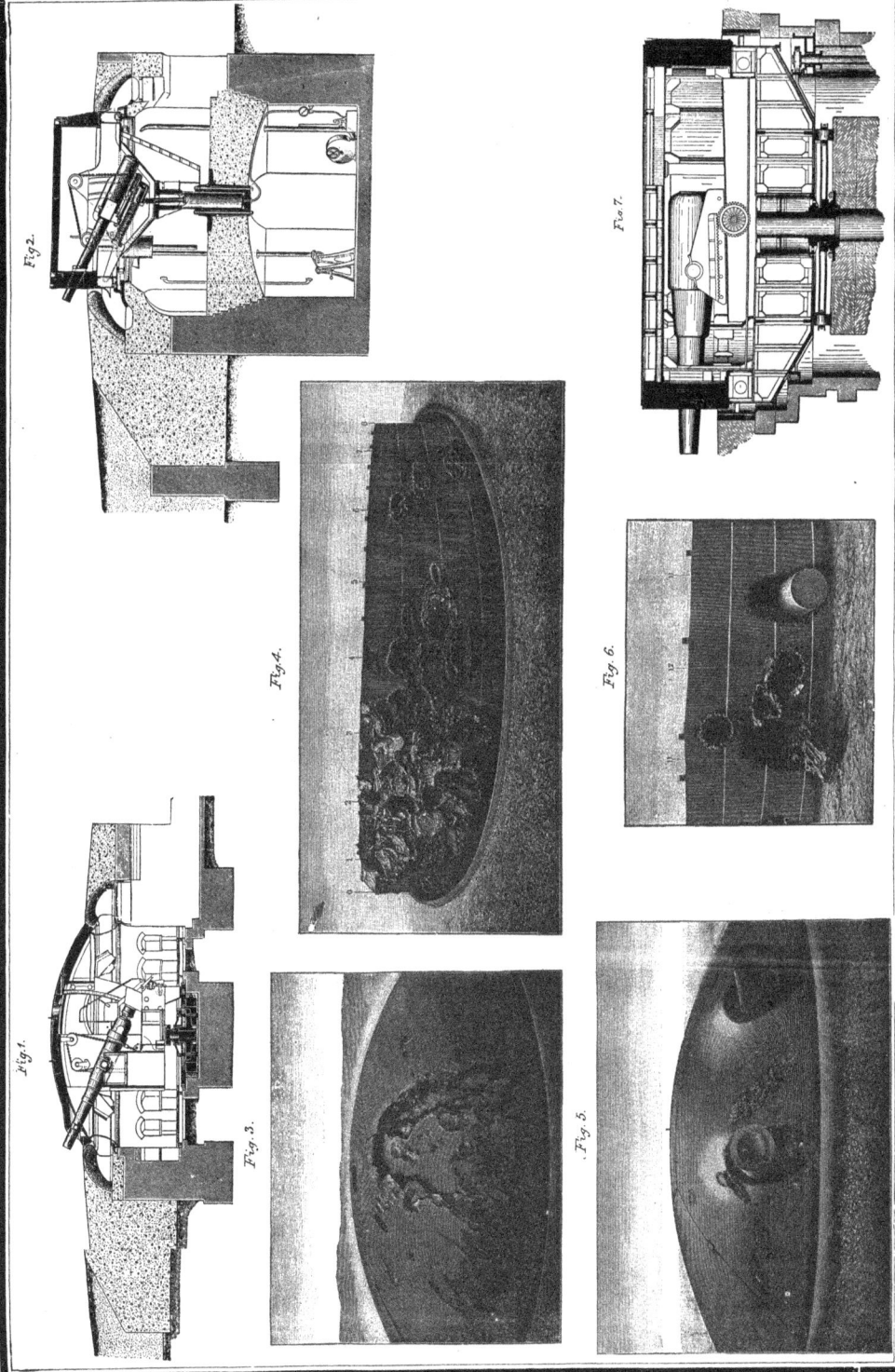

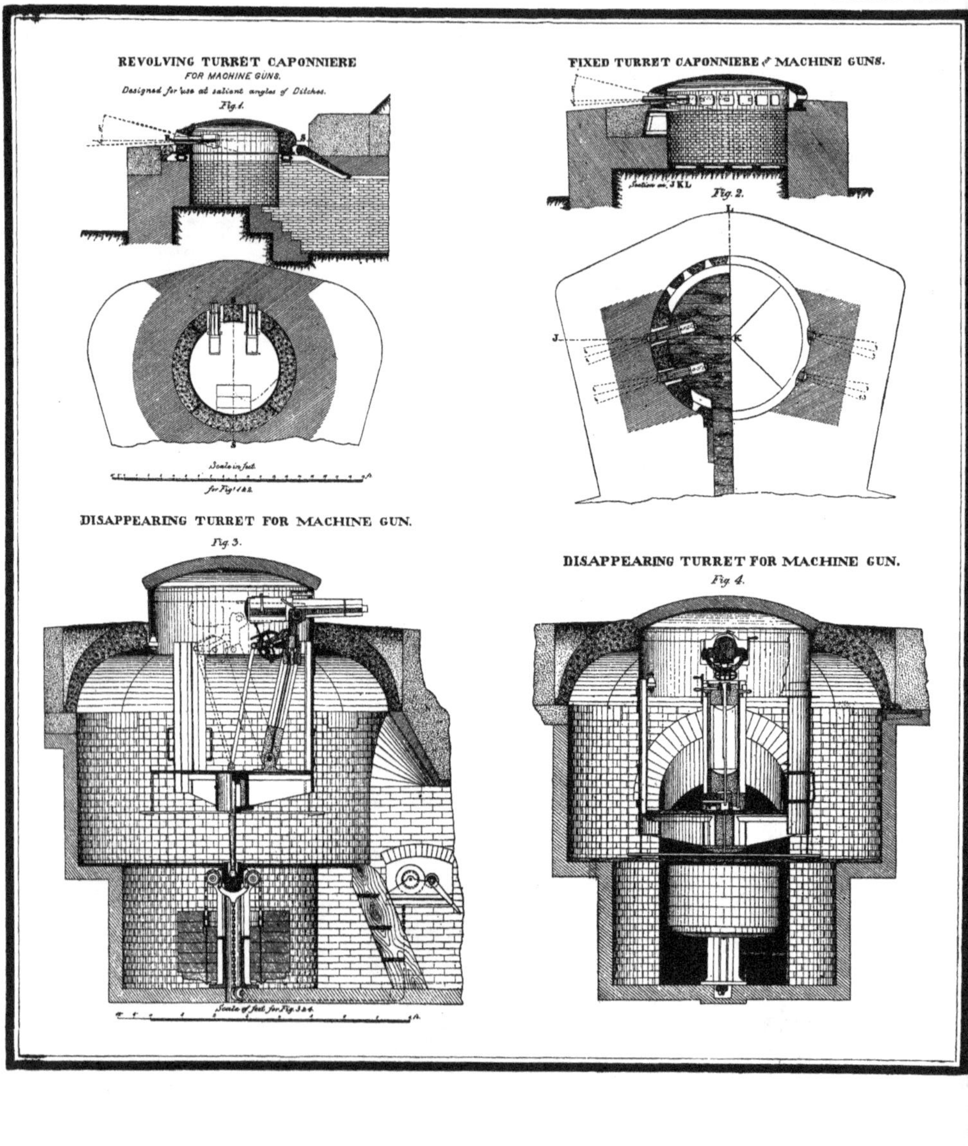

PLATE 19.

REVOLVING TURRET CAPONNIERE
FOR MACHINE GUNS.
Designed for use at salient angles of Ditches.
Fig. 1.

FIXED TURRET CAPONNIERE & MACHINE GUNS.
Fig. 2.

DISAPPEARING TURRET FOR MACHINE GUN.
Fig. 3.

DISAPPEARING TURRET FOR MACHINE GUN.
Fig. 4.

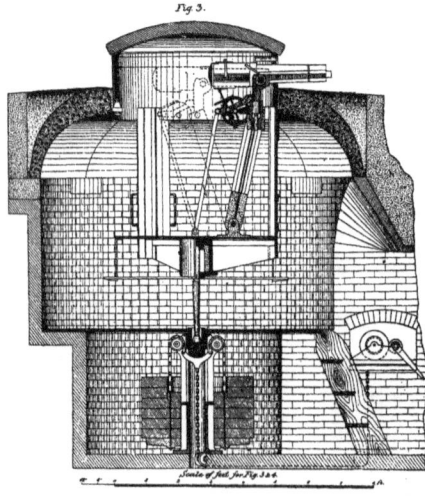
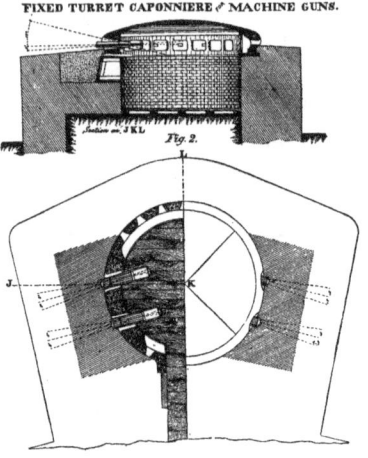
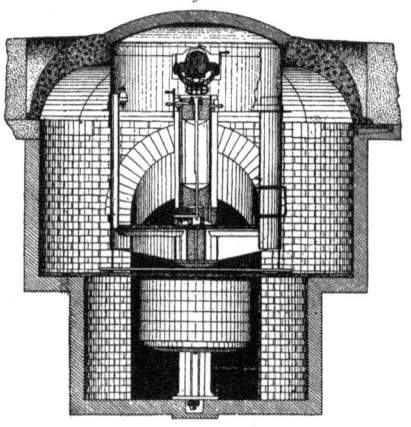

www.ingramcontent.com/pod-product-compliance
Lightning Source LLC
Chambersburg PA
CBHW032225080426
42735CB00008B/716